WHEN ANIMALS SPEAK

ANIMALS IN CONTEXT
General Editor: Colin Jerolmack

When Animals Speak: Toward an Interspecies Democracy
Eva Meijer

When Animals Speak

Toward an Interspecies Democracy

Eva Meijer

NEW YORK UNIVERSITY PRESS

New York

NEW YORK UNIVERSITY PRESS
New York
www.nyupress.org

References to Internet websites (URLs) were accurate at the time of writing. Neither the author nor New York University Press is responsible for URLs that may have expired or changed since the manuscript was prepared.

Library of Congress Cataloging-in-Publication Data
Names: Meijer, Eva, 1980–   author.
Title: When animals speak : toward an interspecies democracy / Eva Meijer.
Description: New York : New York University Press, [2019] |
Includes bibliographical references and index.
Identifiers: LCCN 2019001462| ISBN 9781479859351 (cl : alk. paper) |
ISBN 9781479863136 (pb : alk. paper)
Subjects: LCSH: Human-animal communication. | Animals—Social aspects.
Classification: LCC QL776 .M45 2019 | DDC 591.59—dc23
LC record available at https://lccn.loc.gov/2019001462

New York University Press books are printed on acid-free paper, and their binding materials are chosen for strength and durability. We strive to use environmentally responsible suppliers and materials to the greatest extent possible in publishing our books.

Manufactured in the United States of America

10 9 8 7 6 5 4 3 2 1

Also available as an ebook

For Pika and Putih

CONTENTS

Introduction

Orangutan Ken Allen was born in the San Diego Zoo. While still in the nursery he was already trying to unscrew every nut he could get his hands on, and he used humans as objects to climb on in order to escape the room. In the years that followed, he perfected his techniques, which led him to escape his enclosure many times. This forced the zoo to alter the fences around the orangutan enclosure and change their windows and locks. They also tried to distract him by bringing in females, and they hired spies posing as visitors in an attempt to find out how he did it. But Ken Allen was not the only orangutan who had a desire to leave captivity. His mate Vicki once took over from him, unbolting a door after he was caught, and escaped. Kumang and Sara, two sisters from the same group, organized and coordinated their own escapes, for example, by using a mop handle that one of them held in place while the other climbed it. Cooperative orangutan resistance is found in many other zoos as well, including in the Woodland Park Zoo in Seattle, where a group of five orangutans slipped through several security doors and climbed over a high wall. Neither bananas nor water from fire hoses could convince them to go back in, and they had to be tranquilized. These examples are not the only ones available—orangutan resistance is a structural problem for zoos, often leading them to isolate individuals or break up family bonds by relocating orangutans (Hribal 2012).

There are many other examples of non-human animals who challenge their oppression (chapter 7): non-human animal workers refuse to work, captive wild animals use violence against their captors, farm animals escape on their way to slaughterhouses, laboratory animals turn their heads away. Other non-human animals seek out human company, either becoming members of human households or taking up residence in their gardens, cities, or fields. Non-human animals may also care for humans or work side by side with them; human and non-human animals can have meaningful encounters, develop friendships, or simply co-exist as neighbors.

Non-human animals are individuals with their own perspectives on life, who form relations with human and non-human others. In current human legal and political systems, and in many cultural practices, they are seen and used as objects. Animal rights theorists have challenged this since the 1970s, arguing that non-human animals are sentient beings, who are similar to humans in morally relevant aspects and who should therefore be seen as part of our moral communities. Drawing on these views, and on insights provided by social justice movements that focus on democratic inclusion, recent work in political philosophy proposes to view non-human animals as political groups, and some of these as members of shared interspecies communities. This movement from ethical consideration to political participation shifts questions about non-human animals from how they should be treated to how more insight can be gained into the ways they want to live their lives, what types of relationships they desire with one another and with humans, and how we can and should share the planet that we all live on (Donaldson and Kymlicka 2011).[1]

Questions about non-human animal political participation, interspecies communication, and political voice have not received much attention in animal philosophy until now.[2] This is unfortunate. Because other animals are subjects with their own perspectives on life, it is not sufficient, either epistemologically or normatively, just to consider them: humans need to reformulate political and social relations in interaction with them in order not to repeat anthropocentrism (see also Donaldson forthcoming). Language plays an important role in thinking about creating better relations with other animals. Learning about the languages of other animals can help humans to understand them better and build new relations with them.[3] Challenging an anthropocentric view of language formed by power relations can help humans to see animals of other species, and their languages, differently. Conceptualizing animal languages can also be significant in addressing certain practical problems between humans and other animals, for example, in border conflicts between groups of wild animals and human groups, or with regard to political participation of those non-human animals who are part of our societies. In this book, I discuss these and other questions concerning language and world, politics and activism, shared and sovereign communities, democracy and difference, in order to develop a theory of political animal voices.

From the Political Animal to Political Animal Voices

In political philosophy, the ability to speak is usually considered a necessary condition for being a political actor and for membership in the political community. Speaking is seen as a human enterprise, one that is clearly distinct from the way that other animals express themselves and use their voices. Being able to speak is seen as necessary for rational deliberation (Habermas 1981), for participation in a (hypothetical) social contract (Rawls 1971), for democratic action (Rancière 2007), for collective intentional action (Pepper 2016), and for other forms of political participation. The view that only humans are political actors has a long history. In Book I of *The Politics*, Aristotle defines man as political animal and the only animal that is endowed with speech, or rather *logos*, which here refers to rational speech, and more specifically the ability to distinguish between right and wrong in a speech act (Aristotle [350BC] 1991, 1253a, 10–18; Derrida 2011, 348). This capacity is necessary for being part of the political community. By attributing *logos* only to humans, he draws a line between humans and other animals. This line functions as a border around the political; only humans can be political animals. It also defines political speech: *logos*, meaning speech informed by reason, is contrasted with *phonè*, the sound of the voice, which can express pain or pleasure. Non-human animals have voices and express themselves, but they cannot speak in the proper sense because they cannot use their voices to decide between just and unjust; they do not have *logos*. What is furthermore important to note is that this move is made inside human language—Aristotle is using human words to argue that using human words is what draws the line between who can speak and who cannot, and between who can be a political actor and who cannot.[4]

Recent work in political philosophy challenges the idea that only humans are part of democratic communities (Cochrane, Garner, and O'Sullivan 2016), as well as the idea that only humans can be political actors (Donaldson and Kymlicka 2011). Animal ethics has, at least since the work of Peter Singer (1975) and Tom Regan (1983), always been a political project, because it challenges the borders of the moral community and focuses on non-human animal rights. These new approaches draw more heavily on the vocabulary developed in political philosophy. They are united by a focus on justice, and on reformulating existing political institutions, practices, and structures to secure just human/non-human animal relations (Cochrane, Garner, and O'Sullivan 2016). Most political animal philosophers focus on including non-human animal interests in existing liberal democratic institutions (Cochrane 2012; Garner 2013; Rowlands 1997; O'Sullivan 2011).

Political philosophers Sue Donaldson and Will Kymlicka (2011) explicitly challenge the view that only humans can be political actors. They are not the first to draw attention to non-human animal agency and the importance of relations for, and between, humans and other animals[5]; Donaldson and Kymlicka are, however, the first to develop a political theory of animal rights based on the relations between groups of non-human animals and human political communities. A focus on political relations implies the need to think about political communication within and between communities. Other animals have languages and communicate, their voices can and should be seen as political—as constituents of or contributions to political processes—and humans can and should attend to and be responsive to these voices as part of a broader conception of interspecies democracy.

As mentioned above, the question of language, and animal voice, including the connection between language, reason, political agency, and political practices and institutions, has not yet received much attention in recent work on political animal philosophy, or animal ethics more broadly. Many animal rights theorists[6] simply assume that other animals do not use language, cannot speak in a way that is relevant to political action, and are destined to stay silent in political and social matters. There are very few animal rights theorists who incorporate the current research on non-human animal, or interspecies, languages in their work, or who investigate how other animals can have a voice in questions that concern their lives in other ways. Activists and philosophers currently often see it as unavoidable that "we" should speak for "them."[7] This is unfortunate, given the strong connections between language and political action in the philosophical tradition and political practice, and given the fact that the political participation of other animals involves communicating with them. Language is an important tool in interacting and building common worlds with others. Furthermore, it glosses over the relationship between how our notions of "subject" and "language" are constructed in relation to *logos* or reason, and the exclusion of other animals. It is also unfortunate because it perpetuates a negative stereotype of other animals as mute, or incapable of speaking, and keeps intact an idealized view of the human and human language.

To challenge this, we need to develop a new understanding of language that can take into account the multitude of non-human animal expressions and ways of creating meaning, and that begins from the idea that other animals are beings who have their own perspective on life and their own ways of communicating this to others of their own and other species.

Animal Languages

Recent research in biology and ethology shows that many non-human animal species have their own complex and nuanced ways of communicating with members of their own and other species, including humans (chapter 2). Dolphins (King and Janik 2013) and parrots (Berg et al. 2011), for example, call each other by their names. African elephants use different alarm calls to distinguish between threats from bees and humans, as well as between different groups of humans (Soltis et al. 2014). Ravens use referential gestures (Pika and Bugnyar 2011). Fork-tailed drongos mimic the alarm calls of other species to scare them away so they can steal their dinner (Flower et al. 2014). We find grammatical structures, including recursion, in the songs of many species of bird (Gentner et al. 2006). The skin patterns of squid can be seen as a language built up of sentences that have a grammar (Moynihan 1991). Prairie dogs, a species of ground squirrel, describe humans in detail, including the color of their T-shirts and hair, the speed at which they are approaching, and objects they might be carrying (Slobodchikoff et al. 2009).

Humans have a long-shared history with many non-human animal species, which has influenced their capacities for understanding one another (chapter 3). Dogs and humans have, for example, co-evolved, and both species have influenced the characteristics of the other—some biologists even think that humans may have started to use language in relation to dogs (Haraway 2003). Research shows that humans can correctly interpret dog moods when they hear them bark or growl on tape or see their facial expressions; dogs can also read human sounds and faces (Hare and Woods 2013). When dogs and humans who are friends gaze into each other's eyes they create oxytocin, the "cuddle hormone," something that also happens between lovers, and parents and babies (ibid.).

In philosophy and biology, language has long been equated with human language. As I will discuss in more detail in chapter 1, many philosophers in the Western tradition have even seen language as a defining characteristic for humans. These empirical studies, along with the aforementioned developments in political philosophy and other fields of study that argue for the recognition of non-human animal subjectivity, challenge this view. They call for us to reconsider the cognitive, social, and linguistic capacities of other animals, and they also ask us to reconsider what language is. Humans do not know currently whether there are any non-human animal languages as complex as human language, neither do they currently understand the full meaning of many non-human animals' expressions or the depth of form of interspecies communication. However, it is clear that the idea that only humans have language as informed by *logos* and that other animals do not is untenable. The insights obtained from recent studies compel us to think differently about non-human animal language, culture, and subjectivity, and perhaps more importantly, about how humans can interact with other animals to discover their attitudes to the questions that concern their lives.[8]

Ludwig Wittgenstein's later work, and in particular his concept "language games," offers a good starting point for thinking about and studying non-human animal and interspecies languages. Wittgenstein argues that the way in which language works and its interconnection to social practices means we can never give a universal definition of language as a whole, or fixed definitions of separate concepts. If we want to study language, we should instead investigate the meaning of different language games (chapter 2) by examining how and where they are used. This method of studying language is well suited to the study of non-human animal and interspecies language games for various reasons. A focus on existing practices and the social context in which language games gain meaning allows us to acknowledge and better understand non-human animal agency in language. Language games also consist of more than words: Wittgenstein emphasizes the importance of gestures and other non-linguistic expressions in creating meaning (PI§7). Gestures, movements, and other non-verbal expressions play an important role in the languages of other animals. Existing human concepts can offer guidelines for understanding the meaning of certain practices, and Wittgenstein's ideas about how language games are related—by means of a family resemblance—can shed light on similarities and relations in human, non-human, and interspecies language games. Finally, Wittgenstein views language as essentially a public practice, arguing that meaning originates from the relation between language and world, which helps us to see why skepticism about the minds of other animals—human and non-human—is misguided (chapters 2 & 3).

My aim in this book is not, however, to present a full theory of non-human animal languages. Humans are only just beginning to learn about many non-human animal languages, and it would be empirically impossible to develop a final theory of animal language. Furthermore, rethinking what language is should not be a solely human endeavor, and it is not up to humans to define what constitutes meaningful communication for others. In order not to repeat anthropocentrism, we need to learn about language in interaction with other animals.

In further developing ideas about language and politics in an interspecies context, it is important to keep in mind that there is, of course, no such thing as the political animal voice or "the animal" (Derrida 2008). There are many different species, communities, and groups of non-human and human animals, and they all have their own languages and cultures. There are also many different relations and encounters between different groups of animals, including those of the human variety. In order to rethink language and politics with other animals, we need to take these differences into account. We also need to be careful not to use the human as a standard for measuring other animals, because this preexcludes many of them, and makes it difficult to see them in their own right. This means we need to challenge human exceptionalism together with the view that there is a binary opposition between "the human" and "the animal." We should pay attention to the variety of ways in which other animals speak and act politically, and search for ways to form new, better relations with them. This should not just be a human project, because other animals have their unique perspectives on their own lives and on their relations with humans, and their own ways of formulating these. Humans and other animals can, and already do, have relations in which species is not the determining factor in achieving understanding or intimacy, and in which humans aim not to oppress the other animals with whom they share households or land. These relations can offer us insights into how change is possible, and can function as starting points for thinking about new forms of coexistence.

Theorizing from the Ground Up: A Note on Method

Until now, the political turn in animal studies has primarily been advanced by philosophers and political theorists working in the tradition of Anglo-American analytical liberal political philosophy (i.e., Cochrane 2012; Donaldson and Kymlicka 2011; Garner 2013; and O'Sullivan 2011). In this book, supported by empirical ethological studies, I bring their ideas into conversation with insights from other philosophical traditions, most notably phenomenology and post-structuralism. I do so because I do not simply defend the view that we need to take animal voices into account politically. This project is also an investigation of what concepts such as "language" and "politics" mean and could mean in relation to other animals, and how they have been constructed. We need to do both because non-human animals have been excluded not only from our political communities, institutions, and conversations, but also from the concepts we use to describe and think about them.

Language is a good example of how this works. Other animals have been excluded from this concept from very early on in Western traditions of thinking. As discussed above, Aristotle famously separated human language from non-human animal use of voice, thereby drawing boundaries around "language" and the political community in one movement. This is not a neutral or natural step: unequal power relations play a role in this process, and we could even say that our view of language has been constructed by excluding other animals. In order to develop a theory of non-human animal and interspecies languages, we cannot, therefore, simply draw on ethological research that investigates the linguistic capacities of other animals and say that other animals "have" language; we also need to investigate how this concept was constructed and how it is used and has been used in relation to other animals. This critical investigation can function as the basis for developing a new phenomenological understanding of language together with other animals. As I argue in more detail below, insights from different traditions can shed light on different aspects of this question.

Recognizing the role that power relations play in constituting the meaning of concepts also has consequences for the political philosophical standpoints adopted in this book. My phenomenological approach to political concepts can perhaps best be described as "from the ground up," meaning I start with non-human animal agency and interspecies relations, as described in the case studies and other examples I use, as the basis for the development of my philosophical views. I do not, for example, start from the basic principles of liberal democratic theory and then argue for including non-human animal interests; rather, I evaluate the relevance of concepts such as citizenship, sovereignty, or deliberation through the lens of non-human animal agency and interspecies politics. Rights, and other liberal democratic institutions, practices, and processes, may play a large role in improving the lives of other animals, and a critical investigation of these can lay the foundation for new interspecies relations. However, as I discuss in more detail in the second part of the book, while rights and other human inventions can be important stepping stones towards better relations, they cannot be the final goal. It is not up to humans to come up with a full political theory into which other animals fit; to do so would be to repeat anthropocentrism (see also chapters 1 & 8). Just relations can only ultimately come into being through interaction with other animals.

Theorizing from the ground up also means that these explorations are rooted in a liberal democratic reality. This is relevant from a material point of view because existing institutions, rights, and practices can be changed to better incorporate animal voices, and this would make a significant difference for many non-human animals. Theoretically, it is also important to start with existing situations in order not to make universal or metaphysical claims about other animals; this would again be a matter of humans deciding what is best for other animals without consulting them. Just as with language, however, while rights and other liberal democratic institutions and practices carry a promise of justice and can make a difference for many non-human animals, one must remain critical of the system in which they are grounded, and bring to light the power relations that helped to create them. This is especially important in the case of non-human animals, who were not just excluded from rights by accident, but were seen as the "other" in relation to which "the human" was constructed (chapter 1, Derrida 2008). In order to move beyond that and conceptualize new futures, we must learn from other animals and from non-Western human cultures (Ko and Ko 2017).

In this book, I therefore discuss existing concepts from different theoretical angles, rooted in existing practices, and explore how we can use these as tools to begin thinking and acting differently. Because thinking and acting differently will need to happen in an interspecies context, and because we do not know how other animals will act once they no longer need to fear humans, the outcome of this is unclear. As Hannah Arendt shows ([1958] 1998), this is also where we find hope.

Political Animal Voices: A Brief Summary

In this book, I develop a theory of political animal voices. I do so in three steps. The first part of the book focuses on language. It offers a critique of viewing language as exclusively human, as well as an alternative to that view. In chapter 1, "The Animal, What a Word! Human Language and Non-Human Animals," I investigate the relation between language and anthropocentrism. By examing the connections between human language and non-human animal exclusion, I argue that, in order to adequately address anthropocentrism, we need to redefine language in and through interaction with non-human animals. Chapter 2, "Animal Languages," turns the focus to non-human animal languages. In this chapter, I draw on empirical studies of animal languages and cultures to provide a better insight into their worlds as a starting point for conceptualizing interspecies interactions and world-building. I draw on Wittgenstein's later work, and specifically on his concept "language games," to develop an alternative way of conceptualizing and studying animal languages and interspecies languages, and I discuss different non-human animal and interspecies language games. In chapter 3, "From Animal Languages to Interspecies Worlds," I investigate how we can conceptualize language between animals of different species, and I explore the role that language plays in constructing common worlds with other animals. The first case study, "Stray Philosophy: Dog-Human Observations on Language, Freedom, and Politics," builds on these insights. In this case study, I draw on my personal experiences with Romanian stray dog Olli to explore philosophical concepts around three themes: language, freedom, and politics. By emphasizing Olli's perspective and actions, I also aim to explore ways to move beyond anthropocentrism in philosophy. This case study concludes the first part of the book about animal languages and interspecies worlds, and opens the door to the second.

The second part of this book focuses on interspecies politics; it challenges an anthropocentric demarcation of the political, and develops an alternative, which takes into account non-human animal agency and interspecies political relations. In chapter 4, "Animal Politics: Justice, Power, and Political Animal Agency," I criticize an anthropocentric view of politics from the perspectives of justice and power relations. I investigate political non-human animal agency and discuss how non-human animal agency can function as a basis for developing new forms of interspecies politics. In chapter 5, "Animals and the State: Citizenship, Sovereignty, and Reformulating Politics," I further explore the relation between groups of non-human animals and human political communities through a discussion of recent proposals for citizenship and sovereignty for non-human animals, and critiques from the perspective of republicanism. I also discuss examples of new ways of relating to other animals, as found in existing institutions, which can function as beginnings for further reformulating laws and political practices such as labor rights, habitat rights, and urban planning. Chapter 6, "Worm Politics," moves the discussion to political relations between humans and earthworms to investigate the relevance of species membership for interaction, and to further clarify the borders of the political and political action. The second case study, "Goose Politics: Resistance, Deliberation, and the Politics of Space," focuses on goose-human relations in the Netherlands. I investigate the goose-human conflict around Schiphol Airport and, based on the insights developed in the second part of this book, I argue that goose agency needs to be taken into account for normative and practical reasons. I also shed light on how goose agency can be translated to existing political practices and institutions.

The third and final part of the book draws on the insights into language and politics developed in the first two parts to investigate how existing political practices and institutions can be extended to incorporate non-human animal political voices, and to explore new ways of interacting with other animals politically. Chapter 7, "Animal Activism and Interspecies Change," focuses on the role of non-human animals as agents of social and political change. Acknowledging this agency is important in order not to reinforce silencing mechanisms, and can open up new ways of thinking about social and political change, as well as contributing to imagining and creating new interspecies communities. In chapter 8, "Animal Democracy and the Challenges of Political Participation," I discuss why political participation is important for different groups of non-human animals, and how we can further improve political non-human animal participation. In the final chapter, "Deliberating Animals: From Multispecies Dialogues to Interspecies Deliberation," I develop an interspecies understanding of deliberation in order to bridge the distance between existing dialogues between human and non-human animals and human political systems. In the conclusion, "Thinking with Animals," I discuss thinking and writing with other animals. I also offer recommendations for further research.

PART I

Speaking with Animals

1

The Animal, What a Word!

Human Language and Non-Human Animals

As cosmographers report, there have been nations that have had a dog as their king. This means that the humans in these countries had to be able to interpret canine voices and actions. According to French Renaissance philosopher Michel de Montaigne ([1595] 1958), who wrote about these nations (1958, 331), this is not really difficult to do—while it is not perfect, we have some tolerable apprehension of what other animals mean, and "so have beasts of us, much the same. They caress us, threaten us, and beg of us, and we do the same to them" (1958, 331). Non-human animals have a full and absolute communication amongst themselves, Montaigne continues, which is not limited to sounds. They also express themselves by actions, and, just as human lovers do, "speak all things by their eyes" (ibid.). Other animals also speak to humans in this manner, as humans do to them.

Brutes are rational animals, who show justice in relations amongst each other, and to whom humans owe justice. At least they are according to the ancient Greek philosopher Porphyry, who wrote one of the first works ever on ethical vegetarianism ([268–70 BC] 1823). He wrote that reason is imperfect in other animals, but they are nevertheless not completely devoid of it (1823, Book 3). Rational capacities also differ between humans, and we should view rationality not as something you either have or do not have, but rather as something you can have more or less of. The same applies to language. When non-human animals "speak to each other, these sounds are manifest and significant to them, though they are not known to all of us" (1823, 79). This is similar for other animals—Porphyry mentions crows who understand each other, and who might see us as irrational because they do not understand all our utterances (1823, 98). Other animals do understand a lot of what we say, and they can learn from one another and from us. If we observe them for a long time, grow up with them, or simply share habitats, we can learn to understand them better. Porphyry gives the example of a shepherd who knows what sheep want by the sound of their voices (1823, 99), and inhabitants of Attica who understand the sounds of crows in their area better than the language of Persians or Syrians (1823, 98). According to him, it is also important to note that silence is not necessarily indicative of a lack of cognitive capacity; the gods also indicate their will silently (1823, 98).

Montaigne's and Porphyry's ideas about the continuity between non-human and human animals, including the use of language and the possibility of relations between humans and other animals, are not common in the Western philosophical tradition. Humans are generally seen as fundamentally different from other animals (Steiner 2010, Tyler 2012), and language is usually defined as human language. Defining language as exclusively human is usually interconnected with seeing a clear break between humans and other animals (Aaltola 2013; Derrida 2008, 2009, 2011). This does not refer to a biological (Darwin 1872) or universal (Derrida 2008) truth, but springs from cultural practices in a discourse that sees humans as more important than other animals, and as the standard by which non-human animals are measured (Calarco 2008, 2015; Derrida 2008). This way of perceiving and interacting with the world is generally known as anthropocentrism: the belief that considers humans to be the most important beings in the universe, and that interprets the world on the basis of human experiences and values. This view is common in Western cultures, in which human superiority over other animals is taken for granted and perceived as neutral and natural (see also chapter 4). Viewing humans as categorically different from, and more important than, other animals is, however, neither natural nor inevitable, but part of cultural practices that have been shaped by power relations (Wadiwel 2015). Viewing language as exclusively human is similarly a cultural construction and not a universal truth (Derrida 2008), as I will discuss in more detail below. Ascribing use of language only to humans is common in the Western philosophical tradition.

Recent research into non-human animal languages supports the view that the differences between human and non-human animals with regard to language, cognition, and culture are differences of degree and not of kind (Bekoff 2002; Crane 2015; Meijer 2016; Peterson 2012; Slobodchikoff 2012; Smuts 2001; see also Darwin 1872). Developing a non-anthropocentric view of language, as well as addressing other forms of non-human animal exclusion more generally, however, means more than simply demonstrating that other animals are like humans in significant respects. It also demands a reformulation of those concepts that are defined by exclusion, such as language. In order to be able to do this, we first need to take a closer look at the history of these concepts to better understand how existing ideas about non-human animals and their languages are formed and how they are connected. This critical investigation can then function as a starting point for the building of new relations with other animals. Including non-human animal perspectives in the processes of such change is necessary, because otherwise it would once again be a matter of humans deciding what is best for other animals. In chapters 2 and 3, I focus on this positive movement, and concentrate on rethinking animal languages, ways to study them, and the building of common worlds with other animals.

In this chapter, I trace the interconnections between the concepts "language" and "animal," to get a better understanding of how existing ideas about non-human animals and language are formed, and of how non-human animal exclusion is intertwined with our understanding of language.[1] I then problematize these understandings and investigate how we can move beyond them, doing so in three steps. In the next section, I focus on the interconnections between language, reason, and "the animal" by discussing the relation between human language and non-human animal exclusion in the work of René Descartes and Martin Heidegger. These philosophers both saw a clear distinction between humans and other animals, partly due to the fact that other animals do not use human language, as well as a view of reason as exclusively human. In the writings of Descartes we find a clear example of how making the perceived rational superiority of humans—as expressed in human language—the standard by which other animals are measured constitutes a discourse in which non-human animals are not able to express themselves meaningfully; they cannot respond to what is asked of them because the questions are framed in such a way that they are excluded. In Heidegger's view, which stems from a very different theoretical starting point than that of Descartes, humans are also separated from all other animals ontologically, again largely due to the defining of language as exclusively human. This leads to a situation in which non-human animals are seen as not having the same privileged understanding of themselves as beings in the world as do humans, which has far reaching consequences for their existence, and leads to a situation in which they cannot build meaningful common worlds with humans and vice versa. In the second section of this chapter, I turn to the work of Jacques Derrida, who provides an alternative way of thinking about non-human animals and language, one which not only complicates the stereotypical views about the animal that we find in part of the philosophical tradition, but also critically examines the construction of the human subject to which it is connected. While his critique is valuable, and offers a good starting point for rethinking relations, it provides only a negative view of non-human animals, language, and human-animal relations. This is unfortunate, because in order to adequately address anthropocentrism, we need first to redefine these concepts in and through interaction with non-human animals. In the final section of the chapter, I therefore sketch the beginnings of an alternative.

Human Language and the Animal

Defining language and reason as solely human capacities is often linked to seeing humans as fundamentally different from non-human animals, and can lead to excluding the latter from the moral and political realms. Perhaps the most extreme conclusions in these regards are found in the work of René Descartes, who introduced certain key questions about human and non-human animals (Derrida 2008; Melehy 2006). Descartes saw non-human animals as a type of machine—he called them "*bêtes-machines*"—because they cannot think, an idea that follows from the fact that they do not speak using human language.[2] In a 1646 letter to the Marquess of Newcastle, he explains this as follows: non-human animals can react to words that are spoken by humans, which is an expression of their passions. For example, a magpie can say goodbye to "its mistress."[3] According to Descartes, the magpie does not think when doing this, but simply expresses the hope of eating. He saw a similar pattern in dogs, horses, and monkeys: what they are taught to perform is always an expression of some passion and therefore they can perform it without any thought. Because other animals can express their passions, they would also be able to express their thoughts if they had any. But they never express thoughts in words, from which we can conclude that they never have thoughts. Descartes understands that not all non-human animals can speak in human language, but the ones who cannot do so physically show no sign of attempting to use any other means to express their thoughts. Non-human animals demonstrate that they lack any language with which to express themselves because they do not respond when a human asks them a question. They might react, but they never respond; they never show humans that they understand what they are saying (Descartes [1638] 1985). In addition to the fact that other animals never respond with words or signs to what is asked of them, they do not learn to imitate humans; they do not try to be as humans are, from which, according to Descartes, we can also conclude that they do not think (ibid.).

Descartes argues that everyone who observes non-human animals sees these two things that set them apart from human actions, namely that they do not respond and do not imitate humans. Therefore no one could judge that there was in them a true sentiment or true passion (see also Derrida 2008, 83). Their passions are, in contrast, purely mechanical reactions to impulses. Descartes compares these to clocks. According to Descartes, perception is unreliable, and this view of non-human animal minds is a judgment, not a sentiment or perception. Another judgment follows from the judgment that other animals do not think: that they do not have true sentiments or passions, from which follows that they function as machines.

These ideas are not just statements about non-human animals. Descartes delineates both what is meant by "animal" and what is meant by "response"—similar to the way in which language, human, and the political community are defined in relation to each other in Aristotle's work (Derrida 2008, 84; Melehy 2006). In one movement, Descartes draws a line between humans and other animals, and between reaction and response, in which "response" is understood as responding to questions asked by humans in such a way as to demonstrate one's capacity to think. He does so not by providing an answer to the question of whether or not non-human animals actually think, but by rephrasing the question, which reformulates the discourse surrounding animals (Derrida 2008, 83). This becomes clear when we compare his views to those of

Montaigne concerning non-human animals. Montaigne ([1595] 1958) argues that different species of animal have their own language, and that communication is possible between members of different species.[4] Humans cannot see or understand the internal motions and secrets of other animals; this is, however, not a defect on the part of the animals, it is mutual, and it would be vanity for humans to think otherwise. Different species have different (complex) languages, as do different groups of humans. The fact that humans might not be able to speak with other animals as they can speak with other humans does not mean that humans are incapable of understanding what they mean, and vice versa. In response, Descartes ([1646] 1991) argues that humans cannot attribute thought or understanding to animals, because they imitate humans only in those actions that are not guided by human thoughts, thereby introducing skepticism as regards their minds, and presenting their minds as closed off from humans because they do not speak in human language. According to Descartes, humans only demonstrate that they are not machines, but have souls and think, by speaking.

The difference between Montaigne and Descartes is not simply a difference in perception or observation, but rather a difference in method and in understanding of the underlying concepts (Melehy 2006). Montaigne writes about other animals as subjects, and compares human groups to groups of non-human animals; for example, he points to the similarities in difficulties in understanding non-human animals, Basques, and the indigenous inhabitants of Brazil. This inability to completely understand others is, furthermore, not just a problem when we encounter other communities: because of the ambiguities in human language, we also cannot have certainty in understanding humans from our own communities. Montaigne twice remarks there is more difference between two humans than between a human and any given beast (1958, 332, 334). In contrast to this phenomenological approach, Descartes searches for an unambiguous truth. He proposes a new method for doing philosophy, by which he aims to find a fundamental set of principles that are true beyond doubt. He shifts the focus from perception to deduction and puts the thinking I—the cogito—at the center of truth and knowledge, separated from the body and expressed in an idealized view of human language. The cogito is immaterial and eternal and is contrasted with the body, which functions as a machine. Other animals are simply bodies that function as machines, without language, thought, or soul. The truth can only be found through reason, expressed in human language, presuming a fixed subject (spirit). In all of these aspects, Descartes sees a clear line between humans and other animals (Derrida 2008; Melehy 2006).

Traces of Descartes's ideas are found in many existing practices and discourses concerning animal sentience, cognition, and language. Here I will focus on two: the concept of "instinct" and the practice of animal experimentation, both of which I will discuss in more detail in the next chapter. It is commonplace to accept the distinction between instinct and intelligence, and to associate "animal" with "instinct" and "human" with "intelligence" (Brentari 2016).[5] So-called "lower desires" are seen as instinctual and as an expression of the animal side of mankind, and instinct is considered a kind of automatic, mechanical drive that is built in to various animals. As with other concepts, however, this concept has a history, and it expresses and has shaped how we view humans and other animals. Seneca wrote about complex animal acts that took place without reflection (Beach 1955), and in early Christian theological work the concept of instinct began to play a role in developing a normative distinction between body and soul (ibid.). We find an early example of this in the work of Thomas Aquinas (Brentari 2016), where the concept was, however, not used exclusively to understand animal behavior, but rather as a motivational term, pointing to an external source of motivation that might range from heavenly inspiration to the influence of the stars. This meaning changed under the influence of Descartes, who as we have seen made a distinction between body and soul, and saw other animals as mechanical beings. This model of two functional systems (Brentari 2016) has led to the view of instinct that we have today, and has also contributed to our view of other animals as automata, who lack thought and act only on passions. This has led not only to privileging humans, and to a too-sharp distinction between human and animal; it has also led to spontaneous behavior being seen as less valuable—in both humans and other animals—while current studies in moral psychology show that much of our moral behavior is habitual and instinctive (see also Donaldson and Kymlicka 2015b). Philosopher Brian Massumi (2014) further nuances the concept of "instinct" by arguing that all so-called "instinctive" behaviors also necessarily have an element of creativity; for example, flight behavior must have an element of improvisation, because if every animal of a certain species were to flee in exactly the same way, predators could learn this and would be able to anticipate it. Expression, or the power of variation and improvisation, is in this view equiprimordial with instinct.

Viewing other animals as mechanical objects has also led humans to develop practices in which using them as such for human goals is acceptable. According to Descartes, non-human animals have no reason and no soul, and are not therefore able to experience pain. He compares them to clockwork: when one sticks a knife into a living dog, the dog will scream, but this is simply a mechanical response. Descartes thus saw no harm in dissecting living non-human animals for the sake of science, and was a proponent of vivisection. Furthermore, his views on non-human animal sentience legitimized certain experiments by scientists of his time (Adams and Donovan 1995, 221; Guerrini 2003). Laboratory animals are still seen and used today as objects that can provide humans with information about human subjects, even though few currently doubt that they are sentient. While scientists need to become attuned to their objects of study and pay close attention to their behavior in order to obtain meaningful results (Haraway 2008), it is the results that primarily matter to humans, and the animals studied are not formally recognized as subjects, so the interaction is asymmetrical (chapter 6). The non-human animals studied are treated as resources, not as cobeings. Viewing other animals as objects whose bodies and minds can be used to answer questions about human subjects also has an effect on the research questions formulated, which in turn has an effect on how we view them, because these questions set the scope for the space in which the other animals can answer. An illustration of this can be found in language research, which I will discuss in more detail in the next chapter. Because humans are taken as the standard, and human language seen as the one authentic language, the capacity for language use in other animals has long been investigated by trying to establish how well the non-human animals in question can learn to speak or understand human language. This served only to reinforce stereotypical views about their ability to speak and think, because many of them obviously did not do well. It also closed off possibilities of finding out about their languages, cultures, and inner lives.

In order to adequately challenge these practices and the views of non-human animals that underpin them, we need to do more than simply argue that other animals are sentient, or similar to humans in significant respects. We must also critically review existing ideas about non-human animal cognition, languages, and cultures, and the role that anthropocentrism has played in how they were constructed. This also implies reconsidering our view of "the human" and exploring the differences and similarities between humans and other animals, a project begun by writers such as Montaigne.

Language and World

One of the things that human and non-human animals have in common is that we share a world—a real world, the planet Earth on which we all live. Other things that we have in common are that we have bodies, are vulnerable, were all born, and that we will all die. In *The Beast and the Sovereign II*, Derrida writes that no one will seriously deny animals the possibility of inhabiting the world, or of co-inhabiting the world with humans (2011, 365). Because of their phenomenological differences, however, humans and other animals often perceive the world differently. Combined with the view discussed above that humans are the only species to possess *logos*, to have reason and the ability to speak, this has led many philosophers in the humanist tradition to argue that humans have a privileged understanding of the world. One of the most prominent proponents of this position was Martin Heidegger, who saw a sharp distinction between humans and other animals, which according to him was interconnected with their perceived lack of language, with clear consequences for their relation to being in the world and our relation to them.

In his lecture series *The Fundamental Concepts of Metaphysics: World, Finitude, Solitude* ([1929] 1995), Heidegger put forward a threefold thesis: the stone is worldless, the animal is poor-in-world, and the human is world-forming.[6] Stones do not have access to the world at all. Animals have access to the world in that they experience it, but they do not have access to the world as such. Heidegger gives the example of a lizard lying on a rock: the lizard experiences lying on something, but "we ought to cross out the word 'rock' in order to indicate that whatever the lizard is lying on is certainly given in some way for the lizard, and yet is not known to the lizard as a rock" (1995, 198). Drawing on the work of biologists of his time, most notably Hans Driesch and Jakob von Uexküll, Heidegger argued that non-human animals are captive in their environment; they cannot break out of the ring that forms their environment because they are absorbed by it. In contrast, (human) Dasein can relate to the world as world, to the Being of things, and to itself as Dasein. Dasein exists, where non-human animals merely live; therefore Dasein can die, while animals simply perish. Because other animals lack the as-such, they also lack *logos*, and, linked to that, language, since *logos* is founded on (or in the possibility of) the as-such.[7] Thus, non-human and human animals are separated by an "abyss" ([1947] 1993, 248). This abyss is the (assumed) lack of as-structure in the non-human animal (Iveson 2010). The difference between humans and other animals is not a difference in degree, but a difference in kind (Calarco 2008, 22). Heidegger, however, stresses this lack is not a "less"; it is not hierarchical or teleological, it is a different mode of being (Derrida 2008, 156).

For Dasein, language is a way of being in the world and having access to that world. Humans are not only living beings who possess language; language is the "house of being in which the human being ek-sists by dwelling, in that he belongs to the truth of being, guarding it" (Heidegger [1947] 1993, 254). This movement works in two directions. Through language, Dasein has access to world and Being; language forms Dasein and is formed by it. Language is not just the expression of an organism, but the "clearing-concealing advent of Being itself" (ibid.), therefore it cannot be thought of in purely symbolic or signifying terms. Instead we should think of language "from its correspondence to being and indeed as this correspondence, that is, as the home of the human being's essence" (1947, 254). Language is here once again seen as human language; other animals might communicate, but they do not have this relation of expressing the world and building the world through their utterances.[8] The consequences of their perceived lack of language for their way of being in the world are far-reaching: they cannot understand themselves as beings in the world, they lack *Mitsein*, the capacity to be with others, and they even cannot die—they simply perish.

The abyss between humans and other animals has been challenged in different ways. The most straightforward seems to be to argue that other animals are similar to humans in significant ways, but this does not challenge the idea of the human norm being used as a standard, nor does it challenge the interpretation of language and reason linked to this image of the human. It also does not do justice to the many differences between various beings—between humans and other animals, between human groups, between individuals, and so on. In this context, Jacques Derrida (2008, 2009, 2011) questions the capacity of the human subject to understand the world as such. He argues that for Heidegger, as for his predecessors, the question of the animal is always intertwined with the question of what it means to think, and the animal is used to demarcate the human subject. He sees problems with this demarcation as being on different levels. First, the idea that "animals" constitute a single category obscures the large differences within this group. Second, Heidegger does not seriously envision *Mitsein* with other animals (2008, 158). Third, the structure Heidegger proposes is, according to Derrida, hierarchical, even though Heidegger claims it is not (Derrida 1991, 55–56). Finally, he questions whether or not human subjects are capable of seeing things as they truly are (Derrida 2008, 160), and he criticizes the existence of a universal "as-such" (Derrida 2008, 459). According to Derrida, to overcome these problems we need a radical reinterpretation of what is living, which calls for a new way of philosophizing.

While Heidegger's views of animals and language may seem radical, non-human animals are still often seen as categorically different from humans and incapable of speaking, in both philosophy and society, and this is interconnected with different forms of epistemic and institutional violence. As mentioned above, animal advocates usually challenge the exclusion of non-human animals by arguing that they are like humans in morally significant respects. While this clearly questions who counts as a subject, and while awarding rights to non-human animals would have far-reaching social and political implications, this approach still takes the human norm as the standard by which the worth of other animals is measured, running the risk of repeating violence to those who are different and of reinforcing anthropocentrism. While many non-human animals share important characteristics with humans with regard to cognition, emotion, language, and culture, and while humans and other animals do form communities, differences remain. Furthermore, using the human norm as the starting point for defining reason and language or for moral consideration is not a neutral step, but is formed by power relations (chapter 4). As we have seen, language has often been defined as human language by excluding other animals, and this has had consequences for the ways in which they are studied and viewed. If we want to address anthropocentrism, we therefore also need to critically review the concept of language in relation to ideas of the human. A good starting point for this can be found in the work of Derrida (2008, 2009, 2011), which I will discuss in the next section.

The Animal, What a Word!

"Animal" and Animals

The starting point for modern animal ethics is often identified in the following words at the end of a footnote by philosopher Jeremy Bentham: "The question is not: can they speak, nor can they reason, but: can they suffer?" ([1823] 1907, 143–144). As a utilitarian, Bentham argued that sentience, and not reason, is what counts in our moral decisions, and he defended the idea that, in moral considerations, equal interests have equal value. The "number of one's legs," or the "villosity of one's skin," should not play a role in this. Philosopher Peter Singer's *Animal Liberation* (1975) stems directly from Bentham's utilitarian principles, and draws on this statement to argue that belonging to a certain species is not in itself morally relevant: discrimination on the basis of belonging to a certain species is speciesism. According to Singer, we should treat equal interests alike, including non-human animal interests. This view forms the foundation of most existing animal rights theories. Derrida (2008, 27) also turns to Bentham's footnote, but he draws attention to the fact that Bentham argues not only for taking non-human animal interests into account morally, but also for the relevance of recognizing suffering. Derrida therefore sees Bentham's footnote as a change in question, which he considers to be at the same time radical and based on common sense, because humans are affected by non-human animal suffering—the counterpoint to Descartes, who moved away from this common sense response to other animals.

Derrida regards this emphasis on suffering as a way to break out of the discourse on the animal through which *logos* is constructed. Bentham's proposal to take suffering as the starting point in our moral relations with other animals has two sides. On the one hand, it refers to the actual suffering of actual animals, and not just of all creatures who fall into the general category of "animal"; it is an appeal to a feeling of compassion for fellow creatures, the possibility of suffering for them and with them. On the other hand, it moves the focus from whatever the animals can and cannot do or be—from their actions and powers—to their responses. According to Derrida, all doubts and questions that surround issues of *logos*, thought, and language disappear when we turn to the notion of suffering. "No one can deny the suffering, fear, or panic, the terror of fright that can seize certain animals and that we humans can witness" (2008, 28). Traditionally, the animal has not only been denied the right to speak, but also the opportunity to answer because of how language is delineated, and because language and reason are seen as powers one either does or does not possess. Taking the ability to suffer as the central notion reframes the question, and allows animals to answer. Suffering is, of course, not completely passive, and there is a contradiction in the question "can they suffer?," because it is at once active (can) and passive (suffer). Humans are also affected, and they can suffer from the suffering of others.

It is important to note that there is no collective "animal" that suffers, acts, or responds. Non-human animals do not and cannot speak as one person with one voice—thinking this would yet again deprive them of a response. Language, and the word "animal," deceives us. The word "animal" categorizes all non-human animals and distances humans from other animals (Derrida 2008, 31). Seeing all other animals as one group in contrast to humans reinforces anthropocentrism, which contributes to the legitimization of practices in which other animals are used for human benefit. Derrida argues that instead of one line between Man on the one side and Animal on the other, there is a multiple and heterogeneous border (2008, 31); beyond the edge of the "so-called human" (ibid.), we find a heterogeneous multiplicity of the living. To account for this multitude, he proposes to use the word "animot." In speech it refers to the plural, the multiplicity of animals, which is necessary because there is no one "animal." The "mot" in "animot" refers to the act of naming and the stakes involved in drawing a distinction between human and animal by the human. It reminds us of the fact that it is a word for animals, not a reference to an existing group of animals.

Acknowledging this multitude of other animals does not, however, mean that philosophy can just throw the difference between humans and other animals overboard. Derrida phrases this as follows: "To suppose that I, or anyone else for that matter, could ignore that rupture, indeed that abyss, would mean first of all blinding oneself to so much contrary evidence; and, as far as my own modest case is concerned, it would mean forgetting all the signs that I have managed to give, tirelessly, of my attention to difference, to differences, to heterogeneities and abyssal ruptures as against the homogeneous and the continuous" (2008, 30). This remark may seem puzzling and problematic in light of Derrida's refusal to see "animal" as one group (Calarco 2008). There are three reasons why it is not. First, Derrida emphasizes the power relations that have formed current interpretations of "the human." A naturalistic ethic, an empirical refutation of empirical claims stating that other animals are like humans, will not suffice. This would leave the structure of the debate intact, and could lead to measuring the worth of other animals on the basis of their resemblance to humans (Wolfe 2003). Second, and relatedly, "the multiple and heterogeneous border of this abyssal rupture" (Derrida 2008, 32) has a history. If we deny the abyss between human and animal that is so prominently present in the history of Western philosophy, we fail to challenge the discourse that produced it, which is necessary for thinking about alternatives. Third, Derrida argues that there is a multiplicity of organizations of relations that are at once "intertwined and abyssal" (ibid.). There is not one difference, not one abyss between human and animal, but a multitude of differences. Forgetting these differences would run the risk of flattening all individuals into the category "same."[9] Instead we need to think about how to interact with those who are different.

Derrida rightly directs our attention to the fact that instead of one difference, there are many differences that must be taken into account in thinking about human and non-human animals. Other animals need to be thought of in their own right, not on the basis of how much they resemble humans or how close they are to humans. It is important to note that in thinking about non-human animals, belonging to a certain species is not the defining characteristic of an individual. Each individual, human or non-human, belongs to different groups, with regard to gender, age, species, race, and so on. Species membership might matter under certain circumstances—for example, in thinking about habitat rights—and be less relevant in others—such as in forming friendships. Humans and other animals sometimes have close relations, and may even form communities. Non-human animals have their own species-specific languages, dialects, and cultural traditions (see chapter 2), but when animals of different species form communities, interspecies cultural norms and ways of creating meaning come into being and evolve. This happens at the level of society, for example, when dogs and humans became attuned to one another in processes of domestication (Haraway 2008); it can also happen on an individual level (Howard 1952; Smuts 2001), or in small interspecies communities (Howard 1952; Kerasote 2008).

While Derrida's critical analysis of the construction of the concepts "animal" and "language" in the philosophical tradition is convincing, he does not offer a framework for thinking about non-human animal languages, interspecies languages, or positive human-animal relations. In his discussion of Heidegger, he argues that addressing unjust power relations cannot be a matter of "giving speech back" to animals.[10] This would, according to him, leave the structure of the problem intact, because by offering this capacity to them, it would again be the human who determines the framework in which other animals can operate. The structure of inclusion and exclusion that this framework relies upon would not be challenged. While his critique of Heidegger is convincing, Derrida does not envision or explicate being with other animals in a different way, nor does he seriously discuss communication with other animals. This follows from his method of deconstruction, in which he shows that certain distinctions that are seen as constitutive are impossible to uphold. But it also seems to exaggerate the importance of species membership in building relations and communities, and in being able to speak.

Because he only focuses on the negative and does not build a positive framework in which we can rethink multispecies relations, Derrida also fails to offer a starting point for rethinking the meaning of concepts with other animals, which is necessary if we want to move beyond anthropocentrism. This runs the risk of reinforcing a view of other animals as silent, which is ontologically problematic and has consequences for the social and political position of other animals. Furthermore, it does not take into account that other animals do speak, whether or not humans acknowledge the fact.

Speaking Back

Derrida's cat sits in the bathroom and looks at him. "I must immediately make it clear," he writes, "the cat I am talking about is a real cat, truly, believe me, a little cat. It isn't the figure of a cat. It doesn't silently enter the bedroom as an allegory for all the cats on the earth, the felines that traverse our myths and religions, literature and fables" (2008, 6). This real cat's gaze makes him uncomfortable, which is the starting point for his reflections. The cat sits there while Derrida writes about human and non-human animals, about the human and the animal—he returns to her every now and then.

In response to Heidegger's view that only human animals understand themselves as being, possess language, and have a world, Derrida argues that there are no such things as a "human" or an "animal," and that we should problematize the kind of understanding that humans have of their own condition—as regards reason, language, death, and so on. There are different ways of understanding one's surroundings, responding to them, and being in the world more generally. This appeal to "pluralizing and varying the 'as such'" (2008, 160) is important, and we should indeed understand that humans do not have the powers they like to think they have—we are as vulnerable as other animals, and our knowledge is always limited by our sensory mechanisms, ways of being situated socially and politically, or more generally, by our specific ways of being. However, Derrida also argues that we should not simply give speech back to animals, an argument that, once we read it together with his interpretation of his cat companion's behavior, seems itself to carry traces of the problem it tries to address. The idea that humans have the power to give speech back to animals implies a hierarchy—the human decides who gets what—and also implies that other animals do not currently speak.[11] For Derrida, this power is never ultimate and can never not be deconstructed, but here he is still seeing language as exclusively human, something that is also evident in how he approaches interaction with other animals. There are three problems with this view.

First of all, it is important to recognize that there is a close relationship between language and intersubjectivity. Speech and language can and do create common, interspecies worlds, and are ways of expressing these. Non-human animals express themselves, and these expressions need to be taken into account if we want to adequately address how they have been silenced in the philosophical tradition, and more especially if we want to move beyond that. Derrida describes in detail how his cat companion looks at him while he is in the bathroom, naked. The gaze of the cat affects him; it makes him feel naked and ashamed. The cat looks at him but does not speak, he looks at the cat but does not speak to her, nor does he touch her or communicate with her in any other way (Haraway 2008; Warkentin 2010). Looking at someone, making eye contact or avoiding eye contact, is an act of communication. Derrida does not mention eye contact with the cat; the situation is fixed and silent like a film still. We see a scene with a naked man and a cat, told from the perspective of the man. We do not know whether the cat wants to leave the room, if she is hungry, upset, or if she wants to play. There is no interaction, and therefore no space for the cat to give meaning to the situation. The cat is merely an animal mirror in which Derrida sees himself reflected, naked. If the human is the only party to the interaction who thinks about their difference, the non-human animal individual remains dependent on the human to interpret and acknowledge her presence. In his discussion of Bentham, Derrida appreciates the change in question, the move to receiving, suffering, answering, and the power in these seemingly passive acts. His response to the gaze of the cat is an illustration of this; he cannot help becoming embarrassed and feeling ashamed. But although he describes many different—real and imaginary—animals in detail,[12] he never mentions an actual non-human animal responding to him, and there is no mention of a dialogue between humans and other animals. This is unfortunate, because other animals do express themselves and can be consulted. In order to create a meaningful dialogue, we need to ask other animals questions and respond to them, not just look at them looking at us.

The second objection to Derrida's remark is that there is political power in explicating animal speech and voice, and in addressing the epistemic dimensions of violence inherent in viewing non-human animals as silent (chapter 4). Who speaks, who is heard, and who determines this are important questions in political interspecies interactions. As we have already seen, there is a strong connection between anthropocentrism—seeing language as exclusively human—and the borders of the political community. Viewing other animals as silent and incapable of language and speech—which is often connected to other negative stereotypes, such as seeing them as unruly, unreasonable, or just plain stupid—reinforces their status as objects that we can treat in any way we wish. Furthermore, defining language as human language and excluding other animals from it by definition leads to a situation in which there is no common language with which they can address the harms done to them,[13] even though they do communicate with us and try to make themselves known (Derrida 2008; Lyotard 1988; Meijer 2016). Investigating how other animals have been silenced as social groups[14] can help to clarify power relations. Animal activists often point out similarities between human and non-human animals, and stress that other animals are subjects with their own views on life. Drawing attention to their languages and bringing to light what they say to us has great potential for improving their social and political status (chapter 7). Speaking for them and letting them speak for themselves are both important, and language is an essential tool in working towards change and developing new forms of political interaction.

The third objection arises as regards the meaning of "speech" in "giving speech back to animals." What is meant by speech—who speaks and who has been allowed to speak—has changed over time, and differs between human and non-human, Western and non-Western cultures. It will change again, under the influence of social movements, cultural changes, and, in the case of non-human animals, empirical research. Exploring the history of existing concepts can function as a tool in envisioning change. In order to move away from anthropocentrism, however, we need to begin to reconsider the meaning of these concepts with other animals.

Rethinking Language with Other Animals

Rethinking language with other animals starts from two directions. First, it is important to recognize that humans and other animals share languages, or language games, in which non-human animals exercise agency. I will discuss this in more detail in the next chapter. Second, existing human concepts are already influenced by animals of different species, because humans and other animals coexist and coevolve. Raimond Gaita (2002) argues for taking the public character of language into account in interspecies communities. He gives the example of intentions (2002, 60) and states that it is wrong to think that this is a human concept that we do, or do not, apply to other animals. Rather, the meaning of "intention" is formed by interaction with, and influenced by, the behavior of different kinds of animals; humans learn what it means by watching the intentions of other animals and humans, by reading about the intentions of others in books, and by understanding their own intentions as intentions. In this view, stating that other animals have intentions is not anthropomorphic, not because of its truth value as a judgment of the mental states of other animals, but because animal intentions are part of what gives the concept "intention" its meaning. Because the meaning of concepts comes into being and can be subject to change in interactions with other animals, communicating with them in new ways can change this meaning. Humans can experience this at an individual level; if one grows up only with humans, a concept such as love might be mostly understood as love in relation to humans, something that a close relationship with an individual of another species in later life can change. But it can also take place at a social and political level; the concept of "rights" changes meaning— the way that it does with women's rights—when animal rights are discussed, and would change meaning again if they were to be implemented in society and were further developed in interaction with other animals (chapter 8).

Rethinking language involves more than rethinking human concepts. Other animals have their own species-specific languages, something that will be discussed in more detail in the next chapter. Using the word "language" to describe communication with and between non-human animals is, however, contentious. It is seen as problematic in animal philosophy because of the anthropocentric history of the concept of "language" (see, for example, Calarco 2008; Derrida 2008) and in other fields of study it is often seen as anthropomorphic. Humans who argue for taking other animals into account in moral and political decisions are often accused of anthropomorphism, of attributing human characteristics to non-human animals (Donaldson and Kymlicka 2013a). This usually refers back to skepticism about other animals' minds, which is often connected to the fact that most of them do not speak in human language (chapter 3). It is argued that humans can never gain insight into the emotions and language of members of other species precisely because they belong to different species and their perception of the world is radically different. A primary problem with this view is that it is unclear why species membership is a relevant characteristic in understanding someone else; there are many differences between individuals from different groups, and while these differences may influence possibilities for understanding, meaning is always generated between different perspectives and comes into being through interaction, not by referring to a pre-given truth. Species membership matters, but so do other characteristics. Second, sharing a language is no guarantee of understanding someone; human language can, for example, also deceive, and the risk of misunderstanding is always inherent in communicating with others. A third objection is that it does not take the public character of language into account (see chapters 2 & 3). Finally, the seemingly neutral stance of denying other animals certain emotions and mental states is also value-laden, and, more specifically, a Western cultural construction (Aaltola 2013; Brooks Pribac 2013; see also chapter 3). "Anthropodenial" (De Waal 2016) is not a neutral stance, and has long colored judgments about other animals (see chapter 2 for its influence on language research).

Seeing non-human animal languages as languages and exploring what language means in the case of non-human animals and in interspecies interactions can help us to see them in a new way and better understand aspects of their behavior; it can also help us get a better grasp of what "language" can mean. Investigating how language and concepts tied to human language use such as grammar, which are thought to be solely human, can also apply to the interactions and expressions of other animals, and can, in a similar way, bring to light elements in species-specific as well as interspecies interactions that have been obscured by denying language to other animals. It offers us a new framework for thinking about them, and presents us with new tools for thinking about and building relationships, which can enable us to gain a richer understanding of the concept used. In the next chapter, I focus on non-human animal languages in order to further develop a non-anthropocentric view of language. In chapter 3, I shift the focus to the relation between language and world, and the role of language in creating common worlds with other animals.

2

Animal Languages

Gua was born in Cuba in 1930. Psychologists Luella and Winthrop Kellogg took her into their house when she was seven and a half months old. They planned to raise her alongside their son, Donald, who was ten months old at the time. Winthrop Kellogg was interested in the comparative psychology of primates, and the Kelloggs had moved to Florida to work with psychologist and primatologist Robert Yerkes of the Yerkes Primate Center. Gua was given to the center with her parents in early 1931, and soon afterwards she moved in with the Kellogg family. They used her to conduct a new type of experiment, one in which they wanted to teach her to speak in human language. The aim of the study was to investigate whether language use was a product of nature or nurture. Even though Gua was a fast learner in many respects and surpassed Donald in many practical tasks (*Montreal Gazette* 1954), she did not learn to speak using human words, and when Donald started to copy her sounds, the Kelloggs ended the experiment. Gua, who was sixteen months old at the time, was taken back to the Yerkes Primate Center for further study, where she died of pneumonia less than a year later. A similar experiment was conducted by scientists Keith and Catherine Hayes, who took chimpanzee Viki into their home and used intensive speech therapy, in which they manually manipulated her lower jaw, to teach her to voice four words: "mama," "papa," "up," and "cup."

Because Gua, Viki, and chimpanzees in other studies—similar experiments were carried out in laboratories—had not learned to speak, it was assumed that non-human primates either lacked the cognitive ability to learn to speak, or were physically incapable of it, which led to a modification of the experiment: instead of speech, chimpanzees were taught sign language. This technique was more successful. Chimpanzee Washoe (Hillix and Rumbaugh 2004) was born in the wild and taken from her parents by the American Air Force, initially to be used in space experiments. Beatrix and Alex Gardner took her into their home and raised her as a human child. They dressed her in human clothes, had her dine at the table with them, took her for rides in the car, and took her to the playground. Washoe had books, toys, and her own toothbrush. She soon learned to use signs, with and without direct instruction—the latter by observing humans—and invented her own: for example, she combined the signs for water and bird when she saw a swan. She could also categorize nouns and form simple sentences. When she was five, the Gardners ended the experiment and brought her to the University of Oklahoma's Institute of Primate Studies, where she lived until her death in 2007. While at the Institute, Washoe learned to use around 350 different signs, which she also used to communicate her emotions and thoughts. She recognized herself in the mirror and showed self-awareness, as well as empathy with others. When new students came to work with her, she slowed down the speed of her signing to help them to understand her.

Chimpanzees were not the only primates used in these experiments. Gorilla Koko, who was born in the San Francisco Zoo, was taught to use over a thousand hand signs in Gorilla Sign Language (a version of American Sign Language, modified to fit gorilla hands) (ibid.). Psychologist Francine Patterson, who taught her to use sign language, reports that Koko also understands over two thousand human words. Koko signs about her emotional state and memories, showing she has episodic memory and narrative identity; she likes to make jokes and sometimes tells lies. She is also famous because she had a pet kitten, and grieved for him when he died.

Bonobo Kanzi, who was born at the Yerkes field station at Emory University, taught himself to sign by watching videos of Koko, something his trainer realized when he saw him sign with an anthropologist (ibid.). He was taught to use lexigrams, symbols on a keyboard that are used in the artificial primate language Yerkish, and he has been observed speaking human words. Kanzi likes to eat omelettes and play Pac-Man, and he is a good toolmaker. Non-human primates have been taught grammar in other language experiments. Chimpanzee Sarah, who was born in Africa, was taught to parse and produce streams of tokens that obeyed a simple grammar. Along with three other chimpanzees, she learned to use a board with plastic symbols to analyze syntactic expressions, including if-then-else (ibid.).

In these language experiments, "language" means human language, and non-human animals are used as objects of study to gain knowledge about human language. Recent research in biology and ethology shows that many other non-human animal species have their own complex and nuanced species-specific ways of communicating with members of their own and other species. These studies ask us to reconsider the cognitive, social, and linguistic capacities of other animals, and to reconsider what language is. In the first chapter of this book, the focus was on the critical part of this investigation, tracing the relation between defining language and excluding non-human animals. In this chapter, I focus on non-human animal languages, studying language and the question of how to define language. I draw on recent empirical research into non-human animal languages on the one hand, and Ludwig Wittgenstein's proposal to view language as a set of language games on the other, to develop a non-anthropocentric way of thinking about language and studying animal languages. My aim is not to provide a full theory of non-human animal languages; humans are only just beginning to learn about many non-human animal languages, so it would be empirically impossible to provide a full description or theory of animal language. This would also be undesirable for political reasons, because rethinking language should not be a human endeavor, and it is not up to humans to define what represents meaningful communication for others. We need to learn about language in interaction with other animals in order not to fall into the trap of repeating anthropocentrism. The following investigations are meant as a first step in this process. Even though my aim is not to provide a full theory of language, I do want to show that the question of whether or not other animals use language is legitimate, point to the complexity of their expressions, and demonstrate the similarities between non-human and human languages. I also want to offer a starting point for a different way of thinking about and studying language in an interspecies context.

If we are to adequately study non-human animal languages and develop a non-anthropocentric view of language, we need to move away from seeing language as exclusively human. Wittgenstein's (1958) proposal to view language as language games offers a good starting point for thinking about non-human animal and interspecies languages, as well as for studying language in an interspecies context. Wittgenstein argues that, because of the way in which language works and its interconnection to social practices, we can never give a universal definition of language as a whole, or fixed definitions of separate concepts. Instead, we should investigate the meaning of different language games by exploring how and where they are used. This method of studying language allows us to acknowledge non-human animal agency in language and recognize how non-human animals co-create meaning in relation to members of their own and other species, including humans. Existing human concepts can offer guidelines for understanding the meaning of certain practices and for illuminating relations between human, non-human, and interspecies language games, without pre-determining what counts as language for other animals. Before discussing different non-human animal and inter-species language games in more detail, I now first turn to this movement from seeing language as exclusively human, and studying it as such, to viewing it as a set of animal language games.

From Human Language to Animal Language Games

Studying Human Language in Other Animals

Although writers and philosophers have always speculated about non-human animal behavior and animal minds—or the absence thereof—animal cognition was not taken seriously in science until the end of the nineteenth century, when Charles Darwin (1872) began writing about animal behavior and animal minds (Bekoff 2002, 2007; Slobodchikoff 2012). Darwin emphasized the continuities between species, and he saw the differences between human animal minds and the minds of other animals as differences of degree and not of kind (Darwin 1872). His approach to animal cognition was anecdotal and drew upon his personal observations, as well as stories about non-human animal behavior, which led to criticism regarding their scientific value. In order to avoid this criticism, and to improve the study of animal cognition, the psychologists Thorndike and Pavlov took their research on animal cognition into the laboratory, where they could study the reactions of non-human animals to stimuli in repeatable experiments (Allen and Bekoff 1999). In this way, they studied operant conditioning and classical conditioning respectively. The design of their experiments was heavily influenced by behaviorism, both in research questions and methods, and became the standard for most research into animal behavior until the 1960s. Behaviorism is a philosophy behind the study of behavior that uses methods from the natural sciences and focuses on functional connections between acts and environment, aiming to predict and control behavior. In behaviorism, human and non-human animal minds are studied as black boxes of which the content is not relevant; only outward reactions that can be measured have scientific value. Description of behaviors or interpretations of acts should be avoided. In the 1960s, a cognitive revolution in the study of human minds took place, which also influenced thinking about the minds of other animals. Mental processes that were not immediately observable became part of the study of animal minds, and other animals were increasingly seen as agents with a level of cognitive complexity. The rise of ethology and animal psychology as scientific disciplines also helped to instigate this process. However, the methods used by Thorndike and Pavlov were, and still are, widely used in animal research, and the view of animal minds as black boxes has continued to influence research methods and objectives to the present day.

How studies are set up, and the research questions asked, have a great influence on the outcomes.[1] For instance, they can reinforce anthropocentrism and stereotypical views about non-human animals with regard to capacities for language use. We find an example of this in Project Nim. Following the Washoe experiment, behavioral psychologist Herbert Terrace set out to investigate whether chimpanzees were able to learn to use grammar, or more precisely, whether they had an innate sense of grammar. The project was inspired by the work of linguist and philosopher Noam Chomsky, who argues that the language use in humans is innate, and terms this innate body of genetic linguistic knowledge "Universal Grammar." According to Chomsky, only humans are capable of using language. In the experiment, a chimpanzee with the name Nim Chimpsky was raised in a human foster family and taught to sign. In his education, much attention was given to sentences, grammar, and linguistic structures.[2] Although Nim learned to use about 125 signs, and could use them in simple sentences, Terrace argued that he only learned them by operant conditioning and had no insight into what they meant. In other words, he did not learn their meaning, but simply performed a trick for a reward. This, however, simply reflected the way in which the experiment had been set up and how Nim had been taught to sign; he was given no opportunity to behave otherwise (Hillix and Rumbaugh 2004; see also Slobodchikoff 2012).

There are also more general problems with studying non-human animal cognition and language in laboratories using experiments that treat non-human animals as objects rather than as subjects to be communicated with. Non-human animals in laboratories are kept in captivity, often in solitary confinement, which is morally problematic. They have not consented to the research, and most of them will not leave the lab alive. Many of the experiments inflict pain on animals—conditioning studies are often particularly cruel, and involve withholding food or giving electric shocks—and lab animals usually suffer from stress, loneliness, emotional problems, and behavioral disorders. This also leads to scientific problems. The conditions under which animals live influence the outcomes of studies. For example, keeping social animals alone or flying animals in cages will influence their capacity for problem-solving. A recent study shows that pigeons make better decisions when they are kept in groups, but they are usually kept in solitary confinement for the purposes of research (Laude et al. 2016).

In the language experiments described above, the behavior of the non-human animals involved was influenced by their captivity, including the lack of social interaction with members of their own species. There is, however, another relevant issue at stake, and that is that language is invariably equated with human language, while the results claim to say something about the capacities of the non-human animals used for study. Studying capacities for speaking, signing, or understanding human language in other animals can, of course, give us information about their ways of learning, non-human animal mimicry, memory, emotions, and attunement to humans. Patterson, for example, emphasizes the understanding between herself and Koko, and describes their interaction as rich and complex, with human words forming a bridge between their worlds in some instances and body language in others (Hillix and Rumbaugh 2004). Eye contact is mentioned as especially important.[3] However, these studies do not tell us much about the species-specific language skills of other animals. Between themselves, for example, chimpanzees (Hobaiter and Byrne 2014) and bonobos (Genty and Zuberbühler 2014) use a great variety of gestures and vocalizations, many of which we do not yet understand in detail. Studying the origins of human language in non-human primates, dolphins, parrots, dogs, and other non-human animals is furthermore often anthropocentric in nature in that it presupposes that humans are a step further along the evolutionary scale, when in fact non-human and human primates have mutual ancestors, and non-human animals have adapted to their particular environments in intelligent ways.

Language research that sees human language as the only true language not only refers to a flawed view of non-human animals and their linguistic capacities, it is also based on a problematic, narrow idea of language. The idea of a universal linguistic structure that can only be located in human animals is part of a tradition in which human language is seen as the only language, and in which language is seen as interconnected with truth (chapter 1; see also Glendinning 1998). Humanism usually sees human language as that which creates and expresses a distinct break between human and non-human animals. This presumes a specific view of language in which language is the expression of objective, determinate meanings which man alone can grasp (see also Glendinning 1998, 77). The definition of language is here connected to the exclusion of non-human animals in two ways: a humanistic view of language pre-excludes their languages and forms of expression because language is explicitly defined as human language, and it further excludes other animals because language is seen as the expression of objective, determinate meanings that are presented as universally true, but which are in fact based on human language, which means that many aspects of other animals' languages will be seen as deviations and of lesser worth. In order to further investigate non-human animal languages and to develop a non-anthropocentric view of language, we therefore need a different perspective on language and studying language.

This different perspective can be found in the later work of Ludwig Wittgenstein. Wittgenstein also searches for clarity about the essence of human language. He rejects the view that words have one objective meaning—as he illustrates with the Augustinian picture of language that he discusses in the beginning of *Philosophical Investigations* (1958). A view of language as fixed and universal comes naturally to humans, and humans need the promise of meaning to communicate; however, if we take a closer look at words, we find that their borders are not clear and limits cannot be drawn around meanings. According to Wittgenstein, we cannot give a single definition of language: there are many different ways in which we use language that are related but do not share one characteristic, so there is therefore no one way to describe them. Here he draws a parallel with the concept "game." This word can refer to many different games that do not have one common characteristic, even though many games resemble each other and have overlapping similarities; something Wittgenstein describes as having a "family resemblance." The same applies to the structure of other concepts and to the concept of language itself. This led Wittgenstein to develop the concept of "language games."

Language as Language Games

Wittgenstein proposes viewing "language" differently, and offers a new way of studying it: instead of defining language, we should find out how it works. This approach is very useful, both in method and in content, for thinking about non-human animal languages and interspecies languages. For empirical and political reasons we cannot yet define what "language" means for all animals; as humans, we do not know enough about non-human animal languages, and it is not up to us alone to decide what counts as language. At the same time, new research forces us to broaden our view of what language is and which species use it. If we follow Wittgenstein's ideas about language, we see that because of the nature of language, or rather because of how language works, we can never define "language" as such. It is always tied to social practices, and meaning is generated by use. In what follows I will use Wittgenstein's idea of language as a starting point for understanding how we can conceptualize non-human animal languages as language, finding new ways of studying them, and exploring how non-human animal languages can contribute to how we view language.

Wittgenstein does not give a definition of language games, but he uses this concept to refer to the whole of our natural language as consisting of a collection of language games, as well as for simple examples of language use (PI§7). He also uses it for the most primitive forms of language (PI§7), which are not only available to humans (PI§25). Because of the close connection between meaning and use, Wittgenstein compares language games to tools (PI§11). He emphasizes the importance of gestures and non-linguistic communication in language games (PI§7, see also Wittgenstein 1969). Wittgenstein stresses that language games are open-ended: there is always the possibility of the realization of new language games and there are many language games we do not even recognize as such because the "clothes of our language" (PI, II xi, 224) make everything look the same. To grasp what language is, we should study language games by examining the practices in which they take place.

In language games, different types of act—such as gestures, facial expressions, and so on—play a role. These are often specific to cultures, and therefore learning about cultural habits and rituals is necessary for an understanding of what words mean. In a famous and often misunderstood statement, Wittgenstein writes that if a lion could speak, we would not understand him (PI, II xi, 224). This is often interpreted as a statement about the otherness of non-human animals (Leahy 1994; De-Grazia 1994), but that interpretation is incorrect (see also Hearne [1986] 2007). Wittgenstein rarely discusses actual animals in his work, but he does often use them as metaphors. In this particular quotation, he uses the image of a lion as a metaphor for someone who is from a completely different cultural background. This becomes clear if we read what precedes it:

> We also say of some people that they are transparent to us. It is, however, important as regards this observation that one human being can be a complete enigma to another. We learn this when we come into a strange country with entirely strange traditions; and, what is more, even given a mastery of the country's language. We do not understand the people. (And not because of not knowing what they are saying to themselves.) We cannot find our feet with them.
>
> "I cannot know what is going on in him" is above all a picture. It is the convincing expression of a conviction. It does not give the reasons for the conviction. They are not readily accessible.
>
> If a lion could talk, we could not understand him. (PI, II xi, 224)

Wittgenstein here connects the otherness of others with not knowing their practices, not being able to "find our feet with them." If all we have is a dictionary, we will not understand humans in a strange country;

for understanding, we need knowledge of practices. It is telling that he chooses a lion as the illustration for these remarks. There were few lions in England when he wrote these words, and in the rest of his work he more usually refers to dogs or cats.

Wittgenstein's views about non-human animals do not reflect close attention to them. They often function as an illustration of a claim about humans, as in the case of the lion above. Another example can be found in this statement about squirrels: "The squirrel does not infer by induction that it is going to need stores next winter as well. And no more do we need a law of induction to justify our actions or our predictions" (1969, §287). Here Wittgenstein does not attempt to understand squirrels or say anything definite about their capacities; he only uses them as an example to say something about humans. Similarly, when he writes that "a dog cannot be a hypocrite, but neither can he be sincere" (PI, Iixi, 229), he does not draw on his experience with actual dogs or aim to shed light on the sincerity of dogs (who can and do deceive humans—see Heberlein et al. 2017 and Gaita 2002 for a discussion[4]), but simply illustrates a series of thoughts about pretending and imponderable evidence in the case of humans (see LaCroix 2014, 66–67, for a similar argument). This ties in with his method in *Philosophical Investigations*, in which he often begins with (seemingly) common sense remarks and then responds to them in order to question our ways of thinking, continuously returning to the ways in which we use language. Examples about non-human animals are usually used in building arguments in this manner as an introduction to a question about human language use (LaCroix 2014),[5] or as a way of bringing out specifically human attributes.

Many commentators (see, for example, DeGrazia 1994, 129–30; Diamond 1978; Gaita 2002; Lynch 1996) draw on these and other examples to argue that Wittgenstein did not see non-human animals as language-users, something that is often used as a stepping stone in determining the moral implications of his work for thinking about non-human animals (Diamond 1978; Leahy 1994; Pleasants 2006).[6] The relevance of his work for thinking about non-human animal languages is underexplored. This is unfortunate, because while Wittgenstein's remarks about non-human animals merely repeat stereotypical views about them, and while he did not seriously consider non-human animals as language-users,[7] his views about human language are valuable for thinking about non-human animal languages and interspecies interactions for several reasons.

In conceptualizing and studying non-human animal languages, we need to pay attention to the practices in which they gain meaning that are similar to the way in which this works in the case of humans; Wittgenstein's plea to study language games by studying the practices in which they are used is relevant in the case of non-human animal language as well. Secondly, we need to look beyond words and understand language as embodied (chapter 3). Human words play a role in some, but not all, language games, and Wittgenstein emphasizes the importance of gestures and other non-linguistic expressions in creating meaning (PI§7). Here we can think of "greeting," for example. This can involve saying "hello," waving, nodding, calling someone's name, and so on. In his discussion of the aesthetic judgments that he considers to be complex and refined, he points to the importance of gestures (1978). A slight move of the head or a nod might be a better expression of a judgment than a word such as "beautiful." Gestures, movements, and other nonverbal expressions play an important role in the languages of other animals. Thinking of language as more than words or sounds is crucial to thinking about animals and language, because humans and other animals have so many different relationships and encounters and because non-human animals express themselves in so many different ways. It is also important to note here that human languages need not consist of words: a good example of a language without words is Silbo Gomero, the whistled language of La Gomera in the Canary Islands, which is based on Spanish and used to communicate over long distances across ravines and through valleys. Other examples include the drum languages of Nigeria and Ghana, which are also used to communicate messages over long distances, and in which drum patterns follow spoken language, including the use of grammar.

Wittgenstein's ideas about how language games are related—by means of a family resemblance—can shed light on similarities and relations in human-animal languages without presenting an *a priori* fixed truth about meaning. His emphasis on the strong relationship between meaning and use, and on the situated character of language—remember: we need to study language games by studying the practices in which they take place—are also relevant in thinking about non-human animals and language. Meaning is strongly interconnected with use for many non-human animals, as we will see in the following sections, and for humans the context in which other animals use language is very important in learning their meaning. Finally, instead of locating meaning in the relation between mind and world, Wittgenstein views language as essentially a public practice. He argues that meaning originates from the relation between language and world. Meaning is not a prefabricated entity that we can give or withhold from others, nor is it a property of words or minds; it is essentially social and tied to interactions between living beings. While, as we have seen, Wittgenstein focuses on human language—even though he writes that simple language games are also found in other animal species—this also applies to non-human animals and our interactions with them.

Thinking about language as language games in which human, non-human, and interspecies interactions can play a role allows us to get a better grasp on non-human and non-human/human linguistic practices without determining what language is for other animals. This can help us to study non-human animal language use. Non-human animals are co-creators of meaning in many different practices, and bringing this to light can help us to broaden our view of what language can entail. Similarities to humans can help humans to better understand other animals; differences require us to reformulate our own fixed ideas about language and meaning. In order to further explore this, I now turn to a discussion of different language games in relation to new ethological research, beginning with mimicry.

Parrots and Mimicry

Experiments in which non-human animals are taught to speak in human language can be seen as a specific set of language games. In the examples discussed above, human language is viewed as the only true language, which obscures forms of language use in non-human animals, but we can also find language games that involve using human language as a tool for interspecies communication in animal language research. A good example is to be found in psychologist Irene Pepperberg's (1995) parrot language research. Parrots use human words. It was long thought that their use of language was restricted to simply repeating words without understanding their meaning; humans even use the word "parroting" to describe the mindless repetition of words. These views fail to do justice to parrot cognition and learning mechanisms, and obscure their capacity for understanding. Ethologist Konrad Lorenz (1949) had already described how parrots can learn to use words or phrases on the right occasion—for example, only saying "good morning" in the morning—and how they can teach themselves words, which is something that is usually connected to strong sensory impressions. In 1978, Pepperberg began the first serious experiment to investigate the linguistic capabilities of parrots. She soon found that for parrots, learning a language is strongly connected to acting. Parrots see words as tools, and their meaning is strongly connected with their use. Pepperberg made use of this in her work with her research partner Alex, an African grey parrot, by letting him choose his rewards. By using words, Alex gained more control over his environment. He could determine what kind of sweets he received as a reward, and could express when he wanted a break or to go outside. Using this method, Alex learned to use over 150 words and could recognize 50 objects. He understood questions about these objects and answered them appropriately. He also learned to recognize the colors, forms, materials, and functions of objects. He knew, for example, what a key was, and could also recognize new keys with different shapes and colors. Alex understood and used concepts such as "same," "different," "yes," "no," and "come here." He would sometimes deliberately give the wrong answer if he thought a question was silly or boring. He could count, understood the number zero, used and understood syntax, and could form new words. Alex once asked Pepperberg what color he was, which is often cited as the only existential question ever asked by a non-human animal. Pepperberg did not claim that Alex spoke English, only that he was able to use English words and concepts and that he showed understanding and intelligence in doing so.

Biologist Joanna Burger (2002) describes a different type of relationship with a parrot. She adopted Tiko, a red-lored parrot, when he was thirty years old. Within a few months Tiko had changed from a hostile and dismissive bird to a loving companion. He saw Burger as his partner, and did not shy away from fighting her husband if he came too near to her during the mating season. Burger did not teach Tiko to speak in human language, and he had not learned it before she adopted him.

Even though his use of human words was limited—he used some regular parrot words, like "hello" and "good boy"—they did develop a rich common language, which included the use of words, sounds, songs, eye contact, gestures, and many other expressions. Tiko liked to whistle, and he whistled duets with Burger's husband, Mike. He instigated duets when Mike played the guitar or when he thought that Mike was angry at him, for example, because he had stolen or broken something. He sometimes spoke gibberish, and expressed his mood with his tone of voice and the intensity of his speech. He liked to speak along loudly when Burger was on the phone.

Alex and Pepperberg, and Tiko and Burger, show how different language games can come into being when humans and parrots interact. Some of these interspecies language games resemble the language games that take place between humans, while others are very different. They can be instigated by the human, or by the parrot; in all of them, animals of both species actively create meaning. Vinciane Despret (2008) describes Pepperberg's work as "rendering capable," or enabling the animal to speak. Donna Haraway (Azeredo 2011) rightly argues that this "rendering capable" is mutual. Alex and Pepperberg show that language games are indeed open-ended; that new language games can come into being when individuals of different species interact. While there are, of course, topics that cannot be discussed between animals of different species, there are many subjects which can. Language is limited, even when it is used between humans; there are always things that cannot be said.

One of the language games that Pepperberg and Burger describe is mimicry: imitation of the behavior of others. Wild parrots often use mimicry (Burger 2002). Recordings of two wild African grey parrots demonstrate that they used over two hundred different motifs in one night, of which twenty-three were imitations of other bird species, and one of a bat species. Imitating other animals' call notes and alarm notes is a tool in manipulating their behavior: it can be used to steal their food, attract them, or scare them away. Mimicry is not just vocal; it can involve using gestures, facial expressions, and so on. In human social psychology, the term "mimicry" is used to describe unconscious imitation of someone else's movements or posture. Humans often spontaneously mirror each other's behavior, for example, by smiling, yawning, or crossing their legs. This mirroring often stops abruptly when a human becomes aware of it. Humans who feel connected to someone will imitate that person more often, and mimicry can also excite connectedness: humans who imitate each other more understand each other better, and their emotions become more attuned to one another (Stel and Vonk 2010). Mimicry has a neurological basis in mirror neurons, neurons that light up when an animal performs a movement or sees someone else perform the same movement (Van Baaren et al. 2004). Neuroscientists argue that these neurons—which are also found in other primates, and similar neurological structures are found in birds—help humans to understand the actions and intentions of others and are at the basis of empathy. The human ability to imitate is also said to be the foundation for our form of language use and learning.[8]

As the examples above show, mimicry also plays a role in the interaction—including learning processes—between parrots and humans. Burger describes how Tiko waves goodbye by using his foot in the same way that humans use their hands or pretends to put on his coat when she leaves. Parrots may also nod or shake their heads at the right moment in a conversation. Mimicry in parrots can have different functions. It can be a form of self-defence, or may be used in hunting. When it is used in a close relationship with another parrot or a human, it might have the same function as between humans: to express the connection that is felt or to deepen the relationship.[9] Because humans and other animals learn to understand the actions and intentions of others through mimicry, because it is the starting point of empathy, and because it is how we learn, and learn to use language, mimicry involves more than just imitating others. It can lead to and express mutual attunement (see Kamphof 2017 for an example of this in chicken-human relations). Parrots who repeat words should not therefore be seen as mindless imitators of humans, but rather as individuals who respond to their surroundings, which is a starting point for dialogue.

Alarm Calls: From Communication to Language

Another set of non-human animal language games long thought to concern simple mechanistic reactions is alarm calls. In alarm calls, the relation between meaning and use is clear and tight, but they often contain more information than a simple calling out of danger. Prairie dogs, a species of ground squirrel, live in tunnels under the ground and do not leave their "village," which makes it easy for predators to find and attack them; all they have to do is wait near the entrance of a tunnel and sooner or later a prairie dog will show up to forage. The prairie dogs have therefore developed a complex warning system (Slobodchikoff et al. 2009; Slobodchikoff 2012), using different sounds to describe different predators.[10] In their calls, they identify whether the predator is coming from the sky or land; this is important because it requires a different type of response. They do not, however, stop there, describing the intruder in detail. When a human approaches, they describe their species, height, color, and the things they might be carrying (such as umbrellas or guns). When dogs approach, they mention their form and color, and may add the speed at which the dog is approaching. Their calls change meaning when the order of elements in a sentence changes, which can be compared to grammar in human sentences. They use verbs, nouns, and adverbs, which they can combine to make new expressions for unknown predators. In addition to alarm calls, they have a form of social chatter that we do not yet know much about, and some species do the jump-yip—a kind of wave that involves throwing their hands up in the air and jumping backward while yelling "yip," which is thought to probably be an expression of joy and enthusiasm; they do this when predators such as snakes leave their territory.

Alarm calls are one of the most studied groups of animal vocalizations. There is much variation between species, both in the types of expressions and in the complexity of the calls. Chickadees use the "chickadee" sound to describe predators, and multiply the "dee" as the danger increases. Chickens use different alarm calls for different intruders, describing whether they come from the sky or the ground (Manser 2001). Vervet monkeys also use different alarm calls for different predators. Research has shown they do not react blindly to the alarm calls of others. When a caller proves to be unreliable—for example, because the caller in question is in fact a recording played back by researchers who want to test responses to different predators—the vervet monkeys stop responding. This demonstrates that they can judge the meaning of the call (Seyfarth et al. 1980). Many species also understand and imitate the alarm calls of other species. Campbell's monkey alarm calls have syntax; the elements hang together as words in a sentence (Zuberbühler

2001). Diana guenon alarm calls do not have this, but they do understand the meaning of the Campbell's monkeys' calls (ibid.). Campbell's
monkeys also use different sounds resembling words in different areas of
the world (ibid.). I have already discussed the ability of parrots to imitate
others, for example, to scare them away and steal their food. Fork-tailed
drongos also use mimicry and can imitate the alarm calls of fifty other
species. They use this skill to warn other animals and to steal their food
(Flower 2011).

Alarm calls are often accompanied by, or consist solely of, visual signals, such as facial expressions, body movements, and gestures. Smell
also plays an important role in the alarm calls of many species. As well as
sounds, snails use smells in their slime when they are in danger (Breure
2015). African bees use scents to alarm others and to summon the whole
swarm for an attack (Slobodchikoff 2012). They can and sometimes do
kill humans in this way when they feel threatened. Research into the
role of pheromones and smell in animal communication is still in its
early stages, but we do know that some smells used as alarm calls consist
of different elements, and that the combination of smells, as well as the
ratio, provides meaning. Californian thrips insects, for example, use different alarm pheromones for different threats (De Bruijn 2015). Thrips
larvae produce a pheromone that consists of two ingredients: decyl acetate and dodecyl acetate. When the danger intensifies, the quantity and
ratio of pheromones produced changes. Larvae who receive the signal
change their behavior accordingly, so meaning is transferred adequately.

Alarm calls were long thought to be simple instinctive responses to
danger, a pre-scripted form of communication, wired into the genetic
makeup of an animal. This refers back to a view of non-human animals
who act solely on instinct (see chapter 1 and the previous section) and
who are not capable of responding intelligently. As ethological research
in which other animals are studied in their own habitats progresses,
along with technological developments,[11] it has been found that in many
species, like the prairie dogs, alarm calls are actually very complex. They
should be seen as expressions of an individual animal's intelligence
rather than as simple mechanistic reactions: as language, rather than as
communication. A single call from a prairie dog shares a large amount
of information with others in a much more precise and efficient way
than a human scream or word. The language of the prairie dog seems to

have a similar structure to human language, including grammar (Slo-bodchikoff et al. 2009); it might also have functions we cannot yet understand because we do not recognize or perceive them. We cannot hear the complexities in their calls—to us they all sound more or less the same—so it is logical that humans formerly perceived their language as simple calls. We are only now beginning to find out what they are saying thanks to the use of technology. This example shows us that there is more to animal calls than we think, and that it is important to move beyond a view of animals as acting solely on instinct and only using signals with a fixed meaning when we study alarm calls and animal languages more generally.

Viewing alarm calls as a set of language games in which non-human animals create meaning in ways that are sometimes similar to humans, and sometimes very different, provides us with a new way of studying their languages. This begins with recognizing them as subjects, rather than as objects who simply follow their instincts (see also chapter 3). Studying their languages is closely interconnected with studying their social relations, and in order to map and interpret these language games, we also need to study the practices and relations in which they gain meaning. Understanding the context helps us to understand the meaning of signals while getting a better grasp on the structures of non-human animal languages; for example, the grammar in prairie dog alarm calls can help us to better interpret their behavior: both are needed to gain an insight into their languages.

Grammar

The structures, or grammars, of most animal languages have not been studied in detail. This relates back to the fact that while animal languages are studied in biology and ethology, in most of these studies human language is taken as the blueprint for what language—as opposed to communication—is (Slobodchikoff 2012), which precludes many non-human animal expressions. The fact that other animals do not use human language cannot, however, lead us to conclude that they do not have language. If we do not understand their expressions, we cannot conclude that they are not complex or meaningful—different does not automatically equal less. Even if we cannot use human language as a blueprint for what language is, concepts used in studying human language can function as tools for understanding the languages of other animals, even those very different from us.

An example of this can be found in research into the language of Caribbean reef squid (Moynihan 1991). Caribbean reef squid speak with their skin. Pigment cells in their skin called chromatophores are attached to muscles that can be contracted or relaxed. This either exposes the pigment or makes it invisible, which allows the squid to change the color patterns on their skin very rapidly. In doing so they create complex visual patterns ranging from white to camouflage, which send sophisticated signals to other squid. Males, for example, use specific color patterns to flirt with females, who in turn use other patterns to respond. When there are other males around, the male can use half of his body to signal to the female, and the other half to tell his opponent to back off. Many different patterns are possible, and they can change in the blink of an eye. Because of the subtlety and speed of the changes, most of the patterns have not yet been deciphered. In addition to the color patterns, squid also use body postures to create meaning. Biologist Moynihan (1991) argues that the visual patterns, together with the postures, constitute a proper language, with nouns, verbs, adjectives, and adverbs. Nouns and verbs are most important; they are, for example, used to establish whether the other wants to mate. Adjectives and adverbs are then used to describe the intensity of the desire to mate. Because of the difficulty in understanding all the elements of this visual language, the precise rules of this grammar are still unknown, but the broad meaning can be grasped from the context. Studying these expressions as a language with a grammar helps us to get a better grasp of how they function; seeing their grammar as grammar can also help us to get a richer view of what grammar can entail.

Another example is bird song. The songs and calls of many species of birds have been studied extensively, and it was long assumed that the most important functions of song were to attract females and to defend territory. However, recent research focusing on grammar shows that bird languages are far more complex than was supposed, both with regard to the content of messages and their structure (Slobodchikoff 2012). Many aspects once thought to be unique features of human language have also been found in bird languages. Humans can, for example, produce new sounds that have meaning for speakers of the same language because they follow certain syntactic rules. A recursive, hierarchical embedding, needed for new utterances to make sense, requires a context-free grammar. Recursion has been found in the language of many birds (and other non-human animal species, such as elephants), including chickadees (Kerschenbaum et al. 2014). Chickadee language consists of a variety of different sounds that can be combined creatively. Single units are combined, like words, into patterns and sentences, of which the combinations become more complex as the intensity of the communication increases (Slobodchikoff 2012). For the Carolina chickadee, the meaning of sentences changes when the order of the elements changes (Kerschenbaum et al. 2014). Starlings have recently been found to classify sentences from embedded, context-free grammar (Gentner et al. 2006). The syntax of the black-chinned hummingbird also has an open system similar to that of starlings and humans (Slobodchikoff 2012).

Grammar is also being studied in the languages of other animals. The songs of humpback whales (Suzuki et al. 2006), which sound improvised and chaotic to the human ear, are formed like sentences, consisting of smaller units that are combined to form songs containing up to 400 elements. Mexican free-tailed bats are currently seen as the species of non-human mammals who have the most complex forms of vocal communication (Gillam and Fenton 2016). Because most of their vocalizations are beyond the range of the human ear, humans long thought their vocal communication was limited. But new technologies show that their songs are complex both in content—they discuss everything from territory to social status, love, raising children, and other social affairs—and in structure, with fixed elements combined using grammar. They are creative as well; males each develop their own songs to sing to females. Technology helps us perceive and interpret the complexities of the languages of other species. Dolphin researcher Denise Herzing has studied dolphin languages for decades, and uses technologically advanced equipment to translate their language into human language, and vice versa. She first managed to communicate a word in this manner—sargassum, a type of seaweed—in 2013, and emphasizes the importance of studying behavior in parallel with language (Herzing 2016). Elephants use low-pitched sounds to communicate over long distances, and these infrasounds give them a private communication system that plays an important role in their complex social life. Researchers from the Elephant Listening Project use recordings to decipher their languages, and have found that they communicate not only information, but also emotions and intentions. They have different words for categories (such as groups of humans, and bees) and for individuals, in which they also express family relations (Elephant Listening Project 2017).

The use of recordings and technology can help to categorize animal vocalizations and map the structure of their languages, but, as has been explained, to only study structures is not enough if we want to understand what they mean. Lizards have four ways to express themselves: by their posture, the number of legs they have on the ground, nodding their head, and displaying or inflating their chin. This may seem fairly simple, but there are 6,864 possible combinations, of which 172 are frequently used (Slobodchikoff 2012). We can map these movements, but to grasp what they mean we need to study the grammar of the wider context in which they are used, including how these expressions stem from and shape social relations. In linguistics, grammar is usually regarded as the set of rules that governs the composition of words, phrases, and clauses in a natural language. It also refers to the study of these rules. Wittgenstein (1958) reminds us of the relevance of the wider network of rules, linked to social practices, that determines whether or not use of language is meaningful. Meaning does not simply spring from technical instructions for the use of words and sentences; it is always also tied to a given context.

In studying non-human animal language games, we should therefore focus on their structure and on context. In both of these aspects we must also avoid taking human language as the blueprint for what qualifies as proper language, and investigate how non-human animals create meaning.

Meta-Communication: Play and Greeting

Non-human animals use language to express and shape social relations. In a similar way to humans, they can also communicate about communication: they are capable of meta-communication, which plays a major role in developing relations with others. We find meta-communication in different language games—humor between humans is one. In this section I will discuss two non-human animal or inter-species language games in which we find meta-communication, play and greeting, in order to shed further light on the connection between using language and constituting social rules, and to show that non-human animal language games that do not involve human language can still be complex and enable non-human animals to discuss situations that transcend the here and now. These examples shed light on the relations between language and world, which I discuss in more detail in the next chapter.

Play behavior is found in many species, not only in placental mammals, but also in marsupials, birds, reptiles, and fish. Play-like behavior has furthermore been found in different invertebrates, such as crustaceans, cephalopods, and insects, including ants, bees, and cockroaches (Burghardt 2005). In play, non-human animals use behaviors and movements that usually form part of other social situations, such as fights, flights, attacks, and sexual advances. Animals of many species use special play behaviors to indicate that they want to play. Dogs, wolves, and coyotes, for example, use the play bow as an invitation to play; they also use it during play, for example, in order to make amends when something rough or unintended happens. The meaning of the bow might be "I want to play" or "sorry about that, I still want to play." During play, dogs often change roles; dominant dogs adopt submissive postures and vice versa, and stronger dogs sometimes self-handicap to make play possible. In dog play, however, certain social conventions remain intact (Smuts 2006); for example, dominant dogs will never lick the mouth of a subordinate dog.

Play can be a form of competition and a form of cooperation. Dogs need to play to learn social rules, but it is more than a learning mechanism; dogs are creative in play, they express themselves and enjoy themselves. Furthermore, as we have seen, dogs in play communicate about communication. When the play gets rough and they accidentally hurt one another, they use the play bow and other play behaviors to explain that they mean no harm, that it was just in fun. They also use play gestures when the preferred partner responds in a serious way to acts that were meant as play. Dogs also communicate about the future in play: they negotiate social hierarchies, can work out tensions and conflicts in a safe way, and form friendships (Bekoff 2002; Smuts 2006). This meta-communication enables them to learn about their own strength and the strength of others in the group, allowing the strengthening or clarification of social bonds.

In play, animals of different kinds can use expressions in new and different ways and create new meaning. Massumi (2014) argues that the reflexivity that is needed for this meta-communication to work, or the space between one meaning and another, creates the conditions for the emergence of language, which he sees as the highest or most developed form of animal expression. According to Massumi, many non-human animals use creativity in play, but only humans use language. Both the relation he sees between play and language and his idea of language as human language are problematic. Play can mean many different things for animals of different species, and the relation between play and language is not simply hierarchical. Play and human words can be connected in many ways, depending on the context and the actors involved; play can take place inside human language, as when making a joke, and human words can play a role in interspecies play, as when a dog is asked to fetch a ball. Non-human animal expressions can have a similar relation with play, and, like humans, non-human animals have their own complex forms of creating meaning through play, in which these different expressions, ranging from eye contact to movements, can play a role. As we have seen, equating language with human language is problematic, and it obscures non-human animal agency with regard to using language. Instead of viewing play and language as separate realms, it is better to understand "play" as a set of language games in which different human and non-human expressions play a role. Viewing play as a set of language games that enable human and non-human animals to discuss social issues helps us obtain a better understanding of how other animals shape relations among each other and with humans, and it also helps us to see how they shape their own futures.

Another example of a set of language games that involves meta-communication, and which can involve human, non-human, or interspecies interactions, is greeting. Certain non-human animals use meta-communication in greeting rituals to discuss the future. The greeting rituals of male baboons illustrate how this works. These rituals serve as a means to establish and learn about social hierarchy (Smuts 2002).

Male baboons often fight, and because their teeth are sharp they get hurt easily. They do not have many friendly encounters such as playing or grooming; their only friendly approach to each other is in greeting, and they often greet each other. When a male approaches another male, the other will usually either avoid or threaten him. When the approach is accompanied by lip-smacking, the "come hither" face, and an exaggerated gait, it is understood as an invitation to greet and answered by the making of eye contact (which is threatening under other circumstances), lip-smacking, and making the come hither face in return. This is then followed by a series of gestures that usually involve one male presenting his hindquarters and allowing the other to mount him, grasp his hips, and/or touch or mouth his genitals—an act of trust, considering their sharp teeth. The pair sometimes nuzzle or embrace, and in rare circumstances may play briefly. Their roles are mostly asymmetrical, and the greeting ritual only lasts for a few seconds.

Ethologist Barbara Smuts (2002) argues that patterns of greeting tend to reflect coalitional behavior: young males do not greet often, nor do they form coalitions; older males, who engage in longer, calm greeting sessions most often form coalitions. Considering the sharpness of baboon teeth, allowing someone else to put one's genitals in their mouth poses a risk, so it demonstrates a willingness to cooperate. Play and greeting behaviors both involve meta-communication: behavioral asymmetries are temporarily suspended in both and the future is discussed. The distinctive approach that announces a greeting functions as meta-communication, which works in a similar way in play behavior; a baboon tells another baboon that he wants to greet rather than fight, which minimizes the chance of aggression. As in play, the safety of the greeting environment allows baboons to learn about the intentions of others and negotiate the future without having to fight. Greetings might change over time, as the baboons get to know the other, or when their position in the hierarchy changes. Play is connected to learning about and negotiating social rules, and is also connected to morality, to learning about right and wrong in one's community (Bekoff and Pierce 2009). Understanding, expressing, and forming rules may take different forms in different communities; for many animals, play is a way of learning about boundaries, and responding to them.

From Thinking about to Thinking with Other Animals

This brief investigation into the language games of mimicry, alarm calls, grammar, and meta-communication shows us that there is great variety in the ways that other animals express themselves, make sense of the world around them, respond, and connect to others. To further develop a non-anthropocentric view of language, however, it is not enough to simply study other animal languages. While existing concepts, such as mimicry and grammar, can function as tools in understanding other animals and working towards better relations, they should rather be seen as starting points, not end points. In this chapter, the focus has mostly been on the scientific study of animal languages, which is itself a specific set of language games. In these language games non-human animals often do not have access to how experiments are set up, even though they clearly exercise agency. However, humans and other animals also live together, and form common worlds in which language often plays a formative role. In the next chapter I turn to investigating these relations further by focusing on the relation between language and world and the building of common interspecies worlds.

3

From Animal Languages to Interspecies Worlds

In 1904, when he was four years old, Hans could solve multiplication and division problems and extract square roots (Allen and Bekoff 1999, 26; Despret 2004). He could spell words and detect intervals in music, and he could discriminate tones and colors. Hans, who was a horse, answered the questions that humans asked him by tapping his right fore-hoof on the ground. Local newspaper articles about Hans and his human, Wilhelm von Osten, drew many humans to the courtyard where he exhibited his talents. Some of them were convinced he was a genius; others thought that he, or rather his human, was a fraud. Von Osten was insulted by the suggestions of fraud, and formed a commission consisting of a veterinarian, a circus manager, a cavalry officer, several schoolteachers, and the director of the Berlin Zoological Garden, to investigate the case. It turned out that Hans could also answer questions correctly in the absence of von Osten, and psychologist Oskar Pfungst was enrolled to solve the mystery. Pfungst soon found that although he could not detect any, Hans was picking up signals, because when the human who asked the question did not know the answer, Hans was also unable to answer. Pfungst continued his investigations, and finally discovered that, without being aware of it, the humans who questioned Hans nodded slightly when he tapped the right number, which allowed Hans to give the correct answer.

Hans was clearly an intelligent horse, but his intelligence lay on a level other than the one investigated: Hans had learned to read movements in the skin and muscle of humans. He also trained the humans he worked with (Despret 2004). By responding to some cues and not to others, he taught humans how to communicate with him. Vinciane Despret (2004) describes this process as a mutual attunement: human and horse learn to read each other through "body language," some of which is intentional and some of which is not. For Despret, the phenomenon of attunement is a positive research method that can allow scientists to collect data beyond the animal as object of research, seeing and show-ing the non-human animal in question as subject. Close interaction with other animals thus produces a type of insight not reducible to the classic canons of scientific knowledge-production (Candea 2013). The scientists who investigated Hans did not share Despret's opinion, and while the public still came in large numbers to watch Hans perform his tricks, scientists in fields such as cognitive and social psychology developed experiments that were double-blind, meaning that neither the experimenter nor the subject knew the condition of the subject or the predicted responses.

Bird scientist Len Howard (1952, 1956) argued against behaviorism, the predominant way of studying birds in her time, both in method and as a theoretical starting point. Howard believed that experiments in lab-oratories could never give us a real insight into bird behavior, because captivity made them nervous. She also argued against a mechanistic view of birds, and instead saw them as conscious and intelligent individ-uals. In order to study their behavior in a more natural setting, Howard opened her cottage in Sussex—literally leaving the windows open—to the birds who lived in the area. She fed them and made nesting places for them in and around the house. Great tits, robins, sparrows, black-birds, thrushes, finches, and birds of many other species soon learned not to be afraid of her, and began to use the house as they pleased. This allowed Howard to get to know them intimately. In her work, she writes about the relations they had with one another and with her, their behav-iors and personalities, which she often wrote down in the form of their biographies. Trained as a musician, she also studied and wrote down their songs. The communication between Howard and the birds was ex-tensive, and included gestures, eye contact, tone of voice, bird songs, and calls, but also human words; the birds usually understood what Howard meant intuitively and otherwise learned fast.

With one of the birds, a female great tit named Star, Howard began an experiment reminiscent of the story of Clever Hans. One morning, instead of giving Star her daily nut, Howard told her to tap for it. Star immediately understood what was required of her and rapped out two taps on the wooden frame of a screen with her beak, copying Howard's tempo. Howard first taught Star to tap numbers in response to her own taps, and then used spoken numbers. Star learned to count to eight in this manner. Howard could not tap fast enough to get to nine. Star sometimes refused the lessons, holding her head up high, and at other times explicitly asked for them by turning her beak towards the wood, or instigated them herself by tapping. Because of her mathematical insight, and because she understood so well what Howard wanted from her, Howard called her an avian genius.

In the experiment with Hans, von Osten was investigating human intelligence in a horse, which limited Hans's options to respond. Even if, following Despret (2004), we understand that Hans was intelligent and that attunement makes the production of knowledge possible, Hans's options for exercising agency were limited. He could not, for example, leave the experiment. Howard was interested in bird intelligence, and shows that it is not necessary to raise other animals or hold them captive in order to gain their trust,[1] build a relationship, and conduct a counting experiment.[2] Howard describes how two animals of different species connect, get to know each other, and derive joy from a specific kind of communication in the form of a working relationship (see also Hearne [1986] 2007), whereas the story of von Osten and Hans primarily seems to be one of use—or even exploitation. As far as we can tell from their life stories, Howard was genuinely moved by and interested in the birds she shared her house and life with, and vice versa. Star was free to come and go as she pleased; both she and Howard initiated the contact. In her house and garden, Howard let the birds co-shape the terms of interaction. She repeatedly mentions that the birds were quite demanding in terms of attention, food, and interior decoration. She was willing to expand her human world to incorporate their forms of creating meaning, and actively searched for ways to build new common worlds with them using human and bird languages. For her personally this meant retreating from the human world; because the birds were scared of other humans, these had to be kept out of the garden and house as much as possible. The birds and Howard created a new community by interacting, and over time. Generations of wild birds taught their children not to be afraid of Howard, so perhaps this can be seen as the beginning of a new interspecies culture. Language played an important role in this process, and in the next section I further explore the relation between language and building a world with others in interspecies relations.

Learning to Read the Darkness: On the Relation between Language and World

Teaching a dog to retrieve may seem like a simple process, guided by human superiority and dog treats. Dog trainer and philosopher Vicki Hearne ([1986] 2007) shows that there is more to it than that. Hearne describes how she taught pointer Salty to fetch a dumbbell, which she conceptualizes as teaching her the language game "to fetch." Teaching a dog the meaning of a word clarifies the interaction between dog and human, both on the side of the dog and on the side of the human, and lays the foundation for further interaction. The precise meaning of retrieval is not given beforehand, but comes into being when both individuals interact, and the outcome will differ between individuals depending on their characters and personalities. The learning process asks something of both sides: the dog has to be willing to learn, but so does the human. In order to teach a dog something, one needs to be open to that particular dog, and this means that there is also a chance of being changed by this individual. There is not one formula that works for all dogs, and Hearne argues that dog trainers, in contrast to behaviorists, recognize and respond to the fact that dogs are complex and layered beings.

Hearne uses Wittgenstein's concept of language games to demonstrate how dogs and humans, who are phenomenologically very different—a dog's perception of the world is mostly olfactory, whereas humans have a primarily ocular experience of the world—can come to an understanding. Retrieving is a language game that describes a dog-human activity: the human tells the dog to fetch an object, and the dog brings it. The exact meaning of the word "fetch" is also formed by Salty. When Salty learns what it means to retrieve something, this enables her to express herself more fully. For example, it gives her the opportunity to make jokes. Salty jokes by fetching the garbage bin or a car tire instead of the dumbbell, or she does fetch the dumbbell, but takes it to someone else. When she does this, her body movements and facial expression are playful and joyful. Because Salty has more options to express herself and to understand Hearne, and vice versa, their relationship deepens, and their understanding, as well as their common world, grows.[3] Hearne expresses this as follows: "When we learn a language game, we learn to read the darkness" ([1986] 2007, 72).

Teaching a dog to retrieve, sit, or stay creates common language games, which lead to a larger common world in which both the dog and the human have more options to express themselves to the other. In order for this interaction to work, dog and human need to follow and respect certain rules; the capacity for rule following is also increased in establishing a greater understanding. In other words: a dog can only learn a new language game in a world in which the concepts "right" and "wrong" make sense, and through learning new language games, this moral understanding also grows. Hearne sees a clear hierarchy between the species in this process: humans set the moral framework in which dogs take part and obey. This does not do justice to dog agency. Bekoff and Pierce (2009) draw on empirical research, especially on dog play and theory of mind in dogs to argue that dogs do act morally, and they emphasize that dog morality is not the same as human morality, but tailored to interaction in dog, and interspecies, communities. Dogs can think about, respond to, and anticipate the mental states of others (Hare and Woods 2013; see also chapter 2), and Hearne is right in arguing that creating dog-human language games serves as a starting point for interspecies moral understanding. Differences between the species are not an obstacle to understanding, but rather enable a different kind of being together, which allows for animals of both species to express themselves more fully and which can also be—for the human at least—a source of beauty.

In thinking about the relation between establishing common language games and a common world, it is important to recognize that we are always already with others. For companion dogs, these others are usually dogs and humans, and sometimes other companion animals. For some humans, this means mostly humans, while others also live with other animals. As we have seen, according to Heidegger, "Being-attuned" to others (1927, 172) is a fundamental characteristic of our structure of being in the world. We are not solitary beings who sometimes meet or engage with others; we are always already with them and *Mitsein* is constitutive for our way of being in the world. This "being with others" is made explicit in discourse, of which hearing and keeping silent—relevant in the interspecies context—are an important part. Discourse—which is expressed in language and is language—is equiprimordial with *Mitsein*, and constitutive for Dasein's existence. In other words: through language we not only express and understand ourselves as beings in the world, we also express and create our relations with others. As we saw in the first chapter, Heidegger regarded other animals as poor-in-world (chapter 1): as beings without language and consequently without the opportunity to experience the world as such. This results not only in the assumption that non-human animals cannot experience the world as world, it also restricts *Mitsein* to humans (ibid.). However, like humans, other animals are "thrown into" a world that consists of meaning-giving structures from the moment they are born. These structures are formed by language, and other animals influence them by language, in interaction with others (Iveson 2010, 2012).

Being with others does not only involve being with members of the same species. Humans are already constantly with other animals and vice versa. We share a world with them, and some of us share our lives with them: this is part of what constitutes our sense of world and our perception of ourselves. Relationships and language games will, of course, vary between groups and individuals. Some non-human animals are very similar to humans in the way in which they express and understand the world, whereas others are very different. The examples of Howard and the birds and Hearne and her dogs show how individuals of different species can add new layers of meaning to their repertoires through interaction, and can together create new forms of language and understanding. The form of this language and the manner of creating meaning are not predetermined; they follow from the situated interaction and are shaped by the agency of the various animals involved.

Speaking Bodies

In creating common interspecies language games and common understanding we need to take the different ways in which animals express themselves into account. Hearne uses words, gestures, and body movements to teach Salty to retrieve; Salty runs and moves, and uses gestures, sounds, and eye contact to reply. Howard and the birds communicate with song, human words, gestures, movements, and other expressions.

The body also plays a major role in human language games (Wittgenstein 1978), but so-called "body language" is often thought of as a weaker or less precise form of communication. Locating language in the mind refers back to Descartes's mind-body dualism, and to an idealized view of language. As we saw in chapters 1 and 2, the image of language as located in the mind can be challenged in different ways, and various philosophers (Derrida 2008; Heidegger 1927; Wittgenstein 1958, 1978) argued for a more situated idea of language, interconnected with relations and social practices. Wittgenstein (1958) also emphasizes that in language games, gestures, movements, ways of using one's voice, and other expressions can be as important, or more important, than words.

In the work of Maurice Merleau-Ponty (1962) we can find some helpful motives for further exploring the embodied aspects of language in an interspecies context. In developing his view of language, Merleau-Ponty focuses strongly on the role of the body, on the basis of which he also sees an ontological connection to other animals. According to Merleau-Ponty (1962), we are not thinking, but speaking subjects. Expression completes thought; speech does not translate thought into words, but rather accomplishes it. A thought is not a representation: speech and thought are interconnected. Thoughts are not internal, and do not exist separately from the words we use and the world in which they are used. Bodies play an important role in language because they form the shape of speech, and thus meaning. Expression brings meaning into existence, and words are so many ways of "singing of the world" (1962, 217). By locating meaning in the words themselves, Merleau-Ponty aims to refute both empiricism—according to which speech is a mechanistic response—and intellectualism (or rationalism) in which words are seen as empty containers for pre-formed thoughts. In contrast to Saussure, who privileged *langue* over *parole*, Merleau-Ponty argues that *parole* precedes *langue*; *langue* is constructed through the spoken form. We perceive and understand others through our bodies, and the reciprocity of intentions creates sense in communication (1962, 215). Different languages are tied up with different cultural expressions; thought and expression are simultaneously constituted, building on a specific culture, in an existing linguistic world. Understanding does not mean understanding or translating a representation, but rather dealing with a speaking subject who has a certain style of being, and with the world to which they direct their aim. In language, we take up a position in the world of meanings where the body makes itself understood to external witnesses. The experience of our body gives us an ambiguous mode of existence; we are both object and consciousness.

For Merleau-Ponty, speech and language connect different subjects, as well as subject and world. Through speaking to others, we produce meaning. Merleau-Ponty refers to this production of meaning through the interplay of self and other, or foreground and background, as depth. The inter-subjectivity thus conceived—as springing forward from contrasting subjects and the relation they have to each other—is, according to him, a space in which differences interact and can "give birth to a sense of the richness and wildness of the world which qualitatively surpasses what the differences are able to present in isolation" (Coles 1992, 133). In thinking about interspecies languages, both the emphasis on the role of the body in creating meaning and this conception of inter-subjectivity, in which sharing experiences should not be conceived as a mechanism that reduces difference but as actually allowing for difference to be articulated, are relevant. If we locate meaning in the act of speaking, and see the body as what makes sense of—and simultaneously expresses—world, we can avoid studying other animals and their languages as objects that express pre-determined meanings, or as subjects stuck in their *Umwelt*, and appreciate their creativity. Instead of seeing language as something that separates us from those who are different, we can see how language connects us.

There are, however, problems with locating language and meaning in the act of speaking. It seems too strong to only locate meaning in the act of speaking itself, and words only make sense against a cultural background and in social practices. To begin with this second point: we can think to ourselves, play music in the absence of others, come to insights in writing and write letters that are never sent; these are expressions of language as well, and the meaning thus produced influences us. We are also tied to the structure that a language has, which we can use creatively, but not change singlehandedly. Second, as we have seen, language consists of more than human words expressed by human bodies in speaking: the image of language as exclusively human is a contingent product of power relations. Merleau-Ponty rightly points to the fact that meaning can be created between two subjects who are very different, and to the cultural differences that are expressed in speech. The idea that understanding does not involve dealing with a representation, but rather with the attitude of a person and the world that they are directed towards, is also helpful. However, in order to be able to apply this to relations with other animals, we of course need to view "speaking" as something broader than using human words, and must take into account the differences in how manifold kinds of animal express themselves. Their bodies determine the form their speech takes, which is not limited to sounds. "Singing the world" (Merleau-Ponty 1962, 378) can just as well refer to the color patterns of the Caribbean reef squid, the gestures of lizards, and the scents in the trails of ants.

This view of language as embodied human language is reflected in Merleau-Ponty's view of the relation between humans and other animals. In his *Nature Lectures*, he introduces the concept of "strange kinship" (2003, 271) that allows humans to be together with other embodied beings, not on the basis of a shared origin or evolution, nor of language or culture, but because humans have bodies that relate to their environment and to other bodies. According to Oliver (2007), this strange kinship allows for "an intimate relation based on shared embodiment without denying differences between life-styles or styles of being" (Oliver 2007, 18). The "thickness of the flesh" and "permeability of the skin" (Merleau-Ponty 2003, 141) make "intercorporiety" (ibid.) possible. The thickness of the flesh allows for relations with others, while the skin ensures that we can distinguish our experience from those of others. In communication, our body is always simultaneously subject and object: we see and are seen, we touch and are touched. Merleau-Ponty calls this "reversibility" (2003, 123). Beings belonging to other species also have flesh and skin, so this "transitivity" also happens between humans and other species of animal (Oliver 2007). According to Merleau-Ponty, the relationship between humanity and animality is lateral, rather than hierarchical; humanity neither emerges from animality teleologically, nor is it cut off from it. The difference between humanity and animality cannot be reduced to evolution, or to an abyss between body and consciousness, or animal and Dasein. However, humanity and animality are still contrasted, and language and culture are seen as species-specific.[4] This is problematic, because while different species of animals do perceive the world differently and have different ways of constructing it as speaking subjects, humans and other animals also form communities, and sometimes even cultures, in which species is not the defining characteristic in creating understanding. Contrasting "human" with "animal" furthermore runs the risk of perpetuating human exceptionalism: of course humans are special, but so are guinea pigs, manta rays, bees, and chickens.

An emphasis on the relevance of species-specific differences is often connected to skepticism about understanding other animals. The examples of squid and ants show that univocal meaning is not easily created between members of all species; it is easier between some animals than between others, and sometimes translation is needed. We cannot hear or map many of the sounds that bats make without using technological equipment, and while certain acts might still be easy to interpret, for example nursing behavior or play, we need to study their behavior or consult an expert in order to adequately grasp the full content of what is being said. In contrast, the messages of companion animals often seem very easy to interpret, especially for the humans who live with them, but there are also dangers of projection and anthropomorphism here. While these dangers are relevant and must be taken into consideration, skepticism about other animals' minds is often an expression of anthropocentrism. Before I turn to conceptualizing living with other animals, in which I again partly draw on Merleau-Ponty's work, I will therefore first briefly discuss the role of skepticism in understanding other animals.

Understanding Other Animals

Knowing non-human animals is often considered to be fundamentally different to knowing human animals. One of the main reasons for this is that they do not speak in human language, which is connected to seeing non-human animals as radically different from humans (as discussed in more detail in chapter 1). Because humans use human language, it is thought that we can gain insight into their minds; other animals lack language and thus this option is not open in our encounters with them. As we have seen, many other animals do have languages and do communicate with us, but simply referring to empirical research that shows continuities with human cognition and language is not enough to address skepticism about their minds, because skepticism about other animals' minds refers to a specific view of reason, laden with cultural values, and to an atomistic view of subjectivity.

In the philosophical tradition, reason has often been equated with human reason (Derrida 2008; Steiner 2010), and has also often been contrasted with emotion (Aaltola 2013; Adams [1990] 2010; Brooks Pribac 2013; Gruen 2015). Non-human animals, as well as women and other marginalized human groups, were long seen as non-rational (chapter 7). The view of reason presented was considered to be universal, even though it is in fact built on a specific view of the human subject, in a similar way to that in which 'language' was constructed as exclusively human. Seeing non-human animal minds as different to human minds, and as inaccessible, reflects cultural values (Aaltola 2013; Brooks Pribac 2013). Certain non-Western cultures see humans and other animals, and humans and nature, as part of a whole rather than as separated realms (Brooks Pribac 2013). Mi'kmaq cosmologies are, for example, shaped through a creation model in which other animals are portrayed as siblings who share personhood with human figures (Robinson 2013). Other animals are seen as active agents capable of creating kinship relations with humans. In Cree communities, non-human animals such as ravens are even cast in the role of the creator in creation stories, or portrayed as the figure through which the creator acts (Belcourt 2015). These ideas are interconnected with cultural practices that do not see the human as separated from other animals, but instead see other animals as members of a connected whole who understand humans, who humans can understand and to whom they speak and listen (ibid.).

Viewing other animals' minds as closed off from humans also mistakes how inter-subjectivity works. In a critique against human skepticism about other minds, Wittgenstein phrases this as follows: "My attitude toward him is an attitude towards a soul: I am not of the *opinion* that he has a soul" (1958, 178). In our everyday dealings, we approach subjects as subjects, which enables us to interact with them. This is one of the certainties that are needed in order to be able to acquire knowledge, even though they cannot be proved (Wittgenstein 1978). According to Wittgenstein, this is also how humans generally acquire knowledge about the world around them: there are certainties, which cannot be proved, that are needed in order to be able to get to know things. With regard to other beings, human and non-human, this means that seeing others as subjects, and not as machines, objects, or automata, enables humans to get to know them, and not the other way around.

Getting to know others is not just a cognitive process. Being with others and seeing others as subjects is intrinsically connected to empathy. Understood as a way of feeling and thinking our way into other animals' (human and non-human) minds and souls, empathy helps us to understand other animals. In our dealings with other animals, we have to recognize that we always already stand in relations to others; we are entangled in webs with them. Other animals are different to us, yet we are connected to them, and species is not a determining characteristic in how we understand and relate to one another. While our perceptions and experiences might sometimes be very different—imagine living your whole life under water, or spending all your days in holes in the earth, or flying vast distances twice each year—there is also often much that binds us, depending on context, species, and social groups. And as Merleau-Ponty rightly points out, difference does not separate us from others: it is what creates meaning.

Humans and other animals are connected on an existential level, if only for the simple reason that we all have bodies, can be wounded, and can die. We are also connected on the level of social bonds—humans and other animals feel love and share their lives with others, sometimes including others of different species. Lori Gruen (2015) argues that there is a normative component to this entanglement with other animals: in order to do justice to those that we are connected to, we have to develop a kind of caring perception—an entangled empathy—that is focused on attending to the wellbeing of others and learning to better understand them. Developing empathy in this manner is a process in which both cognition and emotion have a role to play.

Improving empathic skills can improve relations between human and non-human animals. The work of Simone Weil (2002) offers a starting point for further developing this sensibility, in particular her notion of "attention" (Aaltola 2013). Attention is, according to Weil, the core of human activity. It helps us to see clearly, to understand, and to move beyond prejudice. Elisa Aaltola (2013) argues that this concept can be understood as a moral imperative. In order to perceive truth, we need to set aside our ego, prejudices, and prefabricated opinions and ideas. The same applies in an interspecies context: to get to know other animals, we need to move beyond our own motivations and actually pay attention to them. We can then meet the other animal, begin to see them, and follow their lead. To pay attention also means not immediately trying to understand them from our perspective, but rather taking the time to "look at them till the light suddenly dawns" (Weil 2002, 120). To further explore this in the interspecies context, I now turn to living with other animals, beginning with ethologist Barbara Smuts's relations with baboons.

Living with Other Animals

In order to be able to study a group of baboons, Smuts (2001) had to learn to speak baboon. Scientists working with primates will usually try to ignore them, so that their presence near them will not influence their behavior. Smuts discovered that ignoring baboons is not a neutral act. Baboons who are closely related or who are good friends might sometimes ignore each other's close presence, but under other circumstances, ignoring may express mistrust or tension. Furthermore, Smuts directly experienced critical aspects of their society, such as hierarchy, personal space, and communication, by interacting with them. Because she paid attention to them and adjusted her behavior, the baboons came to accept her as a social being in their midst, as a subject to communicate with instead of an object that had to be avoided. Smuts found that the baboons did their best to understand her, even though she had an "outrageous human accent" (2001, 307). Scientists call the process of getting used to the presence of an observer "habituation," which implies that the baboons changed their ways in order to accept her as a neutral observer, but in Smuts's experience, the opposite happened: the baboons went on with their lives and she had to change her ways to be with them (see also Candea 2013; Despret 2008; Haraway 2008).

Smuts travelled with the Eburru Cliffs troupe, a group of 135 baboons, for two years, from dawn to dusk for around twelve hours a day. For several months she lived completely without the company of other humans. Later on she lived with other researchers, whom she saw in the evenings, but with whom she did not have much contact. By living with the baboons, experiencing their habits and daily life, Smuts became attuned to their movements, which changed her experience of her surroundings.

She felt like she was "turning into a baboon" (2001, 299) as she learned, for example, to read the weather as they did. During the rainy season, Smuts and the baboons could see storms approaching from a great distance. The baboons wanted to keep eating for as long as possible, and knew exactly when to move in order to find shelter in time. For months, Smuts wanted to move long before they did, until one day something shifted, and she suddenly understood clearly when it was the right moment to move. Smuts describes this as a moment where she went from seeing the world analytically to experiencing it directly and intuitively. An important factor in this process was belonging to a group: Smuts stresses the individuality of the baboons, but also emphasizes their group consciousness. She describes the troupe of baboons as a "larger feeling entity" that she gradually became part of (2001, 299).

To understand the world as they did, Smuts only had to "stick with the baboons and attend to what they did and notice how they responded" (2001, 299). Merleau-Ponty (1962) sees the life world not simply as the background of our lived experience, but instead as an *interworld* between subjects (see also Haysom 2009). This interworld is both the shared context of meaning that surrounds subjects in their everyday interaction and that which is the result of these interactions. In other words: we operate in a shared realm of meaning, and through interacting we change this meaning. This not only creates an interworld, it also connects those who do so together through bodily actions and through speech and language. Smuts experienced this very clearly: moving with the baboons and learning about their knowledge in this way—and vice versa, the baboons came to accept and, according to Smuts, understand her—changes their interworld, which simultaneously changed her perception of her surroundings and her state of being. Language plays an important role in this process; speaking their language allowed her to be with the baboons and to learn from them, and physically moving with them in the way that they moved changed her. Difference is not an obstacle to forming an interworld; rather, it allows for this common framework to come into being. The baboons created meaning in ways new to Smuts (for example, by moving as a group) and this enabled her to perceive her surroundings differently. In a human-baboon relationship, the perspective on the situation might be different for members of the different species, but through sharing experiences they constitute a common world that is neither human nor baboon.

Speaking to or with Dogs

Smuts needed to learn the language of the baboons in order to be able to study them. Baboons are not, however, accustomed to close interaction with humans, nor do they particularly desire it, something they show by the fact that they do not seek out contact with humans, and Smuts therefore kept her distance. Her worldview did change, as theirs probably also did, at least to a certain extent; Smuts mentions feelings of companionship and even friendship. However, she tuned into their way of being more than they did to hers, so the interaction was asymmetrical. This is often the case in human/non-human animal relationships, but it is usually the other way around: other animals are forced to fit into human material and ideological structures. Even in close relationships in which humans acknowledge and foster non-human animal agency— with companion animals, for example—humans often determine the wider framework within which other animals can exercise agency. We find an example of this in Hearne's work with Salty: although Salty exercised agency, Hearne determined the framework within which she could do so; Salty could not leave the house or choose not to participate in the interaction.

In dog-human relations, humans often decide on key aspects of the dogs' lives, such as where and with whom they live, when they can go outside, and what they eat. This is unfortunate, because it limits the space in which dogs can develop themselves, as well as possibilities of finding new ways to interact. Dogs are seen as incapable of making their own decisions, and do not therefore get the chance to do so, which reinforces the view that they are not capable of doing so. This is often connected to a specific view of language and interaction in which the human is taken as the standard. This way of viewing language limits the possibilities of building common worlds with dogs. An example of this is dog language research.

The most famous language-using dog is probably the border collie Chaser, who learned and retained the proper-noun names of 1,022 objects over a three-year period of intensive training: 800 cloth animals, 116 balls, 26 Frisbees, and a medley of plastic items (Pilley and Reid 2011). She also learned to categorize these objects. Chaser can learn by deduction and understands grammar (Pilley 2013). It is clear that Chaser has a good memory; psychologist John Pilley had to write the names on the toys with a marker because he could not remember them. It is also clear that she is a fast learner. However, Chaser's accomplishments do not tell us much about dog language, or even dog-human understanding. Learning words, seen by humans as something profound, can contribute to improving dog-human understanding, but it is one form of interaction among many. Chaser and Pilley's use of language is very similar to the Augustinian picture of language referred to by Wittgenstein at the beginning of *Philosophical Investigations*; it is a very specific language game, in which Chaser learns to attach names to objects. It is not the only language game developed in this research; categorizing objects and learning to use grammar are other examples. There are, of course, also language games related to the interaction with Pilley, with whom Chaser lives. However, the language research does not help us to understand Chaser better, nor does it help us to see how dogs express themselves and what they want from us.

Haraway (2003, 2008) puts forward a different perspective on dog-human relations. She draws attention to the processes of domestication in which dogs and humans coevolved, and stresses the importance of material and physical dimensions in dog-human interaction to argue for taking dog agency more seriously, and to present an image of the human as always entangled in relations with others. There are different theories about the domestication of dogs (Zeder et al. 2006). While some scientists think that humans domesticated dogs, others argue that dogs domesticated themselves, or that they played a role in the domestication of humans: some even argue that humans started to use language through calling their dogs (Haraway 2003). Because of their long history together, dogs and humans understand each other quite well. We know that dogs started barking to attract human attention, while wolves only sing (Slobodchickoff 2012). Humans, even those who do not live with dogs, can interpret the barking and growling of dogs correctly, and dogs can do the same for human vocal and facial expressions (Hare and Woods 2013). Recent research has shown that, contrary to popular belief, dogs do understand the words that humans use and do not just respond to their tone of voice (Andics et al. 2016).[5] Living with dogs has also affected the genetic make-up of humans. When a dog and a human who love each other gaze into each other's eyes, both create oxytocin—something that humans also do when they look into the eyes of their child or lover (Nagasawa et al. 2015). These examples show that the human species has not evolved in a vacuum, and that animals of other species have played a role in how we perceive the world, and vice versa, on many levels of our existence. How, exactly, certain species have influenced humans, and humans other animals, differs between cultures and communities and changes over time. While humans in Western societies determine much of the macro framework in which non-human animals live, particularly domesticated animals, at a micro-level, non-human animals can also strongly influence human lives.

By describing how she and her dog companion Cayenne Pepper train for agility (a dog sport), Haraway (2003, 2008) draws attention to how living with dogs can change one individually. Training together increases the knowledge and understanding they have of one another and of the world. This enriches their shared vocabulary and strengthens their common world. Haraway stresses the fact that this is a mutual process in which both dog and human exercise agency, and change. However, even though Cayenne Pepper has options to exercise micro-agency and does change Haraway's life, her macro-agency, understood as her ability to determine key factors of her life—such as where to live, who to live with, and so on—is limited (Donaldson and Kymlicka 2013a, see also chapter 9). She cannot, for example, choose not to participate in the agility training. Developing a common language alters their world, but the altered world remains anthropocentric because the human ultimately holds the strings. In this scenario dogs are invited to participate in some language games, but not all, and humans determine which ones they can take part in. While these humans are affected by the dogs about whom they write, the relationships they describe are still asymmetrical in terms of power relations.

We find an alternative approach in the interaction between Smuts (2001) and her dog companion Safi, which shows us how human and non-human animals can together co-determine the shape of their lives. Smuts adopted Safi from an animal shelter and decided not to train her, but to communicate with her as an equal. Safi and Smuts are each sensitive to the other, and they have reached a high degree of understanding and intimacy. Because Safi has "an inherent sense of appropriate behavior in different circumstances" (2001, 303), Smuts can take her almost anywhere off lead. In the city, she will make most decisions; outside of the city it is Safi who usually decides where to go and what to do. If they disagree, they meet somewhere in the middle. Smuts sees intersubjectivity as the possibility to shape new realities through interaction with others, in which both subjects are not "given" before they meet (see also Haraway 2003, 2008). She aims not only to respect the influence of Safi on her life, but also searches for ways in which Safi can influence the larger structures that determine the conditions under which she lives.

In describing these processes, Smuts emphasizes the embodied dimensions of their interactions. In addition to the development of their common language, she describes how daily rituals—including dog-human yoga in the morning, initiated by Safi—come into being as a result of constant interaction. These habits and rituals are not determined beforehand, but spring from their life together and give it substance. Habits usually unfold without explicitly attending to them (Merleau-Ponty 1962; Weiss 2006). According to Merleau-Ponty (1962, 143), it is the body, and not consciousness, that acts in habitual projects. This does not reduce their value; on the contrary, habits expand the meaning and range of our experiences and widen our access to the world. They offer "a different way of inscribing ourselves in the world and of inscribing the world in our body" (Weiss 2006, 236). The body is seen as "an open system of dynamic exchanges with the world, exchanges that, in their habituality, ground the body ever more firmly within the world, and, in the process, offer us new ways of engaging and transforming it" (ibid.). Safi and Smuts show that this can also happen in relations with beings of another species. They co-shape their common world by each being open to the other and paying attention, using language and habits as tools. In order to be able to do this, Smuts has had to set aside her own ego-directed motivations and to be open to Safi, who does the same in relation to her.

Multispecies Households: Material Interventions and Fostering Non-Human Animal Agency

Safi and Smuts live in the same house, which has enabled them to develop a close relationship. Smuts sees Safi as an individual who co-determines the rules according to which they live together. Many humans share their lives and households with other animals, yet houses, like cities (Wolch 2010), are usually seen as human spaces (see Wolch and Emel 1998 for an analysis). This not only mistakes the moral value of other animals—i.e., their standing as members of the household, or inhabitants of cities—it also obscures the ways in which they exercise agency, and limits opportunities for communication. In human relations with other animals, material interventions and the interactions that follow from them can play a major role. Opening the door for someone is a form of communication; putting a blanket on the floor can be an invitation; installing a cat flap can change the terms of interaction (Driessen 2014). Through these interactions humans can express themselves to other animals, and vice versa.

Writer Julie Ann Smith draws attention to the importance of spatial and material interactions in getting to know rabbits. As a member of the House Rabbit Society, Smith has rescued and lived with over two hundred rabbits. She sees rabbits as individuals with rich inner lives and investigates how living with them, sharing a house, can shed light on their ways of being. Rescuing rabbits involves a good deal of human control over them, including determining where, how, and with whom they live, what they eat, whether they are neutered, and so on. As with many other domesticated species, rabbits are vulnerable, so they cannot simply be left to fend for themselves. This does not mean that the rabbits do not exercise agency. Members of the House Rabbit Society, for example, need to "rabbit-proof" their houses because rabbits chew on furniture and demand certain spatial arrangements. While this may seem like a restriction on the side of the human, it can also be a source of information and a starting point for communication. Smith describes how during the day the rabbits made a mess of their litter boxes and toys, which she would clean up in the evening. At a certain point she began to see a logic to their mess: rabbits like free corridors, and they arranged items so that they fit their idea of how space should be arranged.

This insight enabled her to see the rabbits and the space differently. The rabbits decorated the house in the way they thought was best or necessary; the house was not a mess, there was an order to the arrangement that Smith had to learn before she could see it.

Rabbits experience the world differently to humans. As prey animals, they are cautious in all they do. Their hearing is much sharper than ours, as is their sense of smell. Their eyes are on the side of their heads, rather than forward-facing like those of predators, which gives them a wide peripheral range of vision. There are also characteristics that we share. Rabbits and humans are social animals, and like humans rabbits can have close relationships with members of their own and other species. Smith describes, for example, how they mourn deceased companions, which can be very emotional; responses to death differ largely between individuals. Smith is careful not to impose human values and worldviews on them, and wants to engage with them as much as possible on their terms. She has come to think of her relationship with them as "performance ethics," an ethics in which both rabbits and humans act creatively and thereby shape their life together. The ethical part involves a responsibility towards the rabbits, whereas the performance part allows for animal agency (including her own); the precise relationship comes into being through acting (see also chapter 2).

In describing their habits and lives, Smith shows that rabbits do not act on instinct, but creatively and intentionally. However, she still saw a disconnection between the rabbits' natures and their human surroundings. This eventually led her to create a more natural setting for them outdoors so that they could live in large groups in a fenced part of her garden. This solution, she argues, refers back to a larger tension in her work, which will be familiar for many humans who engage in animal rescue work: domesticated animals often need human care to survive or thrive, while at the same time one does not rescue other animals in order to keep them captive. The shape of human society often makes it difficult to live with other animals on an equal footing, or to enlarge their freedom, because so many spatial, material, ideological, and legal arrangements are human-centered. One cannot, for example, let a dog off the lead in the Netherlands, because humans drive cars that pose danger, and Dutch legislation prohibits it (see Case Study 1). However, Smith's solution of giving the rabbits their own space outside her house also seems problematic. Creating a more natural habitat for rabbits does not challenge human domination of animal space, nor does it further explore how animal agency, and interspecies interaction, can shape the conditions of coexistence.

Experiencing a similar tension between wanting to take care of his non-human companion, and the desire to offer him freedom, Ted Kerasote (2008) installed a dog door in his house. The dog door functioned as a tool to create more freedom for his dog companion Merle. Merle had found Kerasote when he was camping out in the desert. Kerasote had been looking for a dog companion, and took Merle, who was persistent in his attempts to stay with him, home. Kerasote was committed to offering him a full life with as much freedom as possible. He taught Merle the social rules of Kelly, Wyoming, where he lived, so that Merle would know the framework within which he could act. This included dealing with wild non-human animals, cattle, and farmers who would shoot dogs when they trespassed. Kerasote then installed a dog door in his house so that Merle could come and go as he pleased. This enabled Merle to spend time with his canine and human friends in town if he wanted to, and to return home when he was hungry or tired. Sometimes he also brought other dogs home. Most of the dogs in Kelly lived similar lives, and experienced a large amount of freedom. They all made different choices; some stayed closer to home than others, some played with other dogs a lot while others did not, some preferred human company, others preferred the company of dogs. The dogs in Kelly seem to enjoy the best of both worlds. They have the safety of a home, access to food and medical care, and the opportunity to form close bonds with humans and other animals in their households, but they are also free to make their own choices regarding where and with whom to spend their time. Kerasote argues that this not only enriches their lives, but also makes them smarter and more responsible. The dogs have to learn to negotiate risks, some of which will always remain risks (these include being shot by farmers and encountering the wild animals roaming the area), but a safe life is not the same as a good life. In these small, rural towns, it seems to be possible to facilitate this kind of lifestyle for dogs and to offer them wider freedom of movement. This does not necessarily lead to detachment. As Merle's freedom increased, the relationship with Kerasote also deepened. Like Smuts, Kerasote is committed to the flourishing of his dog companion, and searches for ways to contribute to this for Merle's sake, even if it makes life less comfortable for him at times; for example, when he fears that Merle will not return.

Developing New Relations with Other Animals

Interacting with non-human animals in new ways aimed at respecting their agency and enhancing their freedom—as Smuts and Kerasote do—gives them the opportunity to act differently, and offers them a starting point to co-shape the grounds of interaction. Non-human animals have their own unique perspectives on life and their own ideas about the good life. Instead of predetermining what they want on their behalf, we should look for ways to enable the conditions under which they can express themselves more fully. Humans can then respond to this in an open-ended process or dialogue.

There is, of course, a large variety in capacities and relations between human and non-human animals—there is no "animal" who speaks or does not speak. In thinking about communication and language, humans often focus on species membership. Social relations are however just as, or perhaps more, important. While humans and wild non-human animals can build relations—as the examples of the baboons and Smuts, or the birds and Howard show– and wild non-human individuals can sometimes adapt to living in close proximity to humans, domesticated non-human animals are generally more attuned to humans. This is the result of breeding practices, often based on the fact that they were eager to interact with humans in the first place.[6] Domestication is a matter of degree—here we can, for example, think of cats, who are not considered completely domesticated (Bradshaw 2016), but who often live with humans as companions, or of "wild" animals living in circuses or other forms of captivity for generations, who have adapted to their artificial surroundings and working with humans, and are in a sense domesticated (Grazian 2012).[7] Groups and individuals within species can furthermore stand in very different relations to humans: for example, groups of horses or rabbits or dogs can be feral, domesticated, or wild, and may move between categories.

Non-human animals who are on the domesticated end of the spectrum are generally quite attuned to humans. Horses, for example, can

read human emotions from photographs, remember them, and anticipate these emotions when they meet the humans in the pictures later
(Proops et al. 2018). They can use pictograms to tell humans whether
or not they want to wear a blanket, and this system could be used to
speak about many other questions (Mejdell et al. 2016; see chapter 9 for
a longer discussion). They can be taught to tell their rider to dismount
off their backs when they are riding[8] and they know how to maneuver
humans into a certain direction if they know the humans do not know
where the carrots are (Ringhofer and Yamamoto 2017). Above I already
discussed dog-human relations, and there are many other examples of
domesticated non-human animals who developed complex language
games in relation to or with humans, ranging from chickens who name
their humans (Montgomery 2016) to cats who teach themselves to meow
if they want to gain their human's attention (Bradshaw 2016).[9] Instead of
using this attunement for human benefit or profit, it can be used to consult other animals about the design of new interspecies communities.

To do justice to non-human animal agency, existing interactions
should form the basis for theorizing non-anthropocentric relations.
Language plays a large part in the formulation of new relations and the
creation of new forms of coexistence, because it is through language that
we can learn to better understand others, and they us, which can serve
as a starting point for strengthening common worlds or coming to more
distant agreements or arrangements. Developing a common understanding through teaching a dog the rules of a town does not restrict the
dog's life; in fact, the opposite happens: it enables them to be more free.

In animal liberation theories, non-human animal freedom is often
conceptualized as freedom from humans. Relational approaches, such
as the political theory of animal rights developed by Sue Donaldson and
Will Kymlicka in *Zoopolis*, or the interspecies encounters described by
Haraway, direct our attention to the many ways in which the lives of
human and non-human animals are intertwined. These approaches also
show that freedom does not have only one form: it may mean something
different to a rabbit than it does to a dog, and it may mean something
other to Safi than to Merle or Chaser. Humans and other animals have
not evolved separately, nor do they live in separate realms. Our lives
are interconnected on many levels: historically, materially, discursively,
and so on. Human influence, ranging from encroaching on the habitats

of wild animals to genetically altering the bodies of domesticated animals, often sets limits on the freedom of non-human animals. It also sets limits on human freedom, and animal oppression shares characteristics with the oppression of marginalized human groups.

In order to envision animal freedom or liberation, it is not enough to criticize exploitation or only work towards abolishing oppressive relationships; we also need to work towards new ways of interacting with other animals. We find examples of this in the work of Howard, Kerasote, and Smuts, who all take the idea of creating new ways of living with other animals seriously. Working towards expanding the freedom of other animals should not be imagined as a single, linear movement guided by humans, but rather as a set of open-ended interspecies freedom practices (Foucault 1998), which can inform political institutions and practices from the ground up (see also part III of this book). Further developing these situated interspecies practices aimed at enlarging freedom for all involved not only helps us to conceptualize practices that challenge the oppression of non-human animals, but also to imagine new, positive, interspecies ways of living with them.

Case Study 1

Stray Philosophy

Dog-Human Observations on Language, Freedom, and Politics

Olli arrived at Schiphol Airport in the early evening of November 17, 2013. By that time he had been travelling for over twenty-four hours. He had left Pascani, in the North of Romania, on Saturday afternoon, arrived in Bucharest early on Sunday morning, waited at the airport for several hours, and then flown to the Netherlands, where I was waiting for him. I was not the only nervous person at arrivals. Olli was one of ten dogs who had travelled to the Netherlands that evening, accompanied by two volunteers from a small Dutch animal welfare organization, Dierenhulp Orfa. My aunt had offered to drive us home, and she chatted cheerfully to the other waiting humans while I watched the door.

The first dogs to arrive were young and very good-looking, with long hair and fluffy ears. Olli was the last dog to come out of the door, and I recognized his black and white fur immediately from the photographs I had seen of him. I had already heard him wagging his tail loudly against the sides of his crate before I could see him. The volunteers put the crate down in front of me, and I sat down on the floor to speak to Olli. He was panting nervously, his eyes were red, and he smelt really bad, but it was clear that he was extremely enthusiastic about all this human attention. He was also quite a bit larger than I had expected. One of the volunteers opened the door of his crate and put a collar and a harness on him. She handed me the two leads, and Olli stepped out of the crate. Overwhelmed by the lights and people, he instantly lay down on the floor. I sat down next to him and told him how happy I was that he was here. He stood up, greeted some of the other dogs, and then lay down again, still wagging his tail.

When most of the other dogs had left, I told Olli we were going home. He refused to get up. My aunt's car was parked in front of the airport and we needed to cross the main hall to get to it. I tried to tempt Olli

FIGURE CS1.1. Olli at the airport 1

FIGURE CS1.2. Olli at the airport 2

with dog treats, but he was far too nervous to eat. So I picked him up, said goodbye to the other humans, and off we went. Olli was not only quite a bit larger than I had expected, he was also rather heavy.[1] I had to put him down a few times, and each time he again made himself as flat and small as possible—all the time still wagging his tail as if his life depended on it. It took us about fifteen minutes to get to the car in this way. By the time we got there, we had already both decided to trust each other—because we needed to.

This case study is a philosophical exploration of the experiences Olli and I had in the first three months we spent together. During this time, we created the beginnings of a common language, we developed habits, and we established a certain degree of freedom for Olli, who learned to deal with living in a house and moving around a city. Both of us put a lot of effort into this, and although I am the one who is writing down what happened, Olli's voice is as important as mine. This chapter is divided into three sections: language and habits, freedom and walking on the lead, and politics. I end with some remarks about Olli's influence on me, and about how these experiences can shed light on new forms of living together.

Language and Habits

Olli joined a small multispecies household consisting of one human, one eleven-year-old former stray dog from Greece, Pika, and one eight-year-old cat from Lebanon, Putih. In the first five years of his life, Olli had never lived in a house or walked on a lead, neither had he experienced a close relationship with a human. He had spent his first two or three years as a stray dog in his hometown of Pascani until he was brought to the new municipal shelter there by dog catchers. Dogs were not treated well in this shelter and over a third of the dogs there died of malnutrition and fights within the first year of its existence. After about a year, the remaining dogs were rescued by an animal welfare organization and taken to a private shelter. A few of them died of exhaustion on the way to this shelter and others caught canine distemper. The brother of the man who transported the dogs also killed some of them. Circumstances were slightly better for the surviving dogs at the new shelter, but there were nevertheless shortages of food, extreme cold in the winter, and fights between the dogs. In the week before Olli came to the Netherlands, he escaped the shelter with a small group of other dogs because they were scared by hunters. The hunters tried to shoot the dogs, and one of the dogs did not survive.

Olli is probably the descendant of generations of stray dogs (although no information is available about his parentage). He is quite different from the domesticated dogs who live in the Netherlands in behavior and appearance. He is very fit and strong, he can run for hours, jump onto a 1.8m wall without a run-up, and he uses his paws and mouth to open doors, boxes, and plastic bags that contain food. When he arrived in the Netherlands, however, he was not in a good shape. He had been neutered in the week before he came, and the vet had not performed the operation correctly; the wound was large and infected. In addition to being very tired from the traveling and all the new experiences, he was ill and dealing with hormonal changes.

In his first days here, he slept during the daytime and was alert at night. I kept the radio on to filter out sounds, but could still hear him jumping up every few hours, scratching at the doors to get out with every sound that scared him. After a couple of days he realized that the house was a safe place, and he has slept well since.[2] The biggest challenge in these first days was going outside and walking on the lead. He was scared of walking out of the door (he disliked doors for a long time), of traffic, humans, and of walking on the lead. Dog treats helped, but he often lay down on the street and refused to walk further. He mostly did this when too much happened at the same time, for example, when we crossed the street and traffic came from all sides, or when bicycles and humans and other dogs passed us as we walked on the pavement, or when there were loud noises in different places. Usually he plucked up courage after a while, but sometimes I had to carry him home. He spent a lot of time smelling everything. We also encountered problems inside the house: Olli liked human attention, but close contact with me was difficult for him. It made him nervous to have me near him all the time, and he and I did not understand each other well—for example, he growls if he wants to go outside or wants to be petted, which I found quite intimidating at first. I had to learn not to touch his head (something I can do now) and to stay away from him while he slept.

In his first weeks here, Pika was Olli's main guide. She accepted him immediately, and from the first moment they got along well. He

FIGURE CS1.3. The first day

stayed close to her, both inside and outside the house. If we crossed the street—a scary moment—he often walked so close to her that the sides of their bodies touched. He copied her actions inside the house, for example, in trying out new food: if Pika ate a piece of food that was new to him, he would also eat it.[3] He needed a lot of physical contact, and Pika did not mind if he lay very close to her; she always remained calm when he was nervous. I followed her example. His nervousness sometimes made me nervous, or anxious about the future, and Pika helped both of us to remain calm. She truly was my partner in this. Many fireworks are let off on New Year's Eve and in the week leading up to it in the Netherlands. Because of the incident with the hunters before he came here, the loud noises frightened Olli so much that he no longer dared to go outside. I was afraid that Olli would not get used to living here, that his fear was too much. Pika helped him to regain his confidence, and she helped me to deal with Olli's panic.

Words and Bodies

From the first moment, Olli and I tried to understand each other. We both had some idea: Olli had met many humans, good and bad; I had experience with dogs and other animals. Barbara Smuts (2002) writes about the experience of adopting dog Safi from a shelter, and describes her as having "an inherent sense of appropriate behavior." This was not the case with Olli, even though he was never unfriendly to me—not even in moments of great fear. His behavior was geared to survival; he was always looking to escape, steal food, and please humans so that they would give him food. For instance, he jumped onto the counter in the kitchen to eat the cat food—Olli is not a small dog—onto the table to eat my food, and he also jumped over the fence into my neighbor's garden to escape and chased Putih around the house.

Many of the movements I made frightened him, and it often seemed as if he could not predict what I might do. In walking past each other in the house, for example, usually both creatures adjust so that they can pass without bumping into each other. Olli clearly lacked the experience to navigate this type of space and he could not read human bodies well. There might also be differences in how Romanian humans and Dutch humans behave. Although he was eager to respond in the right manner, he often did not understand my questions, and I did not know how to frame them in a way he could understand. We both tried hard to convince the other that we meant well. I spoke to him in a friendly tone of voice and touched his body in ways he appreciated; he wagged his tail all the time and kept offering me his paw. I held his hand a lot.[4]

The first word I taught him was "no", mostly for intuitive reasons. I needed to make it clear that Olli could not chase or bite Putih, jump onto the counter or over the fence. The word "no" has never attained the meaning "stop this" in our relationship, but it does tell Olli that I would like him to stop doing whatever he is doing; it gives him information about my position, which clarifies situations for him. If I need him to stop doing something immediately I have to offer him an alternative, a toy or something to eat, or I can give him a hug.[5] Olli proved to be an exceptionally fast learner, and within a few days we developed a simple language, including the use of words such as "no," "here," "dog bed," "food," "cookies," "yes," "go," "wait," and "sorry." These words were tools we worked with to get to know each other, and they helped me to show Olli the way. In addition to using simple words as tools, I spoke to him in full sentences, as I do to Pika, and he soon started to understand these as well. He also understands that words can have different meanings in different situations. As our vocabulary grew, Olli's confidence grew. He is especially fond of words that describe his behavior in a positive way, such as "good" and "sweet." The most important word was, of course, "Olli." Olli very much enjoys having a name. He likes it when neighbors or humans in the park call him by his name. He likes it when I do so too. It makes him feel appreciated, which is part of belonging here. Humans who use his name show that they see him and appreciate him being here. It is also an important instrument between us: I can ask for his attention and he can choose to respond. Because he likes to respond to his name I was later able to let him off the lead.

As well as words, Olli had to learn to read my gestures and body movements. He expressed a strong desire to have physical contact, but in the first weeks he could not relax when he was close to me, which resulted in him standing next to me as I sat on the couch, petting my leg, his body stiff and uneasy. We spent a lot of time on the couch together. Olli showed me how he liked to be touched and by responding to him I could show him that I meant well. From standing next to me he began to sit down, then after a week or so he lay down next to me. If I made a wrong move, he jumped up. Paradoxically, touching him also helped him to relax, particularly softly stroking his neck. He now lies on his back all the time and demands that I rub his tummy, and if I do not respond fast enough he might growl or bark.

Moving together helped to get to know each other and build trust. Because Olli was nervous and wanted to run, I took him with me when I went running. This helped him to get used to the city and to my body. In the beginning, he walked from left to right in front of me, so I often had to stop and jump to the side or over him. We did not run long distances; we would run for a few minutes, stand still because Olli had picked up a scent or was afraid, move again. I went along with what made him most comfortable. Running was more comfortable for him than walking; if we walked he had too much time to see things around him and become nervous. It also made him tired, which helped him relax inside the house.

I had to learn to read Olli as well. Some actions were quite clear from the beginning: if he wanted me to pet him, he would take my hand in his.[6] But I did not automatically understand what he meant when he growled (this usually meant that he was bored, but it sometimes meant my head was too close to his) or barked (this could be an invitation to play or a strong expression of the desire to go outside). Wagging his tail was a way to communicate that he meant well—or even a plea not to harm him—more than of expressing joy, as it is often perceived. These days he wags his tail much less than in those first months, even though he is much happier now.

After a few weeks, Olli started to make eye contact with me inside our house; after a few months he also started to do so outside.[7] His posture changed. At first he held his tail and ears low, whether inside or out, and I thought this was the default position of his body. But after two months his tail went up in a curl and he now walks around proudly. He was afraid of humans and masked his fear by acting very friendly: wagging his tail, holding his body and ears low. He now approaches humans differently, and feels confident enough to ignore them in the park. His attitude towards me changed as well. He stopped asking for attention and comfort all the time. He does make small gestures, such as touching the inside of my hand with his nose, to make contact during the day. In the process of getting to know each other, misunderstandings helped to create understanding (see also Pepperberg 1995, Despret 2006). I once accidentally kicked Olli in the face with my foot because he tried to eat something from the street on our first walk of the day; I was still sleepy and responded too slowly when he walked in front of me. This scared him, but I immediately told him I was sorry and comforted him. In the beginning he was also afraid of me dropping plates and pans, but he learned that this was not directed towards him and that I am just a clumsy human who means well. Olli and I also had to learn to listen to each other in more than one sense: we had to learn to hear each other and follow each other.

Although Pika and Olli got along immediately, he had some trouble communicating with other dogs. This was partly due to suddenly having to walk on a lead, which made him feel uncomfortable and therefore defensive. He was also unaccustomed to meeting so many new dogs all the time, many of whom had to be ignored or who did not act in accordance with their position in the hierarchy. This changed after a few weeks as he became used to the new situation. But there were still miscommunications once he was used to walking on the lead and could play off the lead in the park. Olli uses his voice a lot as he plays (he growls loudly) and he likes to play rough, something that can scare smaller or more timid dogs. We usually go to a park where there are other rescue dogs, and Olli gets along with them fine. He learned to play with the shyer dogs, and they learned not to be afraid of him. Some of them learned to invite him to play on their terms. There is, for example, one young female dog who likes to play slowly with a lot of touching. She was afraid of Olli's rough manners at first, but when she got to know him better, she started inviting him to play in the way she likes. Olli understands this, and is more careful with her than with the others. Now, after three years, he is one of the calmest and gentlest dogs around; he helps other dogs feel comfortable, and is friendly towards all creatures—including humans, dogs, children, birds, cats, and mice.

New Languages and Habits

Olli and I became attuned to each other and created a frame of reference through developing a common language and creating new habits. We expressed ourselves through language, understood in a broad sense (Meijer 2013; Wittgenstein 1958), and this functioned as a bridge to span the distance between us. It created a common world and a way to express understanding of it. We did this together: the content was not pre-determined. Both Olli and I brought our histories and ways of giving meaning to the relationship; through interacting, we created something new that changed both of us (Haraway 2008, 6; Smuts 2006). Developing habits also helped us to understand each other. Doing the same thing at the same time of day every day gave us something to hold onto, and understanding the routines of the house and engaging in daily rituals made Olli feel more secure. It also gave us something to refer to: after he had learned the routine, we could change it. We always take our daily long walk in the morning, but because Olli know this, we can go in the afternoon: I can tell him we will take a long walk later. We have many habits, concerning when and where to sleep, when and where to walk, when and what to eat. Pika and Olli both exercise agency in this.

FIGURE CS1.4. Olli and Pika 1

FIGURE CS1.5. Olli and Pika 2

FIGURE CS1.6. To the park

Before Olli came, Pika and I took the long walk in the afternoon. In the first months, because Olli had so much energy after sleeping through the night and he expressed a strong interest in walking early in the morning (by growling and barking), we moved the long afternoon walk to the morning. He is much calmer now, but we have all gotten used to walking in the morning, so we have kept that routine. Other examples concern the sharing of space. Olli prefers to sleep for a while on a chair in the front room of the house after his breakfast while Pika and I are in the living room. After the long walk, Olli chews his bone on the bed while Pika lies on the couch. They share the couch in the evening until Pika goes to bed. If Olli gets bored in the morning he comes into the living room, where he greets me before moving to the couch with Pika. These experiences are embodied, often not conscious, and create meaning and understanding in a physical way (Merleau-Ponty 1962, 143; see also Weiss 2006). The habits we developed structured experiences and added new layers of meaning to our life together for both Olli and me.

After a few weeks, I taught Olli to walk next to the bicycle. Pika and I usually travel to our favorite park with a cargo bike because it is too far for her to walk; we have small parks nearby, but we do not like them so much. Olli soon learned to run next to the cargo bike while Pika sat in it. This bike is quite heavy, especially with Pika in it, and Olli was still learning to walk on the lead and afraid of the city, so going to the park like this was quite a challenge for both Olli and me. Going to the same park every day, walking next to the bicycle, and taking the same route soon became familiar, making life more familiar. Creating habits like these helped to make Olli feel more at home in his new life. This particular habit gives us the freedom to travel. Through moving with Olli and learning about his responses, I gained an insight into his way of navigating the environment and his view on his surroundings; I learned to see through his eyes. I can reflect on my responses and switch between our perspectives, but when we cycle to the park and encounter something that frightens Olli, my response is physical and immediate in the way Merleau-Ponty describes.[8]

Learning to Walk on the Lead

In his first weeks here, Olli was very eager to escape. One afternoon, he chewed on his lead while I was speaking to a neighbor. It took him about ten seconds to break it—luckily, he was wearing both a collar and a harness. Later that week he jumped over a 1.6m fence into our neighbor's garden. There's a high brick wall between my garden and the street, so there was no real risk of him running away, but the message was clear: he wanted to run away. The city made him nervous and he wanted to get out of it; he also had a strong desire to scavenge for food. Being with me made him nervous as well. He had to watch me all the time to make sure I would not hurt him. After a while he started to relax inside the house, but outside he was still nervous and did not make much contact with me, although he did watch Pika. He did not turn to me for help or comfort when something frightened him, as Pika does, but retreated even more into his own world. Walking on the lead made him extra insecure; he felt handicapped by it. Looking at his behavior, one could conclude that Olli understood freedom in a negative sense: he longed to be free from external restraints, and he felt very passionate about enlarging this freedom.

Olli's desire to escape was, of course, connected to his past experience. He had lived in a cage about six meters square, with two or three other dogs, for over a year. Someone came to feed the dogs once a day, and once or twice a week a volunteer visited the dogs, but most of the human attention went to the dogs that had health problems. In the municipal shelter where he had lived previously, he had shared one large space with about thirty dogs who were not given enough food. Many dogs died, and so escape was high on their list of priorities. Before that, Olli had lived on the streets. He was free in the sense that he could decide where to go, what to eat, and who to be with, but there are many dangers for stray dogs in Romania and this had meant that he had to be on guard constantly. Olli had clearly had bad experiences with humans, and fear constrains freedom.

His desire to escape also revealed that Olli has a strong will. Making his own choices about where to go, who to be with, and what to eat is important to him. I wanted to respect this and treat him as an equal as much as possible, but I was limited by the circumstances; I had to make him walk on the lead. Dogs are obliged to walk on a lead in the Netherlands by law, except in certain designated areas, such as some beaches and dog parks. There is also a lot of traffic in the part of the country where we live, which makes it unsafe to walk off-lead. And, as I mentioned, Olli was scared and wanted to run away, so I had to restrict his freedom in order to be able to expand it later.

In the first weeks I made Olli wear both a collar and harness outside for reasons of safety. He slowly became used to the neighborhood and to our routines, which allowed me to take off the collar. If we did something difficult, such as running next to the bicycle or taking the tram, I made him wear his collar as well. After about a month I felt secure enough to take him and Pika to our favorite off-lead, unfenced dog park. This park is large, relatively quiet, and visited by friendly dogs. I bought a lunge line so that Olli could play with the other dogs and behave more naturally. Although he began to feel more at ease in the weeks that followed, he still really wanted to get away and did not pay much attention to me outside the house—he came when I offered him food, but he did not make eye contact and his stress levels were quite high. This was the most difficult period in terms of negotiating freedom. Olli was still nervous, yet eager to move and to play with the other dogs. I wanted to let him off the lead, but could not, because our relationship was too fragile and there was too much traffic nearby. It was physically difficult

FIGURE CS1.7. The curl in his tail

FIGURE CS1.8. Making eye contact

for both of us as well: Olli is a strong dog, and it hurt his body and my hand if he ran to the end of the lead and jerked it. It was hard for him to behave normally towards other dogs. He felt handicapped by the physical restraints and this made him more defensive and sometimes slightly agitated. Although he did not seem to hold it against me, it made me feel sad to be the one who was restraining his freedom. I wanted him to be as happy as possible—running and playing with other dogs made him happy—and I seemed only to be making things more difficult for him.

In February, three months after he came to live with us, he started to make eye contact with me in the park. We always go to the park at around the same time, so Olli got to know the dogs and the humans that were usually there well, and they him, which made him feel safe and connected. At that time, he always came to me when I called his name, even when other dogs distracted him. I decided to take the next step, and I sometimes let go of the long lead for a while. After that, I left a short lead on the harness, and eventually I took him off the lead completely. This process was a positive spiral: I was able to start it because he was more at ease, and it made him more at ease because he could use his body freely. This improved his relationships with the other dogs in the park and helped him to relax, which also changed his attitude towards me.

Discipline and Deliberation

The lead had multiple meanings in the relationship between Olli and me. On the one hand, it constrained Olli's freedom of movement and expression. On the other hand, it was a tool between us, similar to words, an instrument for what animal geographer Clemens Driessen (2016) calls "interspecies deliberation," and as such helpful in his education. In order to further conceptualize this, I first want to make a distinction between the process of learning to walk on the lead and the lead as an institute. As an institute, leads very clearly restrict the freedom of dogs. The lead is an instrument developed to control the bodies of non-human animals, to tame or train them and make them internalize power: to discipline them (Foucault [1975] 2010). Many humans in Western societies have strict ideas about how dogs should behave, and some even use instruments such as shock collars, in which fear of pain is the main learning mechanism, to control their bodies and behavior. If there had been a choice, I would have chosen not to use a lead, because it represented my power over Olli, symbolically and literally.[9] Being forced to walk on the lead reinforced his fear of humans and his low self-esteem, and made it harder for him to behave as he thought best in a situation that was already difficult. Olli is now used to it, but he does not particularly enjoy walking on the lead—he prefers to be able to roam the surroundings at his own tempo. He does not make a big deal of it, and we usually mutually adjust, and wait for the other if necessary. Unfortunately, for reasons already mentioned, we had and have no choice. I am forced, on legal grounds, to keep my dog companions on the lead, and Olli really wanted to escape, which meant there was a risk of him being hurt or even killed. Both aspects, the legal obligation to keep dogs on the lead and the threats to safety, are expressions of an anthropocentric society.

Some authors (Haraway 2003; Hearne [1986] 2007) view learning processes such as learning to walk on a lead, learning to retrieve, and practicing for sports, as training (see chapter 3). Olli and I both changed during the time when he learned to walk on the lead, but our experiences differed from the processes of "training" that Haraway and Hearne describe. We had no common ground to start from and our communication was aimed at living together on a basic level, not sport or games. Second, for Hearne, the human trains the animal, sometimes using harsh methods, and this was not the case with Olli and me—I asked him things and taught him things, and he asked me things and taught me. Both Hearne and Haraway focus on asking the dog in question to obey commands from their human without question. I do not expect this kind of attitude from Olli and I do not think complete obedience is necessary—or even preferable—for a strong connection. Like Pika and Putih, Olli is extremely attentive, even though he has his own preferences and views.

The process might be better understood as education. In the political theory of animal rights they put forward in *Zoopolis* (2011), Sue Donaldson and Will Kymlicka mention the right of domesticated animals and humans to be educated in multispecies societies. I taught Olli things, Pika taught him many things as well, and he educated himself by paying close attention to his surroundings. This included, for example, paying close attention to the behavior of other dogs in the park; he taught himself to play with a human and a ball, as the other dogs did, and then stopped doing it after a few weeks because it didn't really interest him. He enjoys learning new skills and displaying them. Learning to walk on the lead was part of his new education, and the lead functioned as a tool in further education; walking on the lead helped him learn to take the tram and the train (although trains still frighten him), to ignore dogs when walking next to the bicycle, to ignore (to some extent) humans who eat food on the street, and so on. I sometimes had to keep him from doing what he wanted within these processes, but there were clear goals, and because Olli learned very fast, many of the problems we encountered were temporary.

However, as I have already mentioned, the lead also made things more difficult, and we two would not have needed it to come to an understanding—Olli would have learned these things without the lead, although the tempo at which he learned them might have been different. Still, the communication we had because of the lead did provide us with extra information about each other. Driessen (2016) draws attention to how material interventions can stir dialogue between human and non-human animals. He discusses the situation in which cows learn to use a milking machine. Confronted with this new machine, cows adapt their views and behavior, as do farmers in response to them. The relationship with the machine enables the cows to display new behavior and the farmers to see them differently; the process can be seen as a dialogue, in which the milking machine is the subject being talked about.[10] The lead can also be regarded in this way. Because of how Olli responded, I learned about him and vice versa. This was a dynamic process, in which power relations were not completely fixed (Foucault 2010; see also Fletcher and Platt 2016) and in which we both exercised agency—I mentioned Olli's strong will earlier. The precise meaning of the lead was not pre-determined. Olli enjoys going out, and he has started to associate the lead with good things such as dog biscuits and going to the park. He often asks for biscuits as we walk, and I often give them to him; sometimes without thinking, sometimes to reward him. I notice the lead most when we have different ideas about where to go. If this happens, we negotiate. Because we return to it often, we have time to adjust our opinions, to give each other reasons and think it over. I watch his behavior and adjust mine as much as I can; he watches me and responds to what I ask.[11]

For these reasons, the lead functions as more than just an instrument of repression.[12] As our understanding grew, Olli started to flourish. His body changed: some of the muscles in his hind legs disappeared, others became stronger; his neck was very thick when he came, now it is of normal size. As I mentioned above, he held his tail and the back of his body low when he arrived. Photographs of him in the shelter show the same posture. After three months, a curl appeared in his tail. His walk became steady, calm, and proud. His attitude towards humans changed as well. In the beginning he greeted all humans; after three months he no longer felt he needed to ask everyone for reassurance, and started to ignore some of the humans we met in the streets and in the park, even though he is still a very friendly dog who teaches many children in our neighborhood not to be afraid of dogs.[13]

Stray Politics

Dog-human relations can be political in different ways. Both of the topics discussed above are political. "Language" is usually understood as exclusively human, and is used as a demarcation line between human and non-human animals in the philosophical tradition (chapter 1). This is a political problem and leads to other political problems, such as anthropocentrism, in laws, discourse, and practices (chapter 4). The lead is an instrument that is used to oppress other animals: a completely accepted form of human domination over other animals. In developing a common language and in learning to walk on the lead, Olli exercised agency. In the next section I further explore Olli's political agency as a Romanian stray dog, and then I turn to political agency more generally, on both the micro- and macro-levels.

A Stray Dog from Romania

In September 2013, following the death of a four-year-old boy allegedly killed by stray dogs (Allen 2014), Romania's highest court ruled in favor of killing thousands of stray dogs. A new law made it legal to "euthanize"[14] dogs who had been in shelters for fourteen days, or sooner if there is not enough food for them. The euthanasia methods used include poisoning with antifreeze, shooting, electrocution, and gassing (ibid.).

Dogs are also often left in cages without food and water to starve. In some towns, the capture and killing of a dog—euphemistically referred to as "dog management"—pays 200 euros per dog. Animal welfare organizations receive 25 euros for capturing and neutering dogs, although neutering dogs is the only effective way of reducing populations (ibid.). Dogs wearing the ear tags of animal welfare organizations showing that they have been neutered are also captured and killed. In addition to the killings of hundreds of dogs a day by companies working for the government, dogs are beaten to death on the streets, poisoned, and burned alive by angry citizens (ibid.).

My decision to adopt a stray dog from Romania was influenced by this political situation,[15] and in addition to offering Olli a home, I decided to use my work to create awareness about the situation. I did so by writing about, drawing, and photographing Olli, as well as by writing about the situation in Romania. The work was published on my website, and Olli was mentioned in interviews. Olli had no influence on his move to the Netherlands, but he did influence my work, directly through his actions and indirectly because my perspective changed through our interaction.

Olli exercises agency in a number of other ways. In Romania, he invented a little dance to ask humans for food, attention, and sympathy—he sometimes still does this when we meet strangers, mostly with adult males—and is generally extremely friendly. Through this behavior, he challenges stereotypes about stray dogs. Iris Young (1990) writes about the role of stereotypes in what she calls "cultural imperialism," the situation in which the dominant group, in this case humans, sets the standards for socially acceptable behavior. She points to the fact that the "other" is, in the same movement, singled out and rendered invisible. We see this with stray dogs. On the one hand, they are voiceless; humans are indifferent towards them. They are part of cities, but they are faceless, worthless. On the other hand, they are seen as dangerous, dirty, and bad. Belonging to the category "stray dog" renders a dog invisible as an individual, and because they are invisible it is easy to project characteristics onto them. Olli challenged this by being visible in a gentle way. In the Netherlands, the attitude towards dogs is different; humans are usually friendly. But here he also challenged stereotypes, for example, about the learning abilities of older dogs, or more generally, the subjecthood of

FIGURE CS1.9. Olli in Romania

animals. Because he is so kind and open, many strangers we encounter on the street want to pet him or say something to him. I tell them he is from Romania and inform them about the situation over there.

From Micro-Practices to Macro-Agency

Taking other animals seriously as subjects and treating them as equals can challenge anthropocentrism. Sociologist Leslie Irvine (2001) proposes seeing play between humans and cats or dogs as a site for political resistance. She argues that in play, humans and dogs, or other companion animals, challenge the current construction of the human-animal divide. Play acknowledges non-human animals' subjectivity and communication skills, through which it challenges "human disregard for non-human life" (2001, 1) and creates interconnection between members of different species. Irvine discusses different aspects of play, such as resisting "the notion of otherness" and "trends to dominate other species" (ibid.). Drawing on the work of Foucault, she sees micro-practices—common everyday practices—as spaces in which power hierarchies and conflicts are revealed and in which common views about human-animal hierarchies are challenged.

Honoring animal agency and subjecthood can indeed function as a basis for new forms of living together; other animals exercise agency in many ways and thereby influence humans' understanding of the world around them. However, as the story of Olli shows, not everything can be fixed at an individual level. A focus on individual relationships leaves intact the frame in which animals can exercise agency, as we saw with walking on the lead and having to navigate city traffic. Donaldson and Kymlicka (2012) make a distinction between micro- and macro-agency. Some authors (Haraway 2008; Hearne [1986] 2007) focus solely on animal agency in personal relationships in which the human ultimately decides what the scope of the animal's choices is. This obscures certain problems and may even legitimize violence because the wider framework of exploitation of non-human animals is not addressed (Weisberg 2009; see also chapter 9). Donaldson and Kymlicka argue that it is often assumed that humans have a wide scope of agency, whereas the macro frame of domesticated animals is "fixed by their evolutionary history and/or species nature, pre-determining a life of rigid dependence on humans and human society" (2015b, 12). As we have seen, this picture of non-human animals is incorrect, and in order to respect their agency in a human-dominated world, humans should provide them with options to expand their macro-framework. An example of this is being able to choose to leave the interspecies community they are a part of. In practice, this would mean that although domesticated animals have a right to be socialized into interspecies communities, they also have a right to opt out of their community, for example, to go and live in a community with members of their own species, or to spend only part of their time with humans. This would require new spatial arrangements and a very different attitude towards the preferences of non-human animals. Taking macro-agency into account does not mean that non-human animals can do whatever they want and can be completely free in what they choose. There will always be constraints on the scope of agency, as there are for humans.

Although I am committed to creating as rich a life as possible for Olli, the scope of his agency is determined by the limits of a human-centered society. This is unfortunate, because he has a strong spirit and it is important for him to be able to make his own decisions. The situation now is sometimes patronizing: Olli is forced to walk on a lead, to follow one human, and so on. While he is an autonomous adult who is very happy with a warm bed, central heating, food at fixed times, and cuddles, he might also like to spend time outside, roam the streets on his own, create friendships with individuals of different species, and maybe be part of a larger community of dogs.

Conclusion

Olli has adapted well to his new life. Remarkably well, considering he is a five-year-old dog who had never lived in this type of situation before. When he arrived, he preferred canine company to human company and would have chosen the former over the latter, even though he did also seek out contact with humans—he is especially fond of children. As we get to know each other better and build a stronger connection, I am not sure about that anymore. He enjoys having a place where he belongs and it is important for him to belong to a group. He is much happier than he was before, much more relaxed and more present.[16]

Olli was not the only one who changed in the months after he came here; I also changed.[17] The physical process was and is rather intense: we spend a lot of time outside, walking and running in rain and wind, through muddy fields and forests, and we have a lot of physical contact, both outside and inside the house. In *The Parrot Who Owns Me*, Joanna Burger writes about preening rituals with parrot Tiko: "As he cared for my body, I felt myself transported into a much more physically attentive kind of life than we're used to in this society" (2002, 107). Although Olli does not preen or groom me—he sometimes licks my foot—I experience something similar because touch is so important to him. He often asks me to rub his tummy by lying next to me on his back and growling or barking, or just to pet him, by sitting next to me and taking my hand in his paws. This way of interacting connects me to him; being together is important to him and what he asks from

FIGURE CS1.10. Olli's first time on the beach

me in that regard makes me feel more connected to the world around us. The connections I have with Pika and Putih are clear and strong; we belong to each other. Olli wants to belong and connect, but the precise meaning of this is still in question and still growing.

On a more general level, the perspective Olli offered me on our society reminded me of certain aspects of our society and human-animal relations, things I knew but that I experienced in a different way. His views, for example, on dog leads, the number of dogs in this city, cars, large noisy machines, humans, and houses has made me experience these in a different way. Olli has very clear preferences regarding food, other dogs, when to walk, where to walk, when to cuddle, where to sleep, and so on, and our discussions about these things help shape our life together. These experiences can function as the starting point for envisioning new ways of interacting and arranging public spaces.

In animal rights theories, there is a strong tendency to view non-human animal freedom solely as negative freedom, as freedom from humans (chapter 3). Although, of course, some other animals prefer to have as little contact with humans as possible, Olli shows that it is possible for a stray dog to change, to gain confidence and adapt to—or even embrace—new circumstances in such a way that freedom is gained. Not just freedom of movement in an anthropocentric world, also freedom in interaction with others, with the possibility of starting to love a human being. And he is not the only one affected: Olli and the others not only teach me about non-human animals, they teach me about all things that really matter.

PART II

Political Animals and Animal Politics

4

Animal Politics

Justice, Power, and Political Animal Agency

Bartholomew Chassenee, a distinguished French jurist of the sixteenth century, owed his reputation to his work as counsel for a group of rats who had been put on trial before the court of Autun on the charge of having eaten up and destroyed the barley crop of that province (Evans 1906). Because his clients were clearly guilty and had a bad reputation, Chassenee was forced to use all manner of different pleas and objections to try and find a loophole in the law so that the rats might escape their sentence. He first argued that it was difficult to address the rats in question, because they lived in different villages. He succeeded in obtaining a citation, to be published in all parishes, to notify the rats of the impending lawsuit.[1] When the time came to make the proclamation, he excused the absence of his clients on the grounds of the difficulty and length of the journey to the court, and the perils that accompanied it, such as the presence of cats. He argued that because it was impossible for the accused to appear before the court, they could not be charged with refusing to obey the writ. We do not know what happened to the rats, but the arguments used in this case probably enjoyed some success, because they were later used in defense of human offenders (Evans 1906).[2]

Animal trials continued until the beginning of the twentieth century. Some of the most notable cases were the electrocution of the elephant Topsy in 1903, and the hanging of the elephant Mary in 1926. Both Topsy and Mary had been forced to work in circuses. Topsy had killed three humans, including a trainer who had forced her to swallow a burning cigarette (Hribal 2010). Mary had killed her trainer after he prodded her behind her ear with a hook when she reached down to eat a watermelon (ibid.). In the Middle Ages, discussions about non-human animal punishment focused on the questions of whether punishment should be retributive or preventive, whether non-human animals could be held morally responsible, and how this related to humans who acted as a result of insanity; the arguments for prosecution were usually motivated by religion, and animal crimes were seen as acts of Satan. Later cases, such as those of Topsy and Mary, focused mostly on legitimizing the practices of circuses and zoos for a human audience. Instead of looking at what had caused them to use violence towards humans—usually their captivity and the violence done to them for economic reasons—the non-human animals in question were blamed for their behavior.

In current legal systems, non-human animals are sometimes consulted as witnesses, but they are not seen as moral, legal, or political agents. In fact, in most countries they have the legal standing of property, and harm done to them is seen only as harm to their owner. The same applies to politics: non-human animals are not seen as political or democratic subjects. Human legal and political decisions do, of course, affect the lives of non-human animals, and the number of animals used by humans keeps growing. Over 56 billion farm animals (this number does not include fish and marine animals) are killed each year for food, for example, and the number of wild animals living on Earth is set to fall by two-thirds by 2020 as compared with 1970 (Carrington 2016), while the human population has almost doubled since that time. The animal trials of the Middle Ages may now seem absurd and cruel to us, but the situation for non-human animals has not improved.

Recent years have seen changes with regard to the legal and political representation of non-human animals. While these changes have mostly been directed towards improving non-human animal welfare, political parties devoted to promoting non-human animal interests have also come into being. The rise of the Dutch Party for the Animals (Partij voor de Dieren), founded in 2002 as the first political party devoted to promoting non-human animal interests, is a good example.[3] The Party for the Animals aims to speak up for non-human animals in a human political framework. While the Party for the Animals has achieved some small successes, their main function has been to put animal issues on the political agenda, forcing other parties to acknowledge these issues as well (Otjes 2016). Apart from the effectiveness of their strategy in terms of results that can be measured, they have been successful in starting and encouraging discussion about the treatment of non-human animals and the planet in general at various levels of society, ranging from par-liament and city councils to old and new media, helping to raise public awareness.

The Party for the Animals focuses on representing other animals and giving them a voice in the human system, but it does not engage politically with non-human animals. In the Netherlands, the Party for the Animals is often equated with animal politics. Seeing this form of representation—which also applies to proposals for reserving seats in parliament for other animals, ombudsmen, designated animal advo-cates, and other models that aim to include non-human animal interests in human politics—as the sole or best form of animal politics is, how-ever, problematic with regard to both "politics" and "animal" (see also chapter 8). It refers to a narrow interpretation of politics and political actors, which is often built on an anthropocentric worldview, and con-structed similarly to the way in which language has been constructed (see chapters 1 & 2). Non-human animals do speak and exercise politi-cal agency, but they cannot usually influence matters that concern their lives directly because the framework within which they act has been constructed to exclude them. This exclusion has an institutional and an epistemic dimension: other animals are not just formally excluded from political and legal structures; they are effectively silenced, because their perspectives and forms of knowledge are not considered valuable within the dominant system of knowledge.

In this chapter, I begin by discussing two critiques of political an-thropocentrism. Political anthropocentrism is usually either challenged by animal advocates with an appeal to justice, or by a critique of power relations. Both shed light on aspects of political human/non-human ani-mal relationships and offer ways to rethink "the political," but they also both fail to adequately take non-human animal agency into account. In order to be able to take non-human animal agency into account and de-velop new forms of non-human animal political participation, we need to reconsider "politics" in an interspecies context and in interaction with other animals. Building on the two critiques of anthropocentrism in politics, in the second half of this chapter I investigate the ways in which non-human animals can act politically, and how political animal agency can function as a basis for developing new forms of interspecies politics. It is not enough to grant other animals rights or improve their position in the existing framework; we also need to rethink politics with them in order not to repeat anthropocentrism. In the next chapter, I draw on these ideas about politics and animals to further explore the relations between groups of non-human animals and human political communities.

Justice for Animals

The publication of Peter Singer's *Animal Liberation* in 1975 is often seen as the beginning of the animal rights movement, and the book remains one of the guiding texts of the movement.[4] As a utilitarian philosopher, Singer argues not for rights but for moral consideration, and according to him, non-human animals should be included in our moral communities because they are sentient beings who have interests of their own. There is no morally relevant characteristic that all humans possess and all other animals do not possess, and failing to take them into account simply on the basis that they are not human is a matter of speciesism, or discrimination on the basis of species, which can be compared to racism and sexism.[5] Singer's utilitarian views would, if accepted, lead to the abolition of many current practices in which non-human animals are exploited, such as factory farming—the suffering of these animals is far greater than the pleasure that humans experience when eating their body parts—and most of animal experimentation. However, this would not lead to inviolable rights for either human or non-human animals because, for utilitarians, the greater good always trumps individual interests.

Philosopher Tom Regan (1983), who is seen as the modern father of animal rights, draws our attention to the fact that in the case of humans most legal and political systems focus on rights, not a utilitarian calculus, and he argues that non-human animals—or subjects-of-a-life, as he calls them—should be granted inviolable rights (see also Cavalieri 2001).[6] Regan criticizes utilitarianism's possible counterintuitive moral imperatives, such as sacrificing an innocent human being when the benefits outweigh the costs, but he accepts the same premises as Singer with regard to speciesism and sentience. Since the publication of Regan's and Singer's seminal works, animal rights theories have primarily been advanced by moral philosophers and scientists studying animal behavior and cognition, and traditionally focus on the intrinsic capacities of animals and their interests, and the moral status and moral rights to which these give rise. Progress in these fields of study has led to a better understanding of animals and their moral rights, as well as to more attention for animals in public debate and legislation. It has, however, also led to a conception of animals as moral objects to be studied rather than subjects who have their own ideas about how they want to live their lives, and to an emphasis on negative rights (Donaldson and Kymlicka 2011). This runs the risk of repeating the anthropocentrism that these approaches aim to challenge, and obscures opportunities for forming new relations. I will discuss both these problems below, and then turn to a more detailed analysis of how power relations have shaped our view of animals and politics.

Problems with Traditional Animal Rights Theories: Negative Rights and the Risk of Anthropocentrism

Implementing negative rights for non-human animals in present-day society (Regan 1983; Francione 1995) would obviously be a great improvement for many non-human animals, as numerous current practices in which they are exploited would have to be abolished. Extending a human framework to include other animals, however, can lead to reinforcing anthropocentrism. We find an example of this in the Great Ape Project (GAP), an organization set up by philosophers and animal scientists (Cavalieri and Singer 1993), which strives to establish a small set of human rights for non-human primates. The GAP argues for the right to life, liberty, and freedom of movement for non-human primates, because they are sentient beings with their own language and culture, and have emotional and cognitive capacities similar to those of human primates. In this line of reasoning, humans recognize other primates ethically not because they are unique others, but because they are a kind of human. If the organization were successful, this strategy could reinforce the humanism that caused the problems in the first place and simply move it to another level; instead of humans versus other animals, it would be a matter of humans and great apes versus other animals.[7] By extending a humanist/anthropocentric framework, such as rights, to incorporate other animals, the structure, which is based on the (metaphysical) distinction between The Animal and The Human, remains intact, with the inherent risk of repeating violent consequences (see Wolfe 2003 for a longer discussion; see also Calarco 2008; Derrida 2008; and Oliver 2007).

While these risks in extending human concepts and institutions to include other animals need to be taken seriously, it is also important to realize that the meaning of these has never been fixed. Rights are tools that we can use to improve the position of non-human animals. Once animal rights are in place, the meaning of the concept of rights, as well as the basic structure of our society, will change. The recent attention for non-human animals in political philosophy shows us that using existing concepts, such as citizenship (see chapter 5), can be fruitful in gaining a better understanding of the relations we have with them, and can help us to imagine new relations. Of the utmost importance, however, are two things: we need to carefully examine the power relations that have shaped the concepts we use, and we need to develop new relations together with other animals. In order to move beyond anthropocentrism, we need to engage with them in new ways, take their perspectives seriously, and develop new forms of political interaction with them. Rights can improve the position of non-human animals in these conversations at a very basic level—for example, by protecting them from being killed and eaten—and can change shape in interaction with them.

This leads us to the second problem with traditional animal rights theories, which is that they mostly focus on extending negative rights, and not on reformulating relations. While this emphasis on negative rights is understandable given the large-scale violence towards other animals, it also leads to normative and pragmatic problems. An example of this can be found in the case of domesticated non-human animals. Abolitionist approaches to animal rights (most notably Francione 1995) start from the idea that humans should stop using other animals, which means ending all relations with them because these relations are built on oppression. This poses a problem for domesticated animals, who may often depend on humans to survive and flourish. For this reason, from the perspective of the abolitionists it would be better if they did not exist at all. This not only means that humans should stop breeding them, it also implies that humans should make sure that they do not procreate; they should be what is euphemistically called "phased out." This view underestimates the relevance of these relations for both the humans and the other animals involved,[8] and does not take the agency of domesticated non-human animals seriously. Donaldson and Kymlicka (2011) show that dependency is not a problem in itself; we are all dependent on others at different stages of our lives and this does not necessarily lead to unjust relations between humans and other animals. Second, they direct our attention to the fact that "phasing out" domesticated animals would again imply that humans need to make decisions regarding their social lives—and other humans' social lives, because humans may also need other animals—for them (see also Donaldson forthcoming and Oliver 2016). They propose instead that we need to look for ways in which they can enhance their freedom, and in which we can foster their agency, so that the power hierarchy changes. How this might work in practice will differ from species to species, and from individual to individual.

We cannot end all forms of human-animal interaction, since humans and other animals are cohabitants of the same planet. Furthermore, this is also unnecessary, since respectful human/non-human animal relationships are possible and already exist. The lives of humans and animals are interconnected in many ways, historically, culturally, and geographically, leading to various relationships, which, in turn, lead to various rights and responsibilities on both sides. In the human situation, universal rights are held to apply to everyone, but humans have additional rights and duties towards specific others based on their moral and political relationships. To evaluate these relations, Donaldson and Kymlicka (2011) turn to citizenship theory. They argue that political philosophy is pre-eminently appropriate to address questions about relations with non-human animals, because it can provide the conceptual tools needed to translate moral insights into an institutional framework in which concepts such as democracy and citizenship can play a key role. They propose extending the idea of universal human rights to include non-human animals using insights developed in animal rights theories. However, although these universal negative rights—such as the right not to be killed, tortured, or enslaved for the benefits of others—are important, they are not enough. We also need to envision just relations. In order to do this, Donaldson and Kymlicka look at how human communities relate to each other in a liberal democratic framework. They use this as the starting point for thinking about political relationships with,

and justice for, animals. In their political theory of animal rights, domesticated animals should be seen as co-citizens, wild animals as sovereign communities, and liminal animals—those who live among humans
but are not domesticated—as denizens. Humans have different rights
and duties with regard to these groups of animals, and animals in these
groups have different rights and duties towards humans.

Both of the problems found in existing animal rights theories—the
risk of anthropocentrism that is involved in extending humanist concepts and a too-strong focus on negative rights—can be resolved with
a relational approach, that understands that human concepts can be a
beginning for thinking and acting differently, but never the final goal,
because their precise meaning should come into being through interacting with other animals. Furthermore, in order to be able to use existing political and legal concepts in the interspecies context, we need to
investigate how power relations have formed what we view as politics,
and how they have also shaped the distinction between humans and
other animals. This is interconnected with the oppression of non-human
animals on the levels of politics, culture, and knowledge. How humans
treat other animals is inextricably linked to the way in which they view
them and think about them; these aspects of human relations with other
animals are also political.

Anthropocentrism and the Links between Epistemic and Institutional Forms of Violence

Different Forms of Violence

"If slaughterhouses had glass walls, everyone would be a vegetarian,"
Paul McCartney once famously said. Non-human animal exploitation
and invisibility are often thought to be interlinked; many believe that if
humans were actually compelled to bear witness to the harms done to
other animals, they would change their behavior. Topographical dimensions are indeed of great importance in addressing violence towards
non-human animals (Pachirat 2011; O'Sullivan 2011). Exposing hidden
practices makes up a large part of animal activism—documenting and
publishing the treatment of animals in barns and laboratories is one
of the most important activist practices—and making the suffering of
non-human animals public through street protests, on social media,

or via independent media outlets is an important step towards social change. These actions can sometimes provoke public outrage (Hribal 2007) and influence legal or political action (ibid.). They can also affect individual choices. For example, research has shown that the way meat is presented by the industry influences the willingness of humans to eat it; how it is described and how it looks both play an important role in this, and activists can change this (Kunst and Hohle 2016). Most humans do, however, know that non-human animals suffer, and that humans make them suffer, and yet they continue to participate in practices that rely on violence to other animals, such as eating parts of their bodies or wearing their skin. This form of cognitive dissonance is sometimes described as the meat-eater's paradox (Aaltola 2015; Joy 2011): humans empathize with non-human animal suffering and think it should be abolished, but they still continue to eat other animals. In order to challenge this, it is important to look beyond individual responsibility and address the structural dimensions of our relations with other animals.

Philosopher Dinesh Wadiwel (2015) sheds light on what is at stake here by distinguishing between three forms of violence that humans commit with regard to other animals. Inter-subjective violence refers to forms of individual, personal violence in which the perpetrator is identifiable and that attacks an entity directly. Institutional violence shapes the power structures of our lives, thus determining opportunities in life and the outcomes of these for that same entity. Epistemic violence concerns our systems of knowledge as expressed in ideology, science, and law. In human/non-human animal relations, these forms of violence have the following shapes. Inter-subjective violence is violence that is directly seen and experienced, for example, when a human directly hurts another animal. Institutional violence is hidden, not because humans literally do not see it, but because they do not perceive it as violence. In a hierarchical society in which white and black humans do not have the same rights, white humans often perceive injustices and violence to black humans as normal, as part of a necessary natural order of society. Similar patterns are found in relations between men and women (Wadiwel 2015). In the case of non-human animals, we find that many if not most humans are aware of the conditions under which other animals live and die, and are familiar with the images that show the violence inflicted on them by humans. One example is intensive farming: images of pigs and chickens crammed into accommodation without daylight, of calves separated from their mothers immediately after birth, and of animal transport and slaughter are familiar to most humans. While extreme violence might still shock humans, these images are in general not new, and most humans have access to them, particularly via social media networks. Many humans also know that the non-human animals living these lives are conscious beings, not so very different from dogs or even humans in terms of cognition and emotion. Yet most of these humans continue to participate in practices that exploit other animals. This is because there is an epistemic dimension to institutional forms of violence.

We live in a society that is shaped by the assumption that humans are superior to other animals. This "epistemological anthropocentrism" (Tyler 2012) refers to the assumption that humans not only come first, but are also ultimately the ones who determine what knowledge is, and that all knowledge begins from a human perspective (Wadiwel 2015). This knowledge claim is the basis for epistemic violence. It frames violence as non-violence, and as such it makes structural or institutional violence possible. A good example of this can be found in Carol Adams's analysis of the eating of animals ([1990] 2010). Through slaughter, other animals are converted into "meat." The animal is absent from "meat," both in name and in form. Adams refers to this process as creating an "absent referent." Living animals are necessary for the production of meat, but they disappear in the process, and humans can then buy their dead body parts in supermarkets without having to be confronted with the reality of their lives. This process takes place in language as well, for example, through the use of the word "meat." It also has a material component: the body parts of dead animals are made into unrecognizable objects which humans can use as they please.

Wadiwel's analysis of the different dimensions of violence helps us to see why humans continue to participate in violence towards other animals, and why it is so difficult to resist. Making an individual choice not to contribute to the industrialized bringing into life and killing of other animals—by practising veganism, for example—only addresses part of the networks of exploitation of animals.[9] It can therefore be only partly effective in dismantling the institutional and epistemic layers of violence against non-human animals, such as by contributing to raising awareness in others. Here we find a clear difference between the solutions of the aforementioned philosophers of animal rights and justice to non-human animal exploitation, and this analysis of power relations. Animal rights philosophers mostly focus on individual choice and believe in the power of liberal democratic political and legal systems to establish change for animals. Wadiwel adds another dimension of analysis, and argues that this dimension is crucial for an understanding of how relations between humans and other animals are formed. Animal rights philosophers often focus on rational arguments to convince other humans of the rightness of their position, drawing attention to the capacities of non-human animals and the inconsistencies in human thinking. According to Wadiwel, the evidence that other animals suffer is already there, and human attitudes towards this violence should be seen as expressions of akrasia: "choosing a course of action that one knows is not 'right' due to a failure of will" (2015, 57), as willful ignorance, or stupidity.[10] The main question here is therefore, he argues, not ethical but political.

With this he means that our ethical systems—both those proposed by theorists of animal rights and justice, and those that are aimed at inter-subjective encounters with other animals or our individual attitudes—are interconnected with, and partly rely on, the distinction between humans and other animals. The production of truth is connected to the production of power: perceiving "knowledge" as a human capacity springs from unequal power relations, and knowledge produced in this system fits a discourse that reflects inequality (we saw an example of this in the language research in chapter 2), and contributes to intensifying practices in which other animals are used (see also chapter 5). So in conjunction with ethical questions, we also need to address this question of power, including how power relations have shaped and continue to shape our understanding of ourselves and others.

Biopolitics and the Intersections of Epistemic and Institutional Violence

Human power over other animals is expressed in a multitude of ways. Violence is not only found in the fact that humans kill other animals, but also in how humans bring them into being and keep them in such a way that they produce the most profit. The concept of "biopolitics" is often used to clarify what is at stake here (Wadiwel 2015; Wolfe 2012). According to Michel Foucault, sovereignty in the modern era evolved from the power to kill others—often to claim territory or resources—into a biopolitical form of government focused on managing the biological life of populations: "The ancient right to take life or let live was replaced by a power to foster life or disallow it to the point of death" (Foucault 1998, 138). This had positive effects for humans with regard to health, education, economy, and other factors that increase wellbeing. Foucault (1998) suggests, however, that this power to let live is always also intrinsically connected to the power to "disallow [life] to the point of death" (Foucault 1998, 138). Intensive farming is a clear illustration of how this works in the case of non-human animals. In intensive farming, humans bring other animals into existence on an unprecedented scale,[11] often altering them genetically to produce more and resist less. Non-human animal bodies are kept artificially healthy using antibiotics, and economic reasoning is used to determine the conditions under which they live and die. Industrialized slaughter depends on industrialized reproduction (Wadiwel 2015). These processes are strongly interconnected with scientific research and informed by insights from fields of study ranging from biochemistry and genetics to studies on economy, health, and technology (chapter 6).

   This biopolitical perspective on relations between humans and other animals helps us to see how epistemic violence towards non-human animals intersects with institutional violence towards them in a dynamic process, which also sheds light on why exposing unacceptable practices and ethical reasoning are not enough to convince humans to change their behavior. Knowledge is produced to further refine animal exploitation and inform legislation, for example, welfare legislation regarding farmed animals. This reinforces a view of animals as usable or eatable objects, and amplifies the differences between humans and other animals that partly spring from and help to legitimize institutional violence. Humans do not see much of the violence towards other animals because it is hidden in farm buildings, but they also often do not perceive the violence they do see as such—after all, they are only pigs, cows, chickens, or others—because of the epistemic system in which these power relations operate. According to Wadiwel (2015), in order to dismantle epistemic violence we need to challenge human superiority, including epistemic superiority. This is a multifaceted project, and does not demand the granting of rights to other animals within the given framework, but rather the challenging of the framework itself (see chapter 5 on sovereignty). However, as I argued in the previous section, rights and other anthropocentric concepts can also function as starting points for change provided they are reformulated in interaction with other animals. Granting rights to other animals would not be the end station of change, but the beginning.

Non-human animal agency, animal languages, and interspecies communication do not usually receive much attention in animal studies scholarship on non-human animals and biopolitics (Wolfe 2003, 2012; Wadiwel 2015). This is unfortunate, because as we have seen, other animals are reduced to bare life—turned into mute bodies—partly through the use of euphemistic human language (Adams [1990] 2010; Wadiwel 2015). More importantly, the distinction between animality and humanity is intrinsically connected with the question of language and *logos*, and with definitions of who can speak and who cannot (Derrida 2008, 2013; see also the introduction and chapters 1 & 2). Other animals suffer from institutional violence and are not heard in the political and legal structures because these are framed by excluding them. Epistemic violence is interconnected with the silencing of non-human animals: they cannot answer the harms done to them because the framework in which they speak is constructed in such a way that their responses are not considered relevant to the conversation, or even heard. In order to criticize these processes of animal exclusion and silencing, we need to address the power relations on both an institutional and an epistemic level and explore their connections. This can also help us envision change. As we have seen, other animals do speak and exercise agency, and we need to take their perspectives into account in reformulating politics in order not to perpetuate anthropocentrism. Before I turn to envisioning new political relations with other animals that will challenge these forms of oppression, I therefore turn to the question of political non-human animal agency.

Political Non-Human Animal Agency

Apes in zoos often throw their feces at humans. Some theorists argue that this is a sign of political resistance (Hribal 2008, 2010). This may seem far-fetched, but research has shown that the throwing of feces is a sign of intelligence in chimpanzees (Hopkins et al. 2012). Furthermore, there seems to be a connection between this throwing and the development of language (ibid.). The same part of the brain is used in throwing and in communicating with others, and the chimpanzees who throw the most are often the better communicators in their group. Throwing feces is an intentional act that communicates a message, one to which the human visitors to zoos respond.[12] If we were to encounter a group of humans who had been imprisoned for no reason and they threw feces at humans or at members of other species who came to look at them for entertainment, we might view this as an expression of resistance and an act of political communication; in this case, we do not.

In most of contemporary political thought, only neurotypical adult humans are seen as capable of exercising political agency (Rawls 1971; Habermas 1981). Political philosopher Angela Pepper defends this view on the grounds that political agents must be able to "intend to effect social change, collectively imagine alternative futures, and act in-concert with others" (2016, 1). According to Pepper, most, if not all, non-human animals lack these capacities and cannot therefore perform political actions, nor hold rights to political participation. Political agency is, in Pepper's view, normatively significant because it comes with a distinct set of rights and responsibilities. Indeed, she argues that appeals to non-human animal political agency might even hinder the project of achieving justice for non-human animals, since a focus on non-human animal political agency would complicate this project and distort our view of both politics and animals. Pepper accepts that non-human animals can have intentions upon which they act, but she argues that they lack the kind of intentional agency—"intentional" here refers to the capacity to have mental states with propositional content such as beliefs, hopes, and doubts—to do so with regard to changing human political institutions. She also argues that they do not have the advanced level of cognition— including capacities for conceptual abstraction, propositional thought, and language—necessary for envisioning alternative futures and for taking part in collective political activity.

With regard to political domesticated non-human animal agency, Donaldson and Kymlicka (2011) present two different models: the so-called "sheer presence model" and the "negotiation model." The sheer presence model refers to cases in which non-human animals influence human decision-making by being present in spaces where they do not belong, or where they co-effect social change with humans, for example, when non-human animals illegally accompany humans on public transport. The non-human animals in question do not intend to change society, they just accompany their humans on the bus, but with their presence and by behaving well they might affect how humans view them, which can lead to change. In the second model, domesticated animals negotiate with their human companions about the conditions under which they live, for example, with regard to where to walk, whether they are allowed to sleep on the couch, or about the food they like to eat. These negotiations can take the form of processes in which non-human animals co-shape their life and that of the humans with whom they live. By negotiating, they express an ability to conform to social norms and to cooperate with others, including humans, in social life.[13] While non-human animals exercise political agency in many different ways, as I will discuss in more detail below—including resisting oppression (chapter 7), cooperating with humans (chapter 8), and taking part in deliberative processes (chapter 9)—and while there is much we do not yet know about non-human animal agency, I will here discuss Pepper's objections to these two models, because they clarify many of the points at stake in evaluating political non-human animal agency.

To these views of political agency Pepper raises four objections that are common in critiques of political animal agency. First, she argues that the sheer presence model leads to a conceptual confusion that makes it impossible to distinguish political agency from non-political agency. For example, if the movements of the sea had a political effect, then the sea would have to be seen as a political agent, which means that there is no longer any meaningful distinction between political agency and a more general capacity to act. Second, the negotiation model is built on a simple expression of preferences. Non-intentional agents might be able to communicate their preferences, but since they are unable to reflect on and revise their preferences, one cannot really speak of political negotiation. Third, human attention or recognition is needed in these models in order for acts to be political. Fourth, the normative value in the concept of political agency gets lost once we weaken the description or definition of it.

There are several general objections to the view of politics and political agency presented by Pepper. This view seems to be built on the old-fashioned image of "the animal" and on the problematic human-animal binary that I discussed in the first part of this book and in the previous section. As we have seen, there is no one "animal," and we find a plurality of capacities, interactions, and political as well as non-political practices, both at the level of species and at the level of social and political relations. Non-human animal capacities for political action are sometimes very similar to those of humans—acts of resistance by mammals are often easy for humans to read—but might at other times be very different—fish for example do not scream when they are in pain. As we saw in chapters 2 and 3, there is much that we do not yet know about the modes of expression, relations, and other significant characteristics of non-human animals. The fact that they express themselves differently does not, however, mean that their expressions and relations are less advanced, less elaborate, or less important than human acts, and the fact that we cannot read their intentions does not automatically imply that they do not have them. Additionally, as recent work in experimental psychology (Brentari 2016; Donaldson and Kymlicka 2013b) reminds us, there are many moral and political acts of both humans and other animals that are not based on careful deliberation or planning; humans also often act habitually instead of after careful reflection in situations that require immediate action (ibid.).

As we saw in the previous section, the image of the political actor described by Pepper is not universal or neutral, but is formed by power relations, and it expresses an anthropocentric worldview. This is also reflected in the understanding of the political that is connected to this view. The scope of politics is broader than human political institutions (see part III of this book) and the question of whether or not certain acts are political, and who decides this, is interconnected with views about the distinction between humans and other animals, and with a specific interpretation of the human subject (see also chapter 5). Furthermore, to state that political non-human animal acts are all non-intentional also ignores the variety of ways in which humans and groups of humans act politically. An example of this is foot voting (see Case Study 2) or more generally, acts in which humans express their dissatisfaction with political conditions without explicitly aiming to change institutions. In these

processes, it is important to remember that pre-existing social and political relations influence how one can express oneself, to what extent
acts can be effective, and what scope we have for political expression.

With these general objections in mind, we find that Pepper's arguments
are not so convincing. Her first point concerns conceptual confusion.
There is, of course, a morally significant difference between the actions of,
for example, orangutans in zoos and thunder. Orangutans in zoos struc-
turally try to escape, something for which they work together and plan
ahead, often forcing zoos to split them up or relocate them (Hribal 2008).
They are part of political and economic systems of exploitation by humans
and their acts often closely resemble human acts, because as a species they
are closely related to us. Thunder does not live under conditions of exploitation and has no intention of improving its own living conditions, nor
does thunder have much to do with what we usually see as political acts.
Between these two poles we find a multitude of different acts of individuals and (sometimes interspecies) groups. This raises the question of where
to draw the line, which is both a question of interpreting acts and of defining what counts as political and what does not. Some non-human animal
acts can easily be read as protest, for example, when an orca whale kills
their trainer, deer leave their territory because of hunters, or elephants refuse to perform tricks in circuses. In other cases resistance is not so clear.
Some non-human animals may just look the other way—think of rabbits
in laboratories—try to flee, or just sit very still. We are still learning how
to decipher the meaning of many non-human animal expressions. We
should also keep in mind that it is not up to humans to define what is political and what is not. At the same time, existing concepts can, of course,
guide our thinking. Here it is useful to return to Wittgenstein. Wittgenstein uses the concept of "family resemblance" to describe the way games
and, mutatis mutandis, linguistic acts, are related. Different games share
characteristics in the way that members of a family do; a grandson and
grandfather might have the same nose, a mother might share the same
sense of humor with her adopted child, cousin Henry might have a face
similar to his dog, and so on. In a concept such as "resistance," we find that
linguistic and non-linguistic acts are interwoven, and that there are many
situations and ways in which we can use this concept. Different situations
may not be the same, but they share certain characteristics. Concepts do
not begin or end at the species line; there is no characteristic that all the

human political language games that we refer to as resistance share and all the non-human animal, or interspecies, political language games lack. Apes who throw their feces are not acting in completely the same way as humans who start a revolution, yet in both instances the concept of "resistance" has meaning.

The second point regards the viewing of human/non-human animal negotiation as a simple expression of preferences. Other animals do indeed have preferences and can express these in their relations with humans in many different ways (see chapters 2 & 3). Their standpoints and the ways in which they express these can evolve over time, and in thinking about political interaction with other animals it is therefore important to take the temporal dimension into account. I will explore the political potential of these processes in more detail later (chapters 7–9). For now, I want only to draw attention to the complex and nuanced ways of political interaction that are possible, and that already exist between humans and other animals in many cases, both at an individual level and at the level of groups. In certain circumstances these can lead to profound understanding (chapters 2 & 3). Viewing these processes solely as a negotiation about preferences offers far too simplistic a view of other animals and languages.

The third objection concerns the fact that human witnesses are necessary in order to be able to speak of politics. Power relations are, of course, found in many non-human animal (intra- and interspecies) communities: between predators and prey, concerning hierarchies within groups and between different groups in dealings about territories and so on (De Waal 2016). In these encounters and relations, other animals can act in ways similar to those of humans, and defining "politics" only in terms of human behavior is a form of speciesism. However, humans do use violence towards other animals on a different scale. While questions about human intervention in the lives of wild, non-human animals are important (Faria 2015; Horta 2010), as humans, our first locus of investigation should be reconsidering our own role towards other animals for reasons of justice. This means both addressing human exceptionalism and violence and reconsidering our relations with other animals—not in order to limit "the political" to human activity and perspectives, but because humans need to begin to act differently in order to bring about social and political change.

Pepper's final objection raises the concern that political agency loses normative strength when it is extended to other animals. This concern is often mentioned when concepts such as citizenship or democracy (Cochrane 2012; Cooke 2014), or even rights, are extended to include other animals. There are several problems with this idea. First, it is not up to "us" to grant "them" political agency—other animals already act politically, whether humans choose to recognize it or not. Second, as we have seen, the image of the human as rational and atomistic—on which this conception of political agency is based—is neither universal nor natural, but is shaped by power relations. Third, it is appropriate to rethink the scope of concepts as we learn to better understand the fact that, and the way in which, other groups act and think. Fourth, in extending concepts to other animals, one could just as easily argue for the opposite: concepts become more meaningful when used in relation to and in interaction with other animals. Thinking about other animals and politics, language, democracy, and so on requires us to approach these concepts anew. This provides us with a new lens through which we can look at their meaning and value and gives us a better grasp of what a concept is actually about and how it works, as well as how it could work.

Redefining Relations with Other Animals

Non-human animals are no longer prosecuted in Western countries, although they are sometimes considered as witnesses in trials. African grey parrot Bud was present when his human Martin Duram was murdered, allegedly by his wife, in Michigan in 2015 following an argument about unpaid bills and her gambling habit. Duram's relatives believe that Bud overheard the argument, because afterwards he repeatedly said, while switching between a male and female voice:

> "Get out."
> "Where will I go?"
> "Don't fucking shoot."

Bud has no legal or political standing; he is nothing more than property. In chapter 2, I discussed how communication between humans and parrots can create understanding (Pepperberg 1995). Lorenz (1949) discusses how events that make a great impression can create lasting memories in parrots. The relatives of the murdered man take Bud's words seriously, but prosecutors did not use his words as evidence, nor was he called as a witness (Crilly 2016).[14]

The case of Bud demonstrates not only that parrots are not taken seriously as legal or political subjects and that humans have stereotypical views of parrots' language and cognition, it also shows a disregard of human-parrot relations, and of parrots as social beings with rich inner lives (chapter 2). Theorists of power draw attention to the power relations in which individuals are constituted and the forms of oppression and inequality that are inherent in them. This is invaluable, because it shows us how the conditions under which we live are shaped and challenges the hierarchies that we take for granted. For social beings, however, power is just one of the lenses through which we can view relations. If we use only this lens, we run the risk of obscuring many other features that make up the lives of human and non-human animals, such as love and friendship, loneliness and loss. We find a similar lack of attention to social structures in animal rights theories that focus on the interests of sentient individuals. Viewing other animals as singular individuals is important because it directs human attention to the often-forgotten fact that other animals are individuals with worth of their own. However, they are more than species-specific containers for intrinsic worth: they are beings who exercise agency, who influence the shape of their own lives, and who benefit from being able to shape social relations.

Discussing the value of relations, love, and sex for captive animals, Clemens Driessen (2016) argues that most ethical theories do not do justice to the full view of life because they do not recognize the value that relations with members of their own and other species have for animals. In neoliberal times, it is standard to view other animals in terms of individual preference satisfaction (ibid.)—as a sort of human-like consumer in a world in which the good life is defined by a right to fulfillment of species-specific needs. In this image, the value of living with others is denied, something that hampers the progression of culture and imagining other ways of living with animals. Even capability theories (Nussbaum 2006) see the fulfillment of social conditions as a prerequisite for individual flourishing, and these conditions are defined by species characteristics. This glosses over how we are already always constituted by others of different species (Haraway 2008), and how we are ethically entangled in relations of question and response (Gruen 2015). Political relations are important in determining how we are situated, but relationships can also be transformed by other factors. We should also focus on these in conceptualizing new relations with other animals. Seeing other animals as communal and social beings asks us to turn our focus to new areas of research—such as how human acts disrupt communities and social bonds (in households, cities, and nations)—as well as to the question of how other relations with them are possible, and the ways in which we can find out how to achieve them.

Understanding that other animals are social beings with whom we live in communities, cultures, and households, whom we affect and who affect us, also has implications for how we see ourselves as humans. Humans are involved in relations with other animals, and share a common animality with them. Matthew Calarco (2015) argues that to overcome anthropocentrism, animal philosophers should start from the fact that humans are also animals instead of drawing attention to how much like humans other animals are. He refers to this approach as "indistinction," and contrasts it on the one hand with utilitarian and rights theories, which argue that non-human animals are like humans (in terms of sentience or cognitive capacities) and therefore deserve the same rights as humans, and on the other hand, the Derridean ways of deconstructing the human-animal binary by problematizing notions of human and animal, and pluralizing difference. "Indistinction" understands human life as grounded in animal life, and turns the focus to non-human animal agency.[15]

In order to take non-human animal agency seriously and reconfigure our position as humans to build better relations, we should determine which power structures are most fundamental in perpetuating violence towards non-human animals and how best to resist them, and we should explore alternatives for living with other animals. If we do not map and critically review relations of power and domination, non-human animal agency will not be taken seriously, and violent relations will be perpetuated. A critique of power relations alone is, however, insufficient: we need to know what to work towards, and to find out what constitutes a good life for different animals. In determining which power structures are most fundamental in perpetuating violence towards non-human animals and how best to resist them, it is useful to turn to Wadiwel's (2015) analysis of forms of violence. We can challenge intersubjective violence with an ethical appeal to veganism, institutional violence by striving for political change, and epistemic violence by aiming to change cultural, legal, and scientific practices.

It is also useful to turn to social and political relations between humans—including the ways in which these are institutionalized—both with regard to challenging power relations and to exploring alternatives. Concepts developed to shed light on relations between human groups can help us to better understand relations with other animals, and can also offer new starting points for living with them. Existing institutions and practices can furthermore be used to improve the lives of other animals. In the next chapter I therefore further explore the relations between groups of non-human animals and human political communities by investigating how concepts such as citizenship and sovereignty can help us to understand and reformulate relations with other animals. I also explore how existing institutions and practices, such as different types of rights, can be expanded in an interspecies context.

5

Animals and the State

Citizenship, Sovereignty, and Reformulating Politics

In February 2017, the Dutch *Raad voor Dieraangelegenheden* (RDA, Council for Animal Affairs) presented a report on so-called "high risk dogs" and incidents of biting (RDA 2017). Such "high risk" (HR) dogs are dogs who have been bred to defend their territory and their humans, or to fight.[1] The RDA advises putting together a national list of the breeds of dog that most frequently bite humans, and they make recommendations with regard to responsible ownership, aimed at preventing incidents. Concerning the dogs, they advise a "one strike out" policy, meaning that dogs, especially HR dogs, whose biting of humans or other dogs results in serious injury or death should be euthanized immediately. Additionally, HR dogs should be kept on short leads and must wear muzzles at all times. They also recommend swift euthanasia procedures in shelters so that dogs who have bitten humans or other dogs cannot repeat their behavior and are not kept alive for too long.[2] Animal welfare organizations responded by arguing that more attention should be given to prevention and the training of humans who buy dogs, as well as to the policies surrounding the breeding and selling of dogs that make it easy for humans to buy a dog without having either the required knowledge or the means to take care of them.

Dogs bite for different reasons: because they were not socialized or educated properly when they were young, out of fear or lack of exercise, and sometimes for reasons we simply do not understand. Training their humans is important in dealing with difficult dogs, but it is also important to take a closer look at the system in which humans and dogs function. Dogs can currently be bought online or in pet shops by anyone with the financial means. Whether or not they are treated well will depend upon the human they end up with; while many dogs lead a fairly decent life and some lead a good life, many others suffer from

boredom, loneliness, or abuse.[3] Dogs are also often abandoned. Around
1.5 million dogs live in the Netherlands, and their average lifespan is ten
years. 150,000 dogs are bought annually, and 12,000 of them are brought
to shelters, with even more sold or given away through special websites.
Some of these dogs are brought to shelters because their humans die or
get sick, but often the humans were simply not prepared for what caring
for dogs or raising them responsibly entails, and get rid of them when
they are no longer puppies. While it is legally forbidden to harm dogs or
other animals without good reason,[4] dogs are property, and humans can
keep them indoors, feed them unhealthy food, and generally use them
for whatever purpose they wish. Dogs cannot address the harms done to
them in a political or legal context and they depend on humans to help
them if they are in need. The "one strike out" measure for dogs who bite
is defended on the grounds that it will help to prevent biting incidents
because it will make the owners of aggressive dogs more careful. Apart
from the doubtful psychological assumption that irresponsible humans
will be made more responsible by the killing of dogs, the dogs themselves are obviously not considered at all. They are not seen as social
beings with histories and futures in which they can learn to behave differently. Neither are they seen as members of a shared community, but
as mere things that can bring humans joy and that can be disposed of
when they no longer fulfill this function.

Dogs are sentient beings with interests and lives that matter to them;
they are also social beings with whom humans share communities and
have relations that matter to all involved (chapter 3). They can exercise
political agency, and in relations with humans, both parties can come
to have different rights and obligations. Dogs who bite are clearly not
respecting social rules, but killing them is morally problematic, because
it only treats the symptoms of an unfair system, and because it disre-
gards the value of their lives. If we accept that dogs are sentient beings
who deserve to be taken into account in our moral and political systems, and that they are social beings with whom we can have different
kinds of relations, we need to think about their status as members of our
shared communities. For biting dogs, recognizing them as members of a
shared community would create a different starting point, based on the
understanding that by breeding HR dogs, humans created a responsibility, and help us aim for a setting in which they can be socialized and

educated properly. When dogs or other non-human animals do bite or cause other problems, humans should help them to change their behavior, in the same way as they would with other humans. Whether or not non-human animals are in the wrong depends for a large part on whether they know that they are wrong, and it is up to the humans or other animals in their pack to teach them that.[5]

In the last chapter I offered a critique of anthropocentrism in politics, and argued that we need to take political non-human animal agency into account in building new political relations. In this chapter, I further conceptualize the relation between groups of non-human animals and human political communities by investigating the relevance of the concepts and institutions currently used to conceptualize political relations between groups of humans to relations with other animals. I first discuss recent proposals to view non-human animals as members of shared interspecies communities, in which I mainly focus on Donaldson and Kymlicka's liberal democratic view of citizenship for domesticated non-human animals. I then turn to groups of non-human animals who are not part of shared communities with humans, and review proposals to view them as sovereign communities, in which I contrast the existing liberal democratic interpretation of sovereignty developed in relation to the nation-state with a more fundamental conception of sovereignty from the perspective of power relations. I specifically focus on non-human animal agency in my discussion of these concepts. In the final section, I turn to examples of new ways of relating to other animals, as found in existing political institutions and practices, which can function as beginnings for further reformulating law and politics with other animals.

Animal Citizens

Building on the view, as argued for by animal rights theorists, that non-human animals are part of our moral community, and new developments in citizenship theory that focus on broadening citizenship to include the agency of new groups such as severely disabled humans and children (Donaldson and Kymlicka 2015b), Donaldson and Kymlicka propose to view domesticated non-human animals—such as companion animals and farm animals—as citizens. They argue that humans are morally obliged to grant citizenship to domesticated animals, because humans brought them into their communities by force and deprived them of the possibility of living elsewhere through confinement, breeding processes, and other forms of violence. Furthermore, because these non-human animals have co-evolved with humans and have undergone processes of domestication (Zeder et al. 2016), they have become attuned to humans, as humans have to them, which enables them to function and participate in mixed human-animal communities. Ending their oppression does not mean ending all relationships; it means we should investigate what types of relationships they want with us and how we can improve those. This includes searching for ways to increase their freedom, and possibly also creating options for them to leave our communities (Donaldson and Kymlicka 2013a, Donaldson forthcoming). In this process, it is important to recognize that dependency is not a problem in itself: we are all dependent on others at certain points in our lives, and political institutions and practices are developed precisely to protect those who are vulnerable (see also chapter 4).

Donaldson and Kymlicka distinguish three functions of citizenship, which according to them should also apply to non-human animals: nationality, popular sovereignty, and democratic political agency. They argue that although nationality and popular sovereignty would be sufficient criteria for them to be regarded as citizens, domesticated animals are also capable of exercising democratic political agency. They discuss three basic capacities, or what Rawls calls "moral powers," that are seen as requirements for citizenship in the case of humans: the capacity to have a subjective good and communicate it, to comply with social norms, and to participate in the co-authoring of laws (2011, 103). Donaldson and Kymlicka do not dispute this list, but they do dispute the overly rationalist or intellectualist manner in which the list is often interpreted. It is, for example, not seen as enough to simply possess a good; it is also expected that individuals can reflectively endorse a conception of the good. Similarly, it is not seen as enough to understand and comply with social norms—one also needs to rationally understand the reasons for them, and, I would add, voice them in human language. If citizenship is interpreted in this manner, non-human animals, along with certain groups of humans, do indeed seem to be incapable of citizenship. This is not the only interpretation of citizenship possible, however, and as we have seen, the standard on which it relies is not universal: it is built on a certain image of the human (see chapters 1–4). Donaldson and Kymlicka instead argue for an embodied citizenship for both human and non-human animals, in which "the appropriate test for animal citizenship . . . is whether animals exhibit norm responsiveness and intersubjective recognition in actual interactions, not whether they engage in rational deliberation" (2014b, 19). They draw on recent work in moral psychology that sees moral agency as primarily habitual and embodied, and studies in ethology that bring to light the continuities between non-human and human animals in these respects.

While not all rights of human citizenship would matter to non-human animals, and while there are differences between species, many citizenship rights are relevant to them. Donaldson and Kymlicka mention, for example:

> rights of residency; rights to protection, both from harm at human hands and from other threats, such as fire and flood; rights to health care; labor rights, such as the right not to work in an unsafe environment, and disability and retirement benefits; and the right to have one's interests taken into account in determining the common good, and in shaping the rules that govern our shared society and activities. (2011, 9)

They also mention civic responsibilities, and argue that non-human animals have a duty of civility towards their co-citizens as well as a duty of contribution, the latter in line with their preferences, instead of working as slaves for humans as currently occurs, for example, in laboratories or on dairy or egg farms.

Challenges for the Citizenship Approach

By drawing on the vocabulary of citizenship theory, Donaldson and Kymlicka show domesticated animals, and possible relations with them, in a new light. Their emphasis on membership, and their views on dependency and the importance of relations in politics, also helps us to see human politics differently. Exploring a liberal democratic framework for thinking about justice for non-human animals is furthermore relevant because we live in liberal democracies, and this gives us concrete tools to work and think with. Some questions, especially with regard to non-human animal agency and political participation and representation, are, however, underexplored in their model. Before I turn to discussing these, I should first note a more general problem with using a group-differentiated model of citizenship for thinking about relations with groups of non-human animals.

It is difficult to categorize other animals for normative and practical reasons (see also chapter 8). First of all, many non-human animals challenge the border between domesticated and liminal—liminality refers to those animals who live amongst humans but who are not domesticated, such as mice, pigeons, or stray dogs. Feral cats can live close to humans and depend on them for food, but might not be willing to interact with them closely. Some might find ways to survive without human assistance, while others might, at a certain point, want to move in with humans. As Donaldson and Kymlicka show, different animals can also move between groups in the course of their lives; domesticated animals can become liminal and vice versa. There are, however, also borderline cases in which rights and duties are not so clear. A second problem is that it is humans who do the categorizing (ibid.). While this can help to develop a new starting point for interaction, a human lens is always colored by human assumptions and cognition. Third, Donaldson and Kymlicka mainly focus on political interaction and communication with domesticated non-human animal citizens, but we also interact politically with non-domesticated animals, especially those who live close to humans. We need to think about how they can have a voice in questions that concern them about the contact within and between communities. A model based on close relations will not work for these animals, so we need to explore different ways to interact with them politically. Questions of borders are not only relevant with regard to political participation and representation, but also with regard to rights. While the citizenship approach can help shed light on positive rights and duties, and can provide us with concrete guidelines for improving relations, we do need to carefully rethink what we mean by citizenship for these reasons if we are to adequately challenge the role of the human and not repeat patterns of exclusion or domination.

In challenging human supremacy, it is important to move from thinking about other animals to thinking and working with them. This leads us back to the question of non-human animal agency, and how we can

ANIMALS AND THE STATE | 139

translate this agency to a political framework. To further conceptualize how we can take non-human animal agency into account in human political systems, Donaldson and Kymlicka turn to recent work in disability theory (Francis and Silvers 2007; Kittay 2005). They discuss theories that focus on how humans with severe mental disabilities can exercise agency through relationships that are based on trust—so-called "dependent agency" (Donaldson and Kymlicka 2011, 104–8). In applying this model to non-human animals, domesticated animals could communicate their standpoints to the humans who know them well, and they in turn could interpret these standpoints and communicate them to other humans. Domesticated animals should also have a right to be represented politically through these forms of interaction. Donaldson and Kymlicka stress that because we have not yet started to see non-human animals as citizens, denizens, or sovereign communities, the exact range and shape of the ways in which they can exercise political agency is as yet unknown. Humans therefore need to look for agency, and should encourage other animals to express themselves; it is unclear how relationships in a safer world for animals will evolve.

Non-human animals can and do exercise political agency through relations with humans. However, basing the representation of domesticated non-human animals solely on forms of dependent agency is problematic for normative and practical reasons. Not all domesticated animals are able to, or would want to, communicate with humans in this manner—for example, because of bad experiences in the past or simply because they do not like humans that much—and some animals, especially those who have been bred to be docile and have grown up in a household in which humans strongly determine their scope for choice, are at risk of forming adaptive preferences. Furthermore, human interpretation of companion animal behavior would have to be drastically improved and monitored, which will require radical interventions in the private lives of humans and other animals. Other animals have their own species-specific languages to communicate with one another, and many domesticated animals have developed tools to communicate with humans (chapters 2 & 3). These forms of interaction are not private or inaccessible, and this knowledge can and should be improved through education; indeed, Donaldson and Kymlicka (2011) emphasize the need for learning about other species in interspecies communities. More attention for non-human animal languages could contribute to a model in which domesticated animals might speak for themselves.

A related problem involves the human representation of other animals in political structures. Having humans represent other animals politically would be a great step forward for these other animals, and humans do need to take the first steps towards social and political change, but as with categorizing animals, there are risks involved in relying on a system of human representation. Some groups are more like humans, or are easier to represent than others, which can lead to biased views. More generally, humans have their own human perspectives, shaped by centuries of oppression of non-human animals, from which they act. Other animals also have their own unique perspective on life, and because of this they have an interest in shaping the conditions under which they live so that they can flourish as individuals (see chapter 8 for a more detailed discussion). While a model based on humans interpreting non-human animal behavior and then translating it to existing human structures might be a starting point, we also need to look beyond this structure to investigate how other animals might co-shape the grounds for interaction more directly (chapters 8 & 9).

Various authors (Von Essen and Allen 2016; Hinchcliffe 2015; Planinc 2014; Rowlands 2017) have argued against Donaldson and Kymlicka's proposal to extend citizenship to domesticated animals on the grounds that such animals cannot exercise meaningful democratic agency, and that democratic communication with non-human animals is not possible. I would argue for the opposite: Donaldson and Kymlicka have not yet explored the full potential of non-human animal political agency and interspecies political interaction, in part because they have not yet explored the question of language and communication in detail.

Non-Human Animal Sovereignty

Around 3,800 fallow deer live in the Amsterdamse Waterleidingduinen and Nationaal Park Zuid-Kennemerland, two nature reserves on the west coast of the Netherlands. They are the descendants of small groups of deer who escaped from petting zoos and individual deer released there by humans. Hunting is prohibited in these nature reserves and the deer are not shy; human visitors to the dunes can get very close to them. The deer also explore the surroundings of their habitat, and some-times end up in the gardens of humans, or even at the railway station in the town of Zandvoort, and a fence was put up around the area in 2013 because they pose a risk to traffic. The years since have seen recurrent debates about shooting the deer, in which different arguments have been raised—they have been accused of trampling farmers' crops, disrupting the peace of female gardeners (Teunissen 2016), posing a threat to biodi-versity, and generally reaching too high of a population. In 2016, the city council of Amsterdam and the province of Noord-Holland ordered the shooting of 3,000 fallow deer because they posed a threat to biodiver-sity, even though expert opinions differ on this topic.[6] In response, the Faunabescherming, the Dutch Organization for the Protection of Fauna, took the council to court. Early in 2017, the court decreed that the deer could be shot, and 1,400 deer were killed in April 2017.

These fallow deer do not require human intervention to survive, and they have no desire to form communities with humans. Donaldson and Kymlicka (2011) propose the viewing of wild animal communities as sovereign communities. In their opinion, the morally relevant charac-teristic for granting non-human animal communities sovereignty is not whether or not they are capable of organizing their communities in the same cognitive or rational manner as humans,[7] but rather that they are capable of living their lives without human intervention, and that they prefer to do so. Being able to lead their lives without human interven-tion is often necessary for them to flourish. Donaldson and Kymlicka compare human encroachment into the habitats of non-human animals to the colonization of the land of indigenous human communities. They draw attention to the way in which conquest and colonization of the lands of these communities was often justified by arguing that they were not competent to govern themselves, or that they did not even exist—for example, when European colonizers defined Australia as "terra nullias." Similarly, humans see land where no humans live as empty land, and do not recognize the presence of wild animals in these areas, which usually leads to such animals being killed or driven away to other areas where they may not be able to flourish or will come into conflict with the non-human animals who already live there.

Recognizing non-human animal sovereignty entails more than just "letting them be." It comes with a set of responsibilities on the human side, as a response to centuries of injustice, and to the practical problems that non-human animals face because of historical and current human intervention. Donaldson and Kymlicka describe four areas of human impact: direct and intentional violence, habitat loss, spillover harms—when human infrastructure and activity impose risks on other animals as an unintended consequence of, for example, building roads, but also as a result of pollution and climate change—and positive interventions, such as in cases of natural disaster. Because humans and other animals share territories, and because many animals travel or migrate, land will often have to be shared, and strict geographical segregation will, in most cases, not be possible. Sovereignty does, however, require the drawing of some boundaries and the assigning of territorial rights, and the process of invading other animals' land should be stopped. In order to secure this, Donaldson and Kymlicka propose a proxy representation in a number of human political institutions. Others have proposed similar models of representation (Goodin et al. 1997), or even property rights for non-human animals to protect their habitats and restrict further human colonization of their land.

Sovereignty before Politics

In Donaldson and Kymlicka's proposal, non-human animal sovereignty is modeled on human sovereignty. This presupposes that this model is, or has the potential to become, just, and it assumes that non-human animal communities are similar enough to human communities to function in this manner. It also presupposes a human power to attribute these characteristics and the political structures that follow from them to non-human animal communities. However, before all the questions about non-human animal capacities, their resemblances to humans, and the political models we should use to think about and interact with them, we find the question of the demarcation of the animal as different from humans, and the political as human territory (chapter 4). Set against the view of sovereignty as a matter of establishing justice for other animals in a process of moral progress working towards the perfection of liberal democratic principles, Wadiwel offers a different interpretation of sovereignty (drawing on Derrida 2009, 2011) as a groundless claim. Sovereignty thus understood does not reflect a rational, just intention, but rather represents a kind of stupidity: it refers to the violence of appropriating another entity and declaring superiority over that entity. There is nothing superior about the sovereign (Derrida 2011) and sovereignty is first of all a claim made through violence; force precedes the epistemic claim of superiority. The systems built on this violence are not just, and cannot be turned into just institutions and knowledge systems: they are an expression of violence—Wadiwel further conceptualizes this in terms of war. Granting other animals rights or sovereignty within this system always ultimately depends on human power, and this interpretation of sovereignty does not, therefore, according to Wadiwel, challenge human superiority.

Wadiwel sees an example of this logic at work in the connection that Donaldson and Kymlicka make between sovereignty and territory, because it relies on the capacity of a group of non-human animals to claim their land and on a deterministic view of territory: this claim then needs to be recognized by humans. He locates a similar problem in Goodin, Pateman, and Pateman's (1997) plea for sovereignty for great apes. The reliance on capability is even stronger in their argument because they focus on non-human animals who allegedly have a capacity for sovereignty based on their resemblance to humans. This "capability" assumption is arbitrary (see also Oliver 2015), and granting sovereignty on the basis of it, like the assignment of land, relies on the human power to decide (Derrida 2009, 2011). In a model in which humans decide which animal communities are granted sovereignty and how they should be represented, there remains a governing authority, the humans, that can always overrule attributions of sovereignty.

The situation of the fallow deer with which I started this section illustrates Wadiwel's analysis of power relations between human and non-human animals, both in its biopolitical aspects (chapter 4) and in the fact that human sovereignty always overrides non-human animal interests. Humans control the size of the population and the deer's behavior, and human superiority is never challenged in this process. It is assumed that the land belongs to humans and that humans are destined to decide upon the fate of other animals. The fallow deer decided to move into this habitat, settled in, have formed their own relations with each other and with human visitors, neighbors, and foresters, and find their own ways to deal with the challenges with which life confronts them. Humans first limited their freedom of movement with a fence, and have now killed most of them, which will disrupt the remaining deer's reproductive cycles,[8] make them fearful of humans, and lead them to experience stress and fear (Bekoff 2009). The situation of the fallow deer, however, also shows how Donaldson and Kymlicka's existing liberal democratic interpretation of sovereignty can be useful in establishing social change for other animals. Granting the deer sovereignty in the way that Donaldson and Kymlicka propose—including a right to territory—would not only change their lives for the better, it would also halt human expansion, and lead to the questioning of human superiority on the level of institutionalized politics, as well as on an epistemic level. Many of the arguments presented for killing the deer—there are too many of them, they walk into places where they are not wanted, and they pose a threat to the plants and insects in the area—are connected to a view of the human as knowing best for all other species, while often humans clearly do not know what is best.[9] While granting the deer sovereignty could never be the end point in developing new models of interspecies politics, it would disrupt the status quo.[10] Such a disruption might lead to unexpected results—change is never unilinear, and in this also lies hope (Arendt [1958] 1998). Wadiwel's analysis can shed light on the power structures on which our interpretations of politics and non-human animals are built, but the proposal of Donaldson and Kymlicka can be seen as offering the first practical steps to bring about change. Change will need to start with humans, and existing concepts and institutions can help us to think and act, provided that we also address the anthropocentrism inherent in them.

Starting Points for Change: Rights as Tools, and Challenging Boundaries

There is a large gap between the way in which political institutions and practices are currently organized and proposals to view other animals as citizens or sovereign communities. This does not, however, mean that there is an opposition between the current situation and the ideal situation. New forms of relating to and interacting with other animals can be found, both in institutions developed as part of modern nation-states, and in practices that take place on different levels of society and government. As a conclusion to this chapter, and as starting points for further thought, I will discuss three examples of this: labor rights, habitat rights, and taking non-human animals into account in urban planning.

Labor Rights

Police dogs in Nottinghamshire receive pensions when they retire. In 2013, the police force instituted a fund to ensure this, which covers costs of up to £300 a year for a maximum of three years. "These dogs give willing and sterling service over the years in protecting the public. This will ensure continuing medical help once their work is done," said Police and Crime Commissioner Paddy Tipping, who was responsible for starting the fund (BBC 2013). In Sweden, the municipal workers' union Kommunal is exploring whether service dogs—those who work in child, elderly, school, and health care—require legal protections in their workplaces, similar to that which human workers have under the Labour Code (CBC Radio 2016). Spokesperson Sofia Berglund explains that in these sectors, animals are asked to form relationships with humans, which can be stressful and exhausting. As the use of non-human animals in these sectors grows, humans need to think about non-human animals' working conditions and what is being asked of them. One example is the hugging of dogs against their will—many dogs do not like being hugged—which raises the question of whether they should be trained to endure it, and how often. Regulations should not only consider abuse, but also focus on what constitutes fair working conditions, for example, with regard to taking breaks, in order to make this a sustainable practice. Finally, the US army has started to recognize war dogs as personnel (Alger and Alger 2013; Kymlicka 2017), which includes the right to re-homing upon retirement.

Non-human animals are an important work force, and have been for a long time. Their position as workers is often not recognized as such, especially in sectors such as intensive farming and experimentation. In working relations, the lives of humans and non-humans are often intertwined; non-human animal labor is still of vital importance, especially for poor people, and more specifically for women in poor countries (Coulter 2016). Developing a historical account of the role of non-human animals in the agricultural and industrial revolutions,

Jason Hribal shows that they played an important role in the development of capitalism (see also Shukin 2009). He argues that they are active agents who co-shape the outcomes of processes (see also Driessen 2014) and even claims that they should be seen as members of the working class. Marx famously argued that there is a clear-cut distinction between human and non-human animal work, but this is untenable, both from the perspective of non-human animals and from the perspective of human animals. Many non-human animals, such as beavers (see Clark 2014; Cochrane 2016; Milburn 2017 for a more detailed analysis of this example), labor in a purposive and planned way, while many forms of human labor lack purposive planning—we can, for example, think of factory workers or bored office workers. Here, as elsewhere, it seems appropriate to view differences in capabilities to work as differences of degree and not of kind. Furthermore, one can also challenge the distinction between active and passive labor. In a discussion of clinical labor, Clark (2014) shows that an opposition between active and passive labor is untenable, and he argues that if humans in clinical trials are seen as workers, laboratory animals should be as well. However, in the current systems, other animals are usually reduced to the status of mere objects of labor (Clark 2014; Weisberg 2009). Seeing them as workers instead of victims, as Haraway (2008) proposes, is insufficient for addressing violence. To do this we need to critically assess the whole system of human-animal relations of production. Other animals are of fundamental importance in capitalist societies (Shukin 2009) and their opportunities to resist are often severely limited.

Working rights can play an important role in changing their position, and as such they can function as a starting point for bridging the distance between the current situation and universal non-human animal rights (see also Cochrane 2016 on working rights). Kymlicka (2017) discusses this movement, and argues that social membership rights, such as working rights, tell us something about the changing position of certain non-human animal groups in society, and might contribute to recognizing them as legal persons. The struggle to improve the legal position of non-human animals is often framed in terms of personhood. Non-human animals are currently seen as property, and advocates of animal rights argue they should instead be seen as persons (Wise 2014).[11] While this has led to some small successes and media exposure, especially with regard to non-human primates and cetaceans (Wise 2010), for the majority of animals, particularly those used in farms and laboratories, there is no real chance of recognition of their personhood in the near future. The aforementioned discussions of working rights also mostly focus on groups who are already privileged, such as dogs, but they still point to the fact that we increasingly recognize at least some non-human animals as members of society. Recognizing other animals as workers and arguing for workers' rights might change their position further, and might change humans' views of them. The recent investigations into non-human animal workers' rights—pensions for police and war dogs, regulated work for care animals—do not stem from ideal theory and are not promoted by animal activists, even though progressing insights about other animals are promoted by activists, who thereby influence society. They arise from the working situations themselves, where humans recognize the non-human animals they work with as fellow workers and members of a shared community. While this is still a long way from recognizing the wrongs done to other animals who work for humans, it may help to contribute to change.

Habitat Rights and Territorial Rights

A second example of a situation in which secondary rights can help to bridge the gap between the current status of non-human animals and the granting of non-human animal personhood rights can be found in recent work on non-human animal habitat, or territorial, rights. One of the greatest threats to non-human animals—especially wild animals—is loss of habitat. As discussed above, humans see land occupied by non-human animals as empty land. Even nature reserves and natural parks are owned by humans, who always have the ultimate right to sell this land or change its designation. In response to this problem, philosopher John Hadley (2005) has developed an account of non-human animal property rights. He aims to reconcile and meet the key moral demands of animal rights and environmentalism, which focuses on the value of ecosystems and natural areas, even when this is at the expense of non-human animals. He argues for extending the scope of property ownership to those other animals who have an interest in using natural goods. A vital interest in using natural resources is generally considered a sufficient reason to attribute a property right in natural resources to human beings, and there is, according to Hadley, no reason why this should not be so in the case of non-human animals. He asserts that a non-human animal property rights regime would not only deliver justice for other animals in this regard, it would also—perhaps most importantly—act as a check on destructive human intervention in natural areas. It could secure the maintenance of ecosystem stability, and ensure that the vital interests of non-human animals are respected; i.e., that they have access to the goods they require to meet their needs and those of their offspring. Ecologists can determine what these goods are, and identify the territories in which non-human animals live, the paths they travel, and other relevant characteristics, in order to be able to determine the scope of these rights. Competent guardians could use this information to take care of the practical aspects in relation to human communities.

Using a similar line of reasoning, Steve Cooke (2017) argues that non-human animals have a right to their habitats because of the strong interest they have in living within them. Certain non-human animals have adapted to living in a specific territory and are dependent on it for food, nesting, or other resources. Traditional models of conservation, such as stewardship, where habitats are protected for their aesthetic value or the value of their ecosystems are, according to Cooke, not adequate for the protection of habitats. In such models, human interests ultimately determine what happens to spaces such as parks, nature reserves, and wilderness areas. Because the territorial rights of non-human animals are not recognized, they can be, and often are, trumped by human interests or used for social human activities such as logging and road-building. Acknowledging non-human animal habitat rights would prohibit this. Because—as with property rights—habitat rights in a nation-state would always be dependent on the whims of that nation-state, and because legal protections often fail to protect wild animals (who in many countries still fall prey to poachers, for example), Cooke proposes to institutionalize habitat rights as territorial rights in the form of an international trusteeship system modeled on the established legal norms associated with the United Nations trust territories (see also Goodin, Pateman, and Pateman 1997). Protectorates and trusteeships allow for proxy representation by humans, through which non-human animal territories could interact with human international legal institutions. This proxy representation should ensure that the habitat interests of non-human animal communities are met. Cooke sketches a model in which an international body, such as the United Nations Trusteeship Council, could charge political or administrative bodies (members of which might include national and NGO representatives) with governing and representing a certain habitat or community. The UN could implement and supervise this body, and determine the terms by which the trusteeship would operate, together with the rights of governance.

Hadley and Cooke show that there are several steps that can be made before adopting full habitat rights and sharing spaces on the basis of equality. Furthermore, adopting habitat rights does not require acceptance of a strong account of animal autonomy—both Cooke and Hadley reject this, as most humans would in the current state of affairs. Finally, we already have different practical tools, such as the UN, capable of playing a role in establishing such rights. As with sovereignty, territorial rights are part of a violent history, and we should be careful not to repeat the anthropocentrism inherent in these rights and the systems that are built to enforce them. While a trusteeship model could never be the end point of establishing better relations with other animals, it could function as an intervention in the current system, which might lead to a situation in which other animals can express themselves more fully, where humans can come see them differently, and where both groups can together find new forms of interacting.

Urban Animals

A final example of a situation in which current legislation and current social practices can function as a starting point for change can be found in the more-than-human practices aimed at greening the city (Hinchliffe and Whatmore 2006). A multitude of human/non-human animal relations exist in cities, but non-human animals do not often feature in urban theory or city planning. Jennifer Wolch (2010) argues that this is because urbanization is based on a view of progress that exploits nature on behalf of culture, and that rests on a problematic dichotomy between nature and culture (as well as, and relatedly, city-country and human-animal) (see also Wolch and Emel 1998). To address this exploitation,

Wolch argues that we need to "re-enchant" the city by acknowledging and fostering the presence there of non-human animals and nature, as well as by building new relationships with them; we need to invite the animals back in. Many non-human animals live in cities, but they are either seen as pests (Jerolmack 2008) or their presence is simply not acknowledged. Existing and future urban spaces, such as houses, gardens, parks, and roads, need to change because they are oppressive and unjust for humans and other animals. Reintegrating humans with animals and nature can "provide urban dwellers with the local, situated, everyday knowledge of animal life required to grasp animal standpoints or ways of being in the world, to interact with them accordingly in particular contexts, and to motivate political action necessary to protect their autonomy as subjects and their life spaces" (Wolch 2010, 226–27). Interacting with other animals in new ways will lead humans to see them differently, and vice versa.

Non-human animals are not completely absent from existing legislation and from urban practices, as the following example concerning nesting water birds in Amsterdam shows. In May 2016, the renovation of the Brandweerbrug, a bridge in Amsterdam, had to be halted because a pair of coots had built their nest in the reeds underneath the bridge. Nesting birds are protected by the behavioral code of the *Flora- en faunawet* (the Flora and Fauna Law) of Amsterdam, and procedures developed for this protection can lead to delayed building processes, or force humans to work around the nests. Nesting birds are also assisted by humans who live in the city. Because there are no natural spaces for the birds to nest, only walls, humans who live on or near the canals provide the birds with purpose-built nesting spaces so that they do not use boats or other human objects for nesting. These nests often have a sign saying "*broedplaats*" (nesting place). Humans create these spaces in response to the presence and behavior of coots and other birds, and the coots use human litter to decorate their nests, often creating beautiful and colorful objects. When nests are disrupted, coots and humans both defend them. The efforts of citizens to provide coots and other birds with nesting spaces, and their formal counterpart in the behavioral code of the *Flora- en faunawet*, contribute to the greening of the city and take non-human animal agency into account in doing so. Hinchliffe and Whatmore (2006) discuss similar examples, such as badgers who change their behaviors and dealings when they have territories in urban spaces, peregrine falcons who nest on towers built by humans, and groups of humans who want to preserve natural areas, which they call "green urban practices." These forms of urban interaction are informed by experience from below, including non-human animal forms of knowledge, and not by existing expert knowledge from above. They can inform policies and can also function as the starting point for new forms of civic engagement aimed at doing justice to the multiplicity of voices and relations present in cities.

In the case of the nesting coots and other examples, we find that there are already different ways in which humans and other animals act together, in which they create new knowledge that can influence other human citizens, as well as the decisions made by city councils and beyond. The next step in re-enchanting the city would be to consult non-human animals more explicitly through material and other interventions, and to acknowledge their influence on practices and thoughts more explicitly. While a shared *zoopolis* is currently a utopian ideal, city animals can and often do instill a sense of wonder and awe in the humans who see them and interact with them, something that can motivate them to further green the city—or that may simply be an annoyance to those who want to renovate bridges. The existing legislation protecting nests offers a form of recognition of the value of their presence, and of care in the landscapes of stone we have created.

Political Concepts as Starting Points for Change

Groups of non-human animals can stand in many different relations to human political communities. Concepts developed to guide and understand relations between groups of humans, such as citizenship, sovereignty, cosmopolitanism, and republicanism, can help to shed light on these relations. They also have practical value: institutions and practices developed to protect humans and promote their interests can do the same for groups of non-human animals, and can thereby offer starting points for change. Even though non-human animal rights—whether in the form of universal negative rights or citizenship rights—are currently far away, many laws and political institutions already regulate relations between human and non-human animals. These political and social institutions and practices should be extended to incorporate non-human animal agency and interests in order to further promote non-human animal political participation. In the third part of this book, I explore further how existing political practices and institutions can be extended to take political non-human animal agency and non-human animal languages into account. Before doing that, I take two other steps. In the next chapter, in order to further clarify the borders of the political and of political agency and to discuss the relevance of species membership for political interaction, I discuss political relations with worms. This chapter is followed by a second case study, which focuses on goose-human relations in the Netherlands. This case study builds on insights developed in part II of this book, and provides an introduction to the themes discussed in the final chapters.

6

Worm Politics

Earthworms use touch to judge the shape of leaves, petioles, and pieces of paper in order to decide on the best way to carry them into their burrows. Charles Darwin (1881) looked at over two hundred fallen rhododendron leaves, and worked out that in two-thirds of the cases, the best way to carry them into a burrow would be by their base, and in one-third by the tip. When he let his earthworm test subjects perform the task, they matched this almost exactly. This led Darwin to conclude that these worms "judged with a considerable degree of correctness how to draw the withered leaves of this foreign plant into their burrows" (1881, 70). Darwin studied earthworms extensively, and he saw them as one of the most influential species of animals in the history of the world.[1] They cultivate the soil and make it possible for plants to grow, which makes the earth a suitable place for humans to live. Long before the plough existed, earthworms ploughed the earth. According to Darwin, their casts preserve ancient buildings, something for which archaeologists should be extremely thankful. Earthworms are timid creatures whose sight and hearing are not well developed. Darwin tested their hearing with whistles, the bassoon, and the piano; they responded to none of these. They did, however, respond when the jar that contained them was placed on the piano; they are very sensitive to vibrations and touch. They also have a lot of muscular power for their size and display a fondness for eating—they particularly like wild cherries and carrots. The experiments with carrying objects led Darwin to conclude that, contrary to popular belief, their acts are not just based on instinct; they also exhibit intelligence. Worms exercise agency—Darwin calls these small agencies (1881, 1)—and their acts can have great effects. The lives of earthworms and humans are interconnected in several ways: they plough the earth, and humans till the land, which affects their lives. Humans also use worms directly for fishing and scientific research.

In animal philosophy, the word "animal" is usually taken to mean mammal, although birds, fish, and certain invertebrates are sometimes included. An important reason for this is that sentience is generally seen as the ground for rights and human obligations.[2] It is argued that sentient non-human animals have interests, and it is therefore wrong to harm them. Small animals, such as snails, worms, and spiders, are often excluded from this concept, because it is unclear whether or not they are sentient. Since there are many non-human animals who are, beyond doubt, sentient and who suffer greatly from human violence, it may indeed seem best to focus on these cases. The lives of earthworms and humans are, however, also intertwined, and humans use them for their benefit. Furthermore, it is problematic to only focus on those animals who are most like us. Because earthworms are so different to humans, and because we know little about them, our relations with them do raise many questions. In this chapter, I discuss some of the questions related to worm politics. I focus on whether and how earthworms can be viewed as political actors, how humans should behave towards them, and how different theoretical approaches—such as new materialism, animal studies, and animal rights philosophy—can all shed light on political human-worm relations.[3]

Small Agencies

Worms not only move leaves, they also move trees. Bruno Latour (1999) discovered this when he followed a group of scientists into the Amazon rainforest. The scientists were puzzled by the presence of trees typical of the savannah at a spot some meters into the rainforest. After thorough investigation, they found that the local earthworms were responsible for the mysterious position of the trees. They had changed the soil by producing large amounts of aluminum, which enabled the savannah trees to encroach into the forest.

Jane Bennett (2010) draws on Darwin's (1881) and Latour's (1999) worm stories in order to investigate the politics of vital materialism. Bennett aims to show that political theory should take the active participation of non-humans in events more seriously. Recognizing the presence of non-humans in politics is ontologically important, and it might contribute to a more responsible, ecologically sound politics, one that moves beyond blaming individuals and sheds light on the relations that shape our world. She argues for a "vital materialism" (2010, 23) in which objects possess power, and agency is located in "assemblages": understood as ad hoc groupings of diverse elements that can consist of human and non-human bodies. Bodies are always tangled up in networks, which Bennett envisions as a web, a "knotted world of vibrant matter" (2010, 13). Objects, or non-humans, are not passive or stable in these networks. They are interconnected with human bodies, which are themselves made of matter and influenced by pressure from the outside world. In order to further conceptualize this pressure, or agency, Bennett turns to Spinoza, who used the term "conatus"—an active impulse or trending tendency to persist. According to Spinoza, non-human bodies share a conative nature with human bodies: "Conatus names a power present in every body" (2010, 2). These bodies are also associative, or even social (2010, 21), in the sense that each body by nature continuously affects and is affected by other bodies. Relations between bodies can be political in different ways—for example, in the effects they produce or because they are affected by political problems.

Darwin shows that earthworms are aware of their surroundings; their acts cannot be reduced to a mechanical instinct. By acting, they impact these surroundings, and directly or indirectly influence human lives; for example, when they plough the earth or move trees. Earthworm agencies may be "small agencies," but in the right circumstances they can make big things happen. For Bennett, worms exercise agency in the vibrant webs of which humans are also part. While there are clear differences in how worms and humans exercise agency—in terms of intentionality, cognitive capacities, and so on—she argues that there is no dichotomy between human and non-human political agency in which one party has all and the other none. Exercising agency is a matter of degree, and the acts of humans and non-humans can never be controlled completely because we always act in webs with others that influence us. In Latour's example we find that trees, worms, and scientists are all connected, and shape the outcomes of each other's actions,[4] either through material influence (the worms) or through the construction of facts (the scientists).

Political agency is often understood as a form of intentional agency (chapter 4). In order to be able to act politically, the actor must be aware of doing so, and act with the intention to change or influence political

systems. Bennett questions this emphasis on intentionality, and challenges the Kantian dichotomy between persons and things. She does
not do so on empirical grounds, or by arguing that non-human animals,
plants, or other beings are similar to humans in any way. Instead she argues for a different ontology, one in which actants influence each other
and make things happen politically. In this view, humans are also less
autonomous than they like to think. Humans always stand in relation to
others and are affected by them, as well as by the fact that they are matter; human acts are influenced by many physical factors such as disease,
food, genetic composition, and so on, and can never be controlled or
predicted rationally.[5]

The image of politics and political actors that Bennett sketches is
helpful in thinking about human-worm relations for several reasons.
She rightly draws our attention to the fact that worms and humans affect
each other's lives, often without being aware of it. Because humans and
worms share habitats, and share a planet, political events that concern
common goods will often affect them both.[6] Bennett also brings to light
the multitude of relations that make up lives, and offers a way to think
about the role, or even value, of others without colonizing them by defining them on the basis of their capacities.

Bennett's notion of political earthworm agency and subjectivity is,
however, problematic. As we saw in chapter 4, with regard to political
agency there are strong differences between the effects of thunder and
the Arab Spring. Political acts take place on a continuum, yet there are
clear normative differences between different types of acts. In the case of
earthworms, Bennett rightly turns the focus to the necessity of more empirical research, and inventing systems that do justice to them. They are
affected by human acts and we should recognize that, as well as recognizing their agency. Arguing that they act politically because they move
things is, however, going too far too fast. This requires a more careful
analysis of their acts, and of the politics of earthworm-human relations,
both from the perspective of justice and from the perspective of power.[7]
I will turn to the latter first.

Worm Power and Knowledge

Neither Bennett (2010) nor Latour (1999) address the power relations that shape the experiments discussed in detail. This is unfortunate, because human views of other animals determine the outcomes of knowledge production, and stereotypical views often heavily influence the outcome of scientific experiments (see chapter 2). In Darwin's earthworm studies and Latour's expedition into the rainforest we find different attitudes towards worms. Darwin is interested in the worms themselves; the scientists in Latour's experiment mostly focus on their ecological impact. The latter approach is the most common in scientific experiments that involve worms; there are very few studies that focus on the worms for the sake of learning about worms. This is the result of an anthropocentric tradition in science, in which humans see themselves as hierarchically above other animals, and view animals who resemble humans more as more valuable. While non-human animals of many species are exploited in laboratories, the smaller ones, or those who resemble humans less, are not usually given much or even any ethical consideration.[8] The connection between knowledge and power in worm science is manifold. We can map this with the use of Foucault's concept apparatus.[9] The elements of an apparatus are "discourses, institutions, architectural forms, regulatory decisions, laws, administrative measures, scientific statements, philosophical, moral and philanthropic propositions—in short, the said as much as the unsaid" (Foucault, as quoted in Thierman 2010, 90); the apparatus itself is the system of relations that can be established between these elements. A description of an apparatus brings an environment into focus, as the following example shows.

In an ecotoxicological experiment, conducted at the Vrije Universiteit in Amsterdam, earthworms were used to understand soil conditions in order to determine the effects of a toxic compound produced by genetically modified broccoli (Bertoni 2013). Earthworms were chosen because they are ecologically significant—earthworms influence soil on a large scale. Central here is the worms' eating of the soil (or perhaps more precisely: the soil's being eaten by the worms); through eating, the worms produced knowledge that no one else could provide. In order for the experiment to be successful, the scientists needed to learn to attend to the worms, and develop procedures and instruments that made knowledge production possible, both with regard to keeping the worms alive and being able to read their behavior.

This experiment does not take place in a vacuum, as a description of its apparatus shows. In the experiment, worms are studied in a university room, in specially designed boxes, with the use of standardized soil; the worms themselves are also "standardized" and their bodies are the result of specific breeding instructions (ibid.).[10] The scientists who work with the worms, as well as those who write about worms in the social sciences, are part of the academic world, and are under influence of its discursive, financial, and moral structures. Research projects are financed only when they are seen as relevant for humans, something that determines the body of knowledge that is constructed; studying worms for the sake of worms is not valued greatly in our society and so there are very few experiments that focus on the worms themselves. Laws that regulate the use of laboratory animals only take into account the welfare of certain species: worms are not protected by welfare regulations. This follows from a worldview in which small animals, who resemble humans less, are thought to matter less morally and politically. It also refers back to a philosophical tradition in which the human is central. Worms are used because humans want to find out more about diseases or ecosystems for the sake of humans. In capitalist and anthropocentric societies, there is a clear relation in worm research between gaining knowledge and exercising power; humans develop techniques to dominate the non-human world, and scientists are part of that process. Worms are used and held captive by humans; their interests are not considered and they are not paid for their scientific labor. While the worms do exercise agency—for example, by eating—they have no opportunity to shape the conditions under which they live. They influence the outcomes of scientific research, but humans determine the form of the experiments and interpret their behavior.

Power relations between earthworms and humans are, of course, not only found in the laboratory: earthworms are kept as companion animals, used as food for birds or as fishing bait, and even those who live their lives in the earth and never encounter a human might be influenced by human behavior, for example, when causing pollution. In many of these cases, humans dominate the lives of earthworms. This brings us to the question of what justice for earthworms would entail.

Justice for Worms

From Sentience to Relations

In animal ethics, sentience is usually seen as both necessary and sufficient for moral consideration. Sentience refers to the subjective capacity to have experiences and is thus related to consciousness, and because sentient non-human animals have interests, it is wrong to harm them. For many small animals such as bees, worms, snails, and spiders, there is doubt as to whether or not they are sentient. There are, however, several problems with focusing only on those animals that are obviously sentient, such as mammals and birds, as well as reasons to also consider small animals such as worms.

First of all, the empirical matter is not settled. It is usually thought that worms respond to stimuli but do not have the consciousness necessary for understanding and actually "feeling" pain, so while they might respond to pain stimuli, they do not suffer. However, we currently know very little about worm cognition, emotion, and other capacities, simply because there has not been much research on the subject.[11] Not so very long ago humans doubted whether fish were sentient, something for which the evidence is now overwhelming (Braithwaite 2010). Before that, Cartesian skepticism about the capacity of non-human animals to feel pain led humans to perform vivisection on dogs, whose screams were seen as simple mechanical responses to stimuli, and not as expressions of pain. Second, it is unclear why sentience should be seen as the sole moral or political value. A virtue ethical approach could argue that the flourishing of animals whose sentience is in doubt has moral worth, and the vital materialist approach argues for a politics in which different types of agency, and actors with different degrees of intentionality, make up political structures. Third, it is difficult to draw lines between different groups of animals. From an empirical perspective, we find that consciousness is notoriously hard to measure in groups of human and non-human animals, and our ideas about consciousness and other animal capacities—including sentience, as the case of fish confirms—are often informed by cultural prejudices (chapter 2). Biologist Frans de Waal (2016) summarizes this nicely by asking whether humans are smart enough to understand how smart other animals are. Progress in science and morality continually challenges the lines that are drawn, and we should—also from a political perspective—be careful in determining for others what they can perceive or not. Finally, focusing on non-human animals who are clearly sentient is often done for pragmatic reasons: there are so many non-human animals who suffer, and in working towards social change it is best to focus on the obvious cases. As Wolfe (2003) has shown, however, favoring those species most like humans is not an ethically sound tactic, and runs the risk of repeating the violence done to other animals on a different level.

Looking at worms from the perspective of justice helps to turn the focus from interpretation of their individual capacities to political relations. When we try to find out what justice for worms entails, and how to envision relations between worm communities and human political communities, we immediately encounter many empirical questions, not just about worm sentience and cognition, but also about worm communities. Recent research has shown that worms form herds and make group decisions (Zirbes et al. 2010). Earthworms of the species *Eisenia fetida* use touch to communicate and influence each other's behavior. When they are taken out of the soil, they frequently cluster and form a patch. Scientists compare this social behavior to the behavior of herds or swarms. One experiment showed that when a group of worms was put into a chamber with two identical arms, they collectively chose to move to one of the arms (ibid.). Another experiment focused on how worms know how to follow their fellow worms. Two worms were put into a soil-filled maze, with two routes to a food source at the end. When the worms could not detect each other at the start, they followed their own routes, but when they were put into the maze together, in two-thirds of the trials they stayed together. The worms sometimes crossed their bodies over each other, and at other times they maximized contact; it was through these types of interaction that they let each other know where they planned to go. Clustering together helps earthworms protect themselves: they secrete proteins and fluids that have antibacterial properties to deter soil pathogens. To deter predatory flatworms, they secrete a yellow fluid. When they are in a group, the quantity of fluid increases, covering the earthworms and offering individuals better protection (ibid.).

Earthworms form their own communities, and neither need nor desire contact with humans, even though they are sometimes used as companion animals, or as laboratory workers. Most of them live underground and mind their own business, although their paths sometimes cross those of humans. However, humans use various types of worms for research, food, or other practices such as fishing, and in doing so they inflict violence and death upon them, or change their bodies. Humans also depend on worms because they enable plants to grow. While earthworms do live near humans, and sometimes come into view, they do not cohabit in cities and houses in the way that liminal animals such as mice, pigeons, or even snails do. Their territories are all around us: in our gardens, parks, woods, and other spaces. Respecting foreign non-human animal communities is, according to Donaldson and Kymlicka (2011), not the same as just "letting them be." Humans often radically influence the lives and territories of other animal communities, and are therefore responsible for limiting spillover effects (such as noise, pollution, building) that may influence their habitats. Humans may also have a duty to intervene, for example, in the case of a natural or man-made catastrophe. These recommendations can also guide our relations with worms. We should respect their physical integrity, i.e., not use or kill them for our own benefit, and not breed them to better fit human experiments. Earthworms who are bred into a form of domestication should be cared for. Humans should also not pollute the earth in which they live and should take their interests into account in considerations regarding new uses of the earth. Because human activity already influences the lives of worms and their habitats, we need to take a more active attitude in learning about worms. Worm communities are very different from human communities, and we have a long way to go in learning to understand them. It is, however, not up to humans to define whether or not they form proper communities, especially since we know so little about their social lives. In this case, sovereignty starts with respecting worms as different to us.

Keep Your Ear to the Ground: Listening to Our Earthworm Neighbors

Learning about earthworms and how to live with them is not just a scientific project; it is also part of the larger cultural, ethical, and political process of developing better relations with our non-human neighbors. Philosopher Ralph Acampora (2004) searches for interspecies engagement and relations without human domination. He sees potential for new relations in different settings, one of which is sharing urban neighborhoods with non-human animals of all kinds. Aiming for a situation in which the goal is flourishing without oppression, he argues that the figure of the neighbor can help us to find the right ethical attitude towards non-human animal others with whom we share urban spaces or "multispecies neighborhoods." Acampora argues that the concept of "neighbor" preserves an intimacy that is lacking in most approaches that focus on citizenship and related notions. Whereas the political approach through which we view non-human animal communities as liminal or sovereign asks us to remain at a respectful distance from these communities, Acampora invites us to explore proximity. This is important for two reasons. Rethinking politics with other animals means more than just extending concepts and practices to include other animals. We also need to think—for democratic reasons—about how they can co-shape the terms of interaction. Second, while understanding them as sovereign communities asks for a respectful attitude, acknowledging them as neighbors—and earthworms are our neighbors—also invites us to attend carefully and listen to them. The figure of the neighbor can thus complement the image of worms as sovereign communities. They live their own lives, often very close to humans.

In order to find out more about earthworm communities and interests we need to listen to them more carefully. Listening can also play a role in incorporating worm interests into existing democratic institutions and practices. Dryzek (2000) points to the political importance of listening. He argues that in a green democracy, there should be recognition of agency in nature, as well as respect for natural objects and ecological processes. Humans and non-humans should, for reasons of justice, be equally represented democratically, and should be able to make equal demands on our capacity to listen. He emphasizes that humans are ecological rather than simply social beings, and that much of our communication already goes beyond human language. Humans use body language, but are also heavily influenced by the workings of pheromones, oxygen, and unintentional chemical processes. Listening means attending to others[12] and translating this into representative structures. Working with earthworms, paying attention to their dealings with the soil and the earth, and listening to them in the broadest sense of the word, as Darwin did, can and should inform human political decision-making, and can help us work towards new ways of coexisting.

Respect and Response

The different approaches to non-human politics discussed above, and those discussed in chapters 4 and 5, have in common that they ask us to see other animals—and politics—differently. Donna Haraway (2008) draws attention to the relation between seeing and respect via the Latin *re-specere*, which means looking back, looking at, taking into account. She connects this to interspecies encounters and the construction of a common reality: "To hold in regard, to respond, to look back reciprocally, to notice, to pay attention, to have courteous regard for, to esteem: all of that is tied to polite greeting, to constituting the polis, where and when species meet" (2008, 19). Because other animals have largely disappeared from the cultural and political picture in anthropocentric and humanist societies, we need to begin to see them again. This "seeing again" takes place in situated encounters in which we are always already entangled with other animals. One of the "first obligations" in these relations is curiosity.[13] Haraway also connects being polite to constituting the polis; treating other species respectfully not only opens the door to change in individual encounters, it also brings about a starting point for imagining new communities, including the promise of developing new forms of political interaction.

Being curious and being polite are important in respecting earthworms—in seeing them anew and treating them with regard. Here we find that a new materialist approach and a justice approach can complement each other. The materialist approach suffers from a lack of political effectiveness and does not adequately take into account non-human animal suffering or the power relations that shape agencies—this might show a lack of the politeness and respect that we do find in theories that focus on justice. Approaches that focus on justice, however, need to more explicitly acknowledge the way in which humans and non-humans are interconnected and influence one another, as well as the fact that existing political institutions, procedures, and concepts might, for many species, not be so adequate—which could refer to a lack of the curiosity that we do find in materialist theories.

Developing a non-anthropocentric view of politics asks us to reconsider the borders of the political and to develop new forms of interacting with other animals. Existing concepts and institutions can play a role in this process, and function as starting points for change. In the third and final part of this book, I investigate how the relation between non-human animals and existing political practices and institutions can be improved with other animals. Non-human animals do not constitute one group; there are major differences between individuals, social groups, and species, and reformulating politics will look very different in different contexts, depending on the animals involved. Treating other animals with respect and regard is the starting point for all of them. Whether earthworms plan to treat humans with regard is a question yet to be answered; Darwin showed that they are curious and willing to engage with humans if we invite them to do so. Haraway (2008) points our attention to the fact that the word "companion" comes from *cum panis*—"with bread"—which tells us something about the importance for relations of sharing food. According to Darwin, earthworms particularly like wild cherries and raw carrots—something to remember on your next picnic.

Case Study 2

Goose Politics

Resistance, Deliberation, and the Politics of Space

Wild geese like the Netherlands. The Dutch population of greylag geese grew from around ten nesting pairs in 1971 (Bijlsma et al. 2001) to over twenty-five thousand in 2005 (SOVON 2017). The main reasons for this are the increasing use of fertilizers by farmers, which has improved the quality of the grass, and restrictions on hunting geese (and not their predators, most notably foxes). Geese were invited to nest in the Oostvaardersplassen, a large nature reserve in the middle of the country. Their job there is to prevent the growth of trees to keep the fields open so that large ungulates can roam the area. A sizable number of greylag geese have settled in the area around Schiphol Airport, close to the

FIGURE CS2.1. A greylag goose. (Source: "Greylag Goose [Anser anser]" by Charles J Sharp. CC BY-SA 3.0)

Oostvaardersplassen. The grasslands and croplands in that area provide them with plenty of food, and there are enough wetland areas for resting and nesting nearby. However, in 2010, a plane from Royal Air Maroc had to return to the airport following a collision with a flock of geese. This led to an investigation by the *Nederlandse Regiegroep Vogelaanvaringen*, the Dutch Group for Bird Collisions, which concluded in 2014 that the presence of geese in the area around the airport poses a major risk to flight safety. They recommended reducing the number of geese, and emphasized the need for new technological solutions to prevent accidents. The *Faunabescherming*, the Dutch Organization for Fauna Protection, offered a different perspective on the situation. They drew attention to the fact that up to now there had been no fatal accidents—the chance of a collision is smaller than 0.001%. Three incidents with birds in 2013 were related to bad weather conditions, and could have been avoided with bird-detection equipment. The Faunabescherming also emphasized that killing the birds would not solve the problem.[1]

In 2013, the Dutch government commissioned the pest control company Duke Faunabeheer to kill 15,000 Schiphol geese.[2] They captured the birds in May, when they were molting and could not fly. The geese were forced into vans, hidden by large black plastic walls, known by activists as "mobile gas chambers," and gassed.[3] (Later that year, a machine was invented to decapitate the geese in order to kill them more efficiently.) Killing geese simply creates space for others to take their place, however, and the extermination of 15,000 Schiphol geese only resulted in a net reduction of the population by 600 as other geese joined the flock. Even though the method of population control was not efficient, large numbers of geese were also killed in 2014, and in 2015 EU legislation was changed to allow for them to be killed in other parts of the country. The Dutch Party for the Animals, various animal welfare organizations, activist groups, and biologists argue that to really address the problem, the land will have to be made less attractive to the birds—as long as there is a superabundance of food, new flocks of geese will continue to settle in the area. For this reason, the Party for the Animals proposed the purchase of six square kilometers of land around Schiphol to be used for solar panels that could be leased by citizens and companies based in Amsterdam. Other more goose-friendly measures included scaring the birds away with lasers, playing recordings of distress calls, radar systems, and robot birds. A 2011 study also showed that sowing green manure after harvesting cereal reduced the food supply so that very few or no birds were seen in the area (CLM 2011).

In most of these proposals, there is little attention to goose agency and goose-human relations. In the conflict around Schiphol, many different parties play a role, including politicians, animal welfare activists, farmers, the airport authorities, and the general public. The geese are not seen as active agents in the matter, even though it is their behavior that causes the problems, and it is well known that geese are intelligent birds who continue to learn for the whole of their lives (Lorenz 1991). Geese exercise political agency at an individual level and as groups, and certain goose-human relations are already political. In this case study, I investigate how goose agency can be taken into account in this and similar conflicts, which offers a new perspective on the situation, and is important for normative reasons (see also chapters 4 & 5).

Goose Politics

The Schiphol geese are typically non-domesticated,[4] but they do seek out human settlements and are often not shy of humans, although they prefer to stay away from them. Between domesticated non-human animals and those wild animals who have almost no contact with humans, we find a wide range of encounters and relations—think, for example, of mice who live in houses, feral cats, or crows. To determine political rights for this group, Donaldson and Kymlicka (2011) introduce the category "liminal animals," by which they mean non-human animals who are not domesticated, but who, like the Schiphol geese, live among or often encounter humans.[5] Liminal animals are a new group in animal rights literature. By introducing this group, Donaldson and Kymlicka underline that there is no dichotomy between wild and domesticated animals; rather, there are many non-human animals who fit into neither of these categories.[6] This is a heterogeneous group, and in determining reciprocal rights and duties, the context is even more important than in the case of domesticated or wild animals. Non-human animals whose habitat has been invaded and who have nowhere else to go should, for example, have different rights to animals who seek out human settlements but who can also thrive elsewhere.

Non-human animals who are neither domesticated nor wild are the least recognized from a legal and moral perspective. They are often seen as intruders or pests in urban environments, which leads to a wide range of abuses and injustices—think, for example, of the treatment of rats. Defining them as a group can clarify these underlying problems and provide structure for government policies. The non-human animals in question are not connected because of a shared identity, but because of their relationships to human political communities. In order to further shed light on living with animals who are not part of our communities but who live close to us, Donaldson and Kymlicka define three general clusters of rights, in addition to the universal negative rights all non-human animals should have: rights of residence, reciprocal rights and duties of denizenship, and anti-stigma safeguards. All three are relevant in thinking about geese. Because geese have the option to settle elsewhere, humans have a right to keep them off their land. However, the geese have a right to live somewhere, and when they have been in a given area for an extended period, it becomes their home, and humans cannot simply relocate them whenever they feel like it. Furthermore, humans invited the geese to nest in the Netherlands, and they helped to construct the Oostvaardersplassen. Rights and duties of denizenship would depend on the specific context, and the relations that humans and geese have in a given territory. Lastly, liminal animals are often stigmatized as pests and, as mentioned in the introduction, geese are no exception. In the case of the Schiphol geese, we find that both the framing of the problem and the proposed solution are anthropocentric. This is visible in the negative stereotyping of geese, in the way risk is assessed, and in the fact that goose agency is not taken into account at all in thinking about potential solutions to this conflict.

The way that geese are currently treated is connected to a change in discourse. In the 1970s, geese were seen as rare wild birds—as welcome guests. As the population grew, and specifically in recent years when Schiphol Airport and farmers started to complain about their presence, politicians, media, and companies began to represent them as pests.[7] This often happens when non-human animal communities become larger. Animal geographer Colin Jerolmack (2008), who describes a similar process with regard to feral pigeons in New York, shows that stigmatization of problem species is intimately tied to a modernist conception of space, which builds on and reaffirms a binary opposition between nature and culture (see also chapter 5; Wolch and Emel 1998; Nagy and Johnson 2013; Wolch 2010). In the example of Schiphol Airport, the land and air around the airport are seen as human spaces, as expressions of human culture, and as belonging to humans. The geese are now portrayed as intruders into this area who pose a risk to humans. They are demonized and portrayed as the enemy, which legitimizes killing them.

The main reason given by humans for the killing of geese near the airport is that they pose a risk to flight safety. If the presence of non-human animals causes a lethal risk to humans, humans may, of course, act in self-defence, but as mentioned above, the risk posed by birds to airplanes is extremely small—there is a greater risk of dying from a bee-sting. Although we like to pretend otherwise, it is impossible to eradicate all risk from our society. We accept this in the case of traffic, and non-Western human communities who live close to large predators are also more willing to accept this in the case of non-human animals (Bakels 2003). Furthermore, as Donaldson and Kymlicka also convincingly argue, there is no reason why other animals need to bear all the costs. Flying—like many other forms of human transport—poses risks to other animals and imposes significant costs on our environment. As Schiphol Airport continues to grow, more accidents will take place.

While accepting the presence of the geese would be the preferred solution in this and similar conflicts, this might not always be possible everywhere; humans and other animals often have to share spaces. We therefore need to consider alternative ways of living with them, including dealing with this kind of conflict. The current focus in the framing of the conflict and the proposed solutions is on the role and perspective of the human actors, and takes no account of the position of the geese, even though they can clearly express themselves and communicate with humans. This is normatively problematic, because the geese are thereby rendered mute in decisions that concern their lives. They are seen and treated as objects, their deaths are normalized, and methods of killing them are discussed in the media as if they were not living, feeling beings. It is also practically problematic: the developments of recent years show that the geese are a "tough enemy"[8] who are quite determined about staying in, and returning to, their preferred spots (Bastiaansen 2013). For both these reasons we need to take their agency into account and begin to interact with them differently. A first step would be to learn about their languages and behavior.

Goose-Human Communication

Geese communicate with each other in many different ways, for example, by using sounds, smells, gestures, physical movements, touch, voice, eye contact, and by performing certain rituals (see Lorenz 1991 for a detailed analysis of goose behavior, language, and culture). Although many geese are conservative and like to return to the same nesting areas, individual geese can and do sometimes make a different choice, which often leads to the whole flock discovering a new area with better options for feeding. Flocks of geese usually make the same journey every year, but as groups they can also deal with disturbances and create new habits. Flexibility can differ between species, communities, and individuals. Geese can learn new things at different times in their lives—the imprinting period in the first days of their lives is perhaps the most important phase, but they are also open to new opportunities at other times, such as when they first go looking for a partner or during their first autumn migration. They develop personal routines, individually and with members of their own species and others. They have cultural traditions and individual inclinations. Not only do geese recognize many members of their own species through sound, sight, and smell, they also recognize individual humans, other animals such as dogs, and objects such as cars. They respond differently to the same stimuli in different contexts: a black car might only mean danger under certain circumstances; a dog off the lead might be considered a threat, but the same dog on a lead might be ignored.

Geese live in pairs, although they sometimes form trios, usually consisting of two males and one female. They stay together for life unless they fall in love with another goose (which occasionally happens, as vividly described by Lorenz 1991). They sometimes seek a new mate when their first partner dies or leaves. They usually live in flocks consisting of approximately twenty geese, and have a hierarchy that changes throughout the year. The geese with the most offspring are highest in the hierarchy—adoption is common among goose families for this reason—and if the numbers of offspring are the same, age matters: the oldest geese will then rank highest. Geese can live up to twenty-five years. There are different ways of communicating within a goose community, and these range from fights and exercises of power by those of higher rank to friendly encounters; geese from the same family may, for example, be close during nesting time and help each other to defend nests. As in other animal species, geese may exhibit very different personalities: some are calm, while others are dominant, some are creative and others are conservative (Lorenz 1991).

Vocalization plays an important role in the communication between couples and between mother and child, as well as in the larger group.[9] Geese have many different calls, including alarm calls, distress calls, lamentation calls, distance calls, contact calls, cackling, rolling, and hissing.[10] Young geese have a specific sound they make when they are cold and want to rest; geese also make soft noises when they eat grass. In addition to sound, geese have good eyesight, which they use in communication. They make many gestures, such as shaking their heads before they leave the ground for flight, neck arching and neck dipping, and different wing movements; they even yawn. They perform different rituals on different occasions; there is, for example, a wide range of greeting rituals, courtship rituals, and triumph ceremonies. Goose behavior changes throughout the year, something most visible during the molt, when geese become more shy because they know they are not able to fly and are in a different hormonal state.

Geese and humans can have many different kinds of relations. Geese who are imprinted by humans form very close relationships with these humans.[11] Lorenz (1991) describes how, if their significant human calls their name, they will come down immediately when they are flying, and how they go to great lengths to be with their human more generally. These observations have led him to say that, after dogs, geese are the animals who make the best friends for humans. Geese who are not imprinted but who live close to humans may still form friendships with them, although never with the same intensity as imprinted geese. According to Lorenz, this applies to both animals: humans respond to goose intimacy and can become greatly attached to geese they have im-

FIGURE CS2.2. Warnings (Source: "Goose tongue" by Squacco. CC BY-SA 2.0)

printed. Geese who live close to human settlements will learn which humans and dogs are to be feared, and which are not. They will typically be less shy than geese who interact less with humans. Domesticated geese will, for example, try to fight humans who come too close to their nests, while wild geese who have never had contact with humans will usually flee. Geese respond to humans who imitate their alarm calls and contact calls, and humans can often interpret the signals of geese—ranging from friendly gestures to hissing and alarm calls—correctly without having any special knowledge of goose behavior (Lorenz 1991).

When humans try to catch or attack geese they will flee or fight. Geese will defend themselves, their nest, and their partner, and sometimes others with whom they have relationships. Goose resistance may take different forms. A goose who is protecting the nest—this is usually the gander—will first give an intruder a warning call. If the intruder continues, he will try to scare them away by hissing, standing upright, and flapping his wings. If the intruder does not leave, the goose will try to hit them with his wings or peck them. He might also use alarm calls to warn other geese in the area. Partners will often come to help defend the nest, which will make the gander, if he was the first to attack, more violent. Goose attacks can cause serious physical injury in humans, such as broken bones and head injuries, as well as emotional distress. Geese are even used as watch animals in some parts of the world; it is reputed that domestic geese defended Rome in this manner. The Schiphol geese also resist. If they are about to be captured by Duke Faunabeheer they try to escape, and they fight when this is not possible. Although the power relation is clearly unequal—the geese are handicapped because they are molting and cannot fly—one out of ten does escape (De Putter 2015). The others try to break out of the enclosure and fight the humans who have captured them (ibid.). Couples often do not molt at the same time, and the goose who can still fly will usually stay close to the partner who is captured, calling to them from the sky and trying to scare away the intruders (ibid.).

Foot Voting, Occupation, Squatting, and Deliberation

Political Goose-Human Interaction

Goose-human interaction also takes place at the level of social groups. For example, human groups and individuals interact with communities of geese by hunting them, by changing the conditions in a given area to persuade geese to relocate, or by relocating them by force. Geese make certain decisions as groups, such as where to go and when to leave. In what follows, I discuss four human forms of political interaction in order to explore how they relate to goose behavior in the Schiphol conflict: foot voting, occupation, squatting, and deliberation. My aim is not to show that geese participate in practices identical to these human practices, but rather to explore the relevance of these concepts for interpreting goose behavior and conceptualizing the group behavior of geese as political behavior.

Foot voting refers to physically leaving situations that are not beneficial. It has been described as "a tool for enhancing political freedom: the ability of the people to choose the political regime under which they wish to live" (Somin 2014, 110). This is connected to the right to emigrate: "For people living under authoritarian regimes, foot voting through international migration is often their only means of exercising any political choice" (Somin 2014, 111). The term is also used within societies and not just in relation to political regimes. In the context of public finance, for example, Tiebout (1956) uses the term to argue that people vote with their feet to move to the community offering their preferred bundle of taxes and public goods. Humans vote with their feet for a variety of reasons in a variety of political contexts. The result of their behavior is not always predictable or intended; marginalized humans may leave certain communities individually for private reasons, but if many of them do it, their behavior as a group will influence the composition of the community or territory concerned, which will in turn influence policy-making and other aspects of society.

Like humans, geese are creatures of habit, and usually travel to the same nesting ground every year. However, food shortages and disruptions such as hunting or the presence of predators might force them to change their route or destination. These two factors resemble human reasons for voting with their feet—the economic climate, i.e., being able to feed one's family, and political regimes, i.e., being able to live somewhere safely. Humans do not leave their land when there is no food in the area with the aim of contributing to a political process; they leave because they are hungry. When members of a social or ethnic group are politically marginalized, oppressed, or prosecuted simply for being a member of that group, they might leave to seek safety. For some, this may constitute a contribution to a political struggle, but the others who leave but for whom this is not a motive will still influence politics with their acts. When geese leave or settle somewhere as a group, they may unwittingly influence the political context in similar ways. Because the political frameworks of human communities are constituted to exclude non-human animal voices, geese do not usually have the opportunity to change their situation or the larger system by voicing their concerns; relocation is often the only option available to them.[12]

The Occupy Wall Street movement and squatting are examples of human actions that claim space, sometimes out of necessity and sometimes to influence politics. Hardt and Negri (2011) argue that instead of just having an economic agenda, the Occupy movement shares political characteristics with other large-scale protests that were happening around the same time, such as the Tahrir Square uprising and the encampments in central squares in Spain. These and other events have their own context and agenda, but, according to Hardt and Negri, they all originate from the point of view that the current representational model of democracy does not adequately address societal problems. They all express a desire for real democracy without specifying what this would look like. While Hardt and Negri are right to emphasize this "political face" of the protest, there is more to it than a critique of democracy, including economic representation. The Occupy movement claimed specific pieces of land, and saw the community formed there as an intentional community where different social rules applied. The enthusiasm that this movement generated was partly related to claiming space for change and finding out what this might mean. Different types of humans—professional activists, students, artists, and others—related to this message, for different reasons. While some criticized the movement for not being clear about what "real democracy" would entail, having different views and discussing them, without offering a clear alternative, is obviously part of their message. An intermingling of political, economic, and other messages and views can be found in the Occupy movement, something that is reflected in the composition of the group of humans who took part in the protest. Some came with a clear democratic goal in mind; others were just expressing discontent with the current economic climate; others were just following their friends.

Geese need to nest and feed somewhere. They recognize the territories of others—geese, humans, or other animals—except when such territory is not actually inhabited (Lorenz 1991). Part of the appeal of the Occupy movement was that by claiming a certain space, the protesters brought to light existing power relations and made themselves visible as a group. While goose intentions in claiming space might lack the symbolic intentions—although these might also not be present in some human protestors, and geese sometimes understand very well that they are not wanted but keep returning—they still challenge human dominance with their presence and persistence, in the same way that they would challenge other communities of geese. Their aim is not to make human society more democratic, but they do challenge the fact that humans are taking up all the land.

Taking up space in this sense also resembles the human practice of squatting, which is often based on an actual human need—particularly, but not exclusively, in developing countries—although for some it is a purely political act. Squatters challenge the existing power hierarchy as expressed in legal and financial constructions, even if they do not explicate this. Their physical act is the protest, not the words used to defend it. Interestingly, human squatters and occupiers are also framed as pests in the media and in public debate, nuisances to an otherwise orderly society. These examples do not show that groups of geese act in the same way as human groups—members of different species have different perspectives on life and express themselves differently—but they do show that certain human political acts resemble the acts of geese, or the other way around, and that there are different ways of claiming given territories.

Goose-Human Deliberation

Discussions about geese take place between farmers and government, activists and politicians, hunters and farmers and politicians, any of these groups and the media, the media and the general public, and other human groups. Part of this communication is formalized and institutionalized; part of it—street protests, sharing images on social media, the disruptions of goose killings—is informal or disruptive. Different forms of communication are interconnected and influence each other. Activists might, for example, influence the general public, and this might exert pressure on the government to act differently. Financial compensation from the government might influence farmers' crop-planting behavior. European legislation limits the way in which the Dutch government can act. The media can expose practices—such as the violence used in gassing the geese—thereby influencing the wider public and the government. One can understand these different forms of political communication as forms of deliberation (see chapter 9 for a detailed analysis of animal deliberation, including a defense of using material interventions as a tool for discussion in human/non-human animal interactions).

Different authors have argued that the Habermasian deliberative ideal is too demanding for human groups because it favors the educated and the dispassionate and excludes the many ways in which people communicate outside of argumentation and formal debate, such as testimony, rhetoric, symbolic disruptions, storytelling, and cultural-, gender-, and species-specific styles of communication (ibid.). In the case of the Schiphol geese, protests, websites, and demonstrations also inform the legislative process and are a form of deliberation. Many of the discussions mentioned above, particularly the ones that do not take place in institutional politics, involve strong emotions on both the side of those humans who want to protect the geese and those humans who feel disadvantaged by the presence of the geese.

The geese themselves also influence the communication on different levels. Goose resistance partially determines whether they and their partners are caught and killed. Film footage of these scenes, made by activists and journalists, influences the general public. The ways in which they resist influences the methods used by pest control companies to catch them. Goose agency not only takes the form of resistance, it also concerns communication regarding the use of the land around Schiphol. Farmers try to make their land less attractive to keep geese away, and the airport uses dogs, solar panels, and robot birds to scare them into changing their behavior. The geese respond in various ways to these threats, after which the strategies may be changed. These experiments influence the opinion of politicians, thereby influencing policy. Sometimes the acts of the geese are inherently political, at other times they might just be trying to survive and find enough to eat (not unlike the farmers), which influences politics indirectly. In both cases the geese are actively shaping the conditions of coexistence; they are not simply passive recipients of human care or terror.

The Politics of Space

More often than not, human maps of land, sky, and water do not correspond to non-human animal maps of these territories. Animal geographer Maan Barua (2014) shows how questions of "geo" and "bio" are closely intertwined in the case of elephants in northeast India. Colonialism brought cartography to India, when a small group of humans mapped and divided the land, and decided which parts of it belonged to whom.[13] This concerned not only human space, it also designated certain areas for other animals. For elephants, this meant that from that point in time they could still roam freely in nature reserves, but not in certain human areas. However, the elephants had their own ancient, culturally transmitted maps of the land that did not correspond with the human maps, leading to unwanted encounters and sometimes to conflicts. With the process of mapping and dividing the land came a new sense of territory and entitlement to the land for humans, as well as a new sense of entitlement over the lives of other animals, including the right to kill them.

Like elephants, geese have their own flight routes and maps.[14] Human legal systems regulate who is allowed to go where[15]; geese often have no way of knowing that they are unwanted until it is too late. In the Netherlands, humans control all space, and they have given themselves the right to do so. Not only do humans determine which non-human animals can live where,[16] they also actively change landscapes. However, it is possible to let geese know where they are wanted and where they are not. The Dutch Hofganzen Foundation helps to solve conflicts between humans and geese in "animal friendly" ways, within the existing political framework. They mostly work for municipalities, and first aim to prevent problems by covering eggs in oil within fourteen days of laying so that they cannot hatch, leaving one of two untouched where possible so that the mother goose can still take care of her young. However, if there are too many geese, they relocate populations to suitable areas nearby and then use litter management in that area; if a group cannot be relocated, the geese are brought to Akka's Ganzenparadijs, a goose shelter run by the Hofganzen Foundation, where they can either stay or be adopted. Families are always kept together. The Hofganzen Foundation maps the complete situation and aims to provide long-term solutions for dealing with goose-human conflicts. They make designated areas of land attractive for those geese who need to relocate, then work to keep the area where they are not wanted unattractive. Implementing their method on a large scale would be a clear improvement for the geese, especially in the short term. However, their approach still functions in a framework that is built on the view that land belongs to humans. In some circumstances humans might know what is best for other animals—when a group of geese lives dangerously close to a busy road, for example, although this could also be solved by changing the course of the road—but in other circumstances accepting the presence of the geese or withdrawing from a territory might be the appropriate solution.

I mentioned above that there is a connection between the negative stereotyping of geese and the injustices from which they suffer. Describing geese as pests legitimizes removing them from one's territory. Similarly, discussions about interactions between humans and wild non-human animals are currently usually anthropocentric—the human is seen as the center of attention, and human inconvenience almost always trumps non-human animal interests (including their right to life, as discussed with regard to fallow deer in chapter 5). Furthermore, problems are often framed in economic terms (Daniel et al. 2005). Although human communities are the more relevant scale (ibid.), discussions about conflicts with non-human animal communities often take place at the level of countries or districts, which makes it easier to forget about non-human animal subjectivity. Conflicts are often one-sided; in many cases humans are the party that experiences a conflict or sees other animals as intruders, while the other animals might just be going about their business. For this reason, wildlife foundations put a lot of energy into building trust and changing human opinions. Political rhetoric often relies on a binary opposition between nature and culture and human and animal (Doremus 2000). Government policies and language influence how the general public conceives of problem situations. For example, policy discourse influences human perception of aircraft noise around Schiphol; the same amount of noise is perceived differently depending on the dominant discourse (Broër 2006). Policy discourse functions as a form of social control, because it sets the parameters for creating and opposing opinions: humans who accept and humans who oppose the discourse both reaffirm it in some sense. When a dominant narrative or discourse is institutionalized, it disciplines citizens' thoughts (Huys and Kroesen 2009). Laws reflect cultural attitudes, and we lack political stories about humans as part of nature and nature as integrated in areas where humans live (Wolch 2010). New political stories that focus on living together and sharing spaces with other animals might help humans to accept a certain amount of risk and see geese in a different light.

FIGURE CS2.3. Flying geese (Source: "Anser anser EM1B5927" by Bengt Nyman. CC BY 2.0)

New Pathways

Goose agency is not taken into account in current political institutions and decision-making processes. Viewing geese as political actors, involved in political communication with humans, can help humans to better understand the situation and envision new, less violent solutions. Seeing geese as sentient individuals who live in networks of social relations and who take care of one another might also help humans to accept the small risk that they pose in terms of flight safety. Taking goose agency and goose-human communication into account is not an all-or-nothing situation; this can happen step by step. Creating safe zones for geese, protecting nesting areas, activism, and research can all contribute to improving the situation. Change can take place in parks, residential areas, city councils, nation-states, or on the internet. While the work of the Hofganzen Foundation cannot be an end point, they do contribute to changing human perceptions of geese and help individual animals. The same applies to advocacy for the Schiphol geese. The next steps might be to combine knowledge about goose behavior with knowledge about politics to develop new models of interaction. In this process, and in developing new narratives, different human groups can play a role. Alongside activists, biologists, and politicians, philosophers can help with thinking through human rights and duties towards geese, and artists and architects can help to imagine change. Experiments with landscape design and architecture can contribute to processes of negotiating space with the geese. Parallel to these, we need to develop new political experiments in which decisions that concern the lives of geese are informed by actual interaction with geese, and communicated back to them in ways that they can understand. If the geese do not accept something, humans need to take this into account and develop a new standpoint. These experiments can inform other layers of decision-making (chapter 9). In addition to ethological-political experiments aimed at improving communication with actual geese, we need to develop new political stories to communicate to other humans. Geese are often perceived as intruders in human territory: they cross borders to enter cities and land used by humans. Instead of trying to keep them out with violence, we should invest in thinking about new models of interaction and coexistence. Both humans and geese are capable of learning new things throughout their whole life. This learning behavior can and should be used to find new solutions. Although the outcome of this process is unpredictable, both humans and geese are curious creatures, and we can and should be able to do better than this.

PART III

From Animal Politics to Interspecies Change

7

Animal Activism and Interspecies Change

In the 1850s, the United States government introduced seventy-five camels into military service. Their job was to transport equipment and human soldiers. The camels resisted by refusing to obey orders or cooperate, and by biting and spitting on the human soldiers, who learned to hate and fear them. Eventually, the army stopped employing camels and returned to using horses and mules. They stated that using camels had been an experiment, although it was the camels who had made it into an experiment by being bad soldiers. Jason Hribal (2007) discusses the resistance of these camels as an example of a situation in which non-human animal agency has directly influenced a human political decision. There are many other examples, some more successful than others.

The role that non-human animals play in social change is usually not acknowledged in theory or in animal activism, because non-human animals are not seen as political actors (chapters 1–5) or agents of social change (Hribal 2007, 2012), even though they can act politically and influence human political institutions and practices. This is problematic for several reasons. It does not recognize non-human animal agency, and reinforces viewing non-human animals as mute in contrast to human actors, which reaffirms anthropocentrism and unequal power relations. It can also lead to the situation, common in animal activism, in which humans speak for other animals. This runs the risk of obscuring their perspective, both in activist practices and with regard to the goals towards which we strive. In this chapter, I further explore non-human animal activism and possibilities for interspecies political change. I draw on existing forms of non-human animal political agency, such as resistance, in order to challenge anthropocentric politics from the ground up. I investigate non-human animal resistance, human-animal disobedience, and the relation between non-human animal oppression and the oppression of human groups, including the question of speaking for others. Building on this, I explore how human activists can assist non-human animals while taking their agency into account, and how non-human animal acts can co-shape goals that human and non-human animals both work towards. Taking non-human animal agency into account in activism can help us to see the existing situation in a different light and open up new ways of thinking about social and political change with other animals,[1] which can contribute to challenging human superiority and anthropocentric political systems. It can also contribute to imagining and creating new interspecies communities.

Non-Human Animal Resistance and Interspecies Civil Disobedience

Non-Human Animal Resistance

After years of abuse, twenty-year-old circus elephant Tyke killed her trainer during a show on August 20, 1994. She then ran into the streets of Hawai'i, where she attacked a clown and another member of the circus, before she was shot and killed by the police. Her death brought about hundreds of lawsuits against the city, the state, and the Hawthorn Corporation, which owned the circus. It inspired other humans to act on behalf of non-human animals in the form of protests against and boycotts of Hawthorn and similar corporations. These acts forced the government to change the legislation concerning circus animals, and sixteen other abused elephants were confiscated from Hawthorn (Hribal 2007).

The stories of the army camels and Tyke may seem to be isolated cases, but while non-human animal acts of resistance are often—though not always—individual responses to human displays of power, they are neither random nor incidental (Hribal 2008). Zoo animals continually escape from their enclosures; working animals systematically refuse to do the work humans order them to do; non-domesticated non-human animals in circuses and aquariums often attack the humans who exploit them (Hribal 2010). Domesticated non-human animals also resist and protest. As a social group or class, working animals were a force that influenced the course of history—both in what they helped to build and in what they resisted (Eisenman 2015, Hribal 2003). Their unreliability as workers forced humans to instigate processes of modernization and industrialization (ibid.). Non-human animal resistance is also sometimes culturally transmitted. Orangutans who are held captive in zoos cooperate with each other in order to escape and share their knowledge with others in their group, forcing zoos to separate and relocate them, which often just results in their continued resistance in the next zoo (Hribal 2008, see also the introduction). Elephants teach their children which houses to break into and how to avoid humans (Barua 2014). Wild and domesticated non-human animals help members of their own group, as well as other animals, to escape from enclosures or teach them how to do it from a distance (Hribal 2008).

Recent neuroscientific and ethological research into non-human animal cognition and emotion has demonstrated that there is evolutionary continuity in humans and other animal species (see, for example, Bekoff 2007, 2009). Art historian Stephen Eisenman (2015) shows that the aggression that prompts non-human animals to resist is very similar to the aggression in human groups that use violence to resist oppression, both on a physiological level and at the level of cognition. He discusses the examples of the itinerant bands who stormed Newgate Prison during the Gordon Riots in 1780, the anti-Irish protesters of 1736, and the Wilkes and Liberty demonstrators of 1768–69 (2015, 347). All of these groups had reason to protest but were also driven by spontaneous feelings. Seeing the non-human acts of resistance discussed above as merely instinctual or automatic while viewing comparable violence in humans as purposeful neglects the depth of non-human animal emotions, and their self-consciousness, and overemphasizes them in humans (Eisenman 2015, 346). Human animals and other animal species are all driven by physiological and emotional responses to abuse, and these responses influence cognitive processes. Different species have different ways of expressing themselves and their anger, and of reflection on their situation.[2] Conceptualizing non-human animal resistance as a form of political resistance therefore means we need to take both species-specific behaviors and the context into account. This requires empirical research into human and non-human animal behavior, as well as further analysis of the concept of resistance. This concept is used to describe a variety of practices that resemble each other in some ways and differ in others; they share a family resemblance but do not have a single characteristic that defines them all. Certain forms of non-human animal resistance are similar to human resistance, while others are very different. Laboratory animals might resist by looking the other way, insect species might use special scents to resist, apes in zoos might throw feces at humans, orca whales might attack their trainer after long periods of abuse.

In an analysis of fish-human relations, Dinesh Wadiwel (2015) argues that resistance is a good lens through which to consider animal advocacy and non-human animal agency, because it allows us to understand and foster non-human animal creativity and makes us see them in a new light. It avoids an emphasis on animal suffering—something especially important for species who are thought by some not to suffer, such as fish (Braithwaite 2010; see also Driessen 2017), insects, and worms (see chapter 6). According to Wadiwel, resistance is a form of political agency that does not need to be grounded in an innate capability or worth. Drawing on the work of Foucault, he sees power as a network of forces, and argues that resistive elements engage as agents in power relations. Examining these power relations through acts of resistance can help us to see whether these relations are just. Through resisting, non-human animals show us their standpoints (Cohen 2015), which helps humans to see their perspective, and these acts can therefore help humans to think about new relations.

From Animal Resistance to Interspecies Disobedience

In chapter 5, I discussed proposals to view domesticated non-human animals as citizens, and showed that there are non-human animals who are part of shared communities with humans. These non-human animals stand in different relations to human political systems and resist their oppression by these systems in various ways. Humans and other animals can also resist oppression together (see, for example, Donaldson and Kymlicka 2011, 114, see also the next section). This relation between non-human animal acts and their moral right to be part of human communities raises the question of whether some of these non-human animal acts of resistance can be seen as civil disobedience, and what requirements must be met for them to be seen as such.

Civil disobedience is often understood as a protest by individual rights bearers aimed at transgressing the limits of existing moral principles and values. Recent critiques (Celikates 2016; Tully 2009) show that this liberal democratic interpretation of civil disobedience underestimates the transformative potential of civil disobedience for democratic systems. They propose to view civil disobedience not as a means to fix existing democratic institutions, but rather as a democratic practice that critiques and challenges state institutions. This view ties in with James Tully's understanding of citizenship as an agonistic and dialogical struggle for freedom (2009). In this conception of citizenship, practices of resistance and contestation—understood as practices of civic freedom—are of great democratic importance, because democratic freedom lies not in participating within a given democratic framework, but in the possibility to change that framework. In representative democracies, the channels through which democratic action and communication take place are often closed off to those not in power. Acts of civil disobedience therefore often explicitly challenge these channels, using other forms of communication and action; those who are not citizens— illegal immigrants, for example—can also participate in these practices (Celikates 2016). What is at stake is no longer the improvement of a pre-fixed liberal image of citizenship: what citizenship is, and can be, is challenged. This challenges the rules of the game of politics, which according to Tully (2009) is an important characteristic of democracy; democracy is not just about participating in existing institutions, it also implies being able to change those institutions.

Non-human animals are currently not seen as citizens or full members of interspecies communities, but in practice many of them do function as members of the community, for example, as companions to humans or as workers. Because working animals have played such an important role in capitalism, and because of their resemblances to human workers, Eisenman (2015) and Hribal (2003, 2007) argue that they should be seen as members of the working class. Their resistance can contribute to social and political processes that might lead to recognition of them as co-workers. Celikates (2016) shows that sometimes groups that are not recognized as citizens, and that fall outside of hegemonic power relations, can participate in civil disobedience by challenging the rules that affect their lives and striving to change them. This might seem more complicated for non-human animal groups than for marginalized human groups, because their political agency differs from human political agency, but we can draw parallels. One example concerns working animals who refuse to follow orders, or who escape their captivity despite knowing that they will be punished. Hribal (2010) shows that every captive non-human animal knows which behaviors are rewarded and which are punished (2010, 25). Animals of different species have different tactics of resistance. Some bite anyone who comes near them, as captive Amazon river dolphin Chuckles did (2010, 133), or as did the camels discussed above. Others escape their captivity collectively, as did two dozen sheep from Danielsville, Georgia, in March 2007. They went on the run and managed to stay out of the hands and paws of border collies and police for three weeks, jumping over fences and a police car, until they were caught and sent back to work (Hribal 2007). These non-human animal workers' practices of resistance and contestation influence human practices (Hribal 2003) and the shape of common societies, and this can inform state procedures, as happened with the camels discussed at the beginning of this chapter. Their disobedience might not be aimed at pointing out the flaws in a liberal democratic system with the aim of improving that system, but it can be seen as a practice—or rather a set of democratic practices—that critiques and challenges the systems under which they, and we, live. These non-human animals aim to change their situation, and want to enlarge their freedom, sometimes assisted by human activists or coworkers (see also chapter 5). Their acts can help us to better understand what they want and imagine new ways of living with them. Similar to the way in which this works with human marginalized groups, groups of non-human animals sometimes need the support or recognition of others to be able to make political claims or to practice civil disobedience.

Many forms of human civil disobedience—tree sitting, forms of sabotage, squatting—also do not present themselves in the language of power or offer reasonable alternatives or arguments. An overly rationalistic view of civil disobedience fails to do justice to many human and non-human acts aimed at changing democratic systems. As discussed in chapters 1 and 4, using a human standard to interpret non-human animal acts is furthermore problematic; we need to learn to value other animals—just as we do other human groups—as different to us. Empirical research can play a role in bringing about this gestalt switch. A group of chimpanzees in captivity developed a cheer to attract the attention of humans (Dolgert 2015; Hopkins et al. 2012). It took the human researchers a while to understand this phenomenon, which is now seen as a form of using a social tool. Stefan Dolgert (2015) connects this insight to Rancière's (2007) view of democracy in which a subordinate group suddenly claims its rights in the language of the law, and by doing so becomes part of the demos. He argues that animal ethicists help other animals to perform this democratic move by showing other humans that they have been speaking to us all along. What is needed in thinking about non-human animals and civil disobedience is not the idea that other animals cross a threshold to make their acts part of this set of political practices, but another way of looking at their acts, and recognizing that they are already in this set. It is also important to recognize that interspecies civil disobedience is not just about adding non-human animals to the groups "citizens" or "political subjects," but also, and perhaps most importantly, about investigating the ways in which they challenge the rules of the game.

New Directions for Animal Activism: Connections between Social Movements, Speaking for or with Other Animals, and Assisting Other Animals

Viewing other animals as political actors or as activists asks for the redefining of animal rights activism and the rethinking of the relation between human activists and non-human animals.[3] In order to determine how to best support other animals, we first need to take a closer look at how different social groups are related. A good starting point for this is investigating how forms of oppression are linked. There are, of course, differences between, for example, homophobia and racism; all forms of discrimination have their own genealogies and characteristics. Certain forms of oppression do, however, share characteristics, or are made possible by shared material conditions.

Eco-feminists have directed attention to the connections between the oppression of women and of non-human animals. In Western thought, a distinction has traditionally been made between the rational and the emotional, and between the civilized and the natural. The rational and the civilized have been elevated above the emotional and the natural. As we saw in chapter 1, viewing reason, or *logos*, only as human reason is interconnected with distinguishing humans from all other animals, and bodies from minds, and is based on a specific image of the human. This image of the human is presented as neutral, but is in fact constructed by power hierarchies. Eco-feminists point out how this mechanism has led to both the oppression of women—who are seen as more natural and emotional than men—and of non-human animals.

The dualism proposed might seem to be an empirical matter that could be solved by arguing that women are as rational as men.[4] Certain humanist feminists have indeed taken this route. The problem with that approach, however, is that this is not just an empirical matter, it is also a normative construction (Gruen 1993; Kheel 2004; MacKinnon 2004). As proponents of care ethics have shown, "nature" and "natural" are not value-neutral concepts (Gruen 2015; Kheel 2004). Furthermore, even though women's supposed irrationality was based on a factual error, this error is part of a construction of social reality (Wyckoff 2014). The use of the concept is, in this context, more important than finding out whether it actually tracks natural categories. Using the argument that women are as rational as men therefore leads to two problems: the criterion is presented as gender-neutral, whereas it is actually masculinist, and secondly, women must be shown to be like men in order to gain moral or political standing. This line of argumentation does not challenge the underlying structure of patriarchy (Gruen 1993). Like women, non-human animals have traditionally been seen as natural and emotional, and here we also find that these concepts are not neutral, but point to a hierarchy (Adams [1990] 2010; Gruen 2015; MacKinnon 2004). Catharine MacKinnon (2004) argues that, in this context, asking whether non-human animals used in experimentation are like humans is asking the wrong question. Non-human animals do not exist for the benefit of humans, and do not have to be like humans in order to make their existence count.

Another example of interconnected oppressions is found in the relationship between the concepts of Blackness and animality.[5] Aph Ko and Syl Ko (2017) argue that the social construction of animality is conceptually prior to the biological human-animal divide. In the distinction between human and animal, many groups of marginalized humans—such as Black people—are not seen as human. "Human" thus does not refer to a biological reality, but to a social construction, formed by power relations. This social construction also determines how we value animals of other species. A truly anti-racist commitment, Ko and Ko argue, would thus also entail a radical reevaluation of non-human animal lives and interests. We cannot reach this by arguing for rights or drawing attention to non-human suffering: violence against Black people in the US shows that human rights matter less in the case of those who historically were not seen as human. To move beyond this, we should instead analyze the power relations involved in their oppression and find new ways of thinking and acting.

The human-animal distinction is also at the basis of oppression of disabled humans. Drawing on her own experiences, Sunaura Taylor (2017) explores the importance of physical and mental abilities in the construction of the human, in relation to animality. Disabled humans and non-human animals are in current anthropocentric worldviews devalued and abused. There are many points of contact between the oppressions of these groups, for example, in language: disabled humans are often compared to other animals, and similar to non-human animals, they are often seen as incapable of meaningful communication. Certain non-human animals, such as broiler chickens, have disabilities because of breeding practices aimed at maximizing human profit. Instead of arguing that disabled humans are also humans, Taylor pleads for recognizing and embracing the fact that humans are also animals. A shared vulnerability connects humans to non-human animals, recognizing this should lead to a greater solidarity with them.

Further investigating structural similarities between the oppression of non-human and human groups is relevant for several reasons (see also Wyckoff 2014). Non-human animal subjectivity is seldom reflected in anti-racist, feminist, or eco-socialist practice, or in environmentalism more generally (Wolch and Emel 1998; Wolch 2010). Donaldson and Kymlicka (2014a) observe a related pattern, and argue that those on the left who care about social justice do not usually take non-human animals into account. This is unfortunate theoretically, and it hinders broad support for non-human animal rights (Calarco 2015). If oppressions share characteristics, they can be regarded as a bundled political problem with other, similar, possibly linked oppressions, which could inform activist strategies. Investigating links between different forms of oppression can be a theoretical and a practical tool in working towards change (Calarco 2015; Wyckoff 2014).

Speaking for or with Other Animals

Examining parallels between different forms of oppression and regard-ing non-human animals as a social group leads us to the question of speaking for, or with, others. The animal advocacy movement is cur-rently mostly framed as humans speaking for other animals or as humans rescuing or liberating other animals.[6] While, from a pragmatic point of view, it might sometimes be justified to stay within an anthropo-centric framework, speaking for other animals in this way runs the risk of leaving the binary between human and non-human animals intact and of reinforcing anthropocentrism (Wolfe 2003; Wadiwel 2015; com-pare Spivak 1988 on human subaltern groups). The practice of humans speaking for other animals often reflects human views about their own superiority with regard to other animals' cognition and understanding. Humans often think they know best, and do not question the power hierarchies behind this mechanism. This leads to re-inscribing the hier-archies involved, and can also lead to erasing the experience of those who are not given the chance to speak (Alcoff 1991). Even those who aim to improve the lives of other animals might fall prey to the idea that they are somehow their saviors. This does not mean that speaking for others should always be avoided. Sometimes a messenger is needed to bring certain issues to the agenda, and refraining from speaking for others—even when this is done with good intentions, for example, in order to respect difference and promote listening as an attitude—might, in certain situations, significantly undercut the possibilities for politi-cal and social effectivity (ibid.). Being completely authentic and fully understanding one's own position is, as philosopher Linda Alcoff (ibid.) shows, a metaphysical illusion, which often only obscures the intellec-tual's power. To address problems with speaking—or not speaking—for others, Alcoff convincingly argues that we should investigate the power relations involved in this process. This includes questioning our right to speak for others, interrogating the effect of our location and context on what we are saying, taking responsibility for what we say and being accountable to criticism, and analyzing the probable or actual effects of what we say in the context in which we speak, materially and discur-sively. In short: we should look beyond the propositional content of our speech and examine where that speech goes and what it does there.

In relation to other animals, this means carefully considering our own position, the power relations involved, and our relation to non-human animal speech. Our cultural ideas are not fixed, and ideas about non-human animals, including their languages, are changing. Speaking about and for other animals can help this process move forward in the right direction. Emphasizing animal agency is also of practical importance in animal advocacy, because it can help other humans to see their individuality. Those who speak for other animals do, however, need to be aware of the power relations involved, and be critical of their own attitudes, privileges, and motives. Where possible, they should look for ways to let their judgments be informed by the acts and perspectives of the animals for whom they speak. This is not a matter of saving them, but rather of supporting them in situations where they cannot raise their voices and be heard so that they can.

Assisting Other Animals

Human activist groups assist groups of non-human animals in different ways—for example, they organize street protests, raise money, create websites, teach courses in animal studies, build shelters, and rescue the non-human animal victims of other humans. Many variations of speaking for and with can be found in these practices. I will now discuss some examples of animal activist practices in order to shed light on how they incorporate non-human animal agency, and how this can be improved.

First, there are acts that involve contact with actual non-human animals: for example, when activists rescue or liberate them from laboratories, farms, and other places where they are held captive. Some of these acts genuinely take the form of humans saving other animals—think, for example, of saving beagles from laboratories and finding new homes for them—while others assist non-human animals. Greenpeace activists in boats stay close to whales to prevent hunters from killing them. The Lobster Liberation Front demolishes fishing boats and releases lobsters back into the ocean. Activists also go to areas where non-human animals are killed en masse—for example, the gassing of geese around Schiphol Airport in the Netherlands from 2011 onwards (see Case Study 2) and the English badger culls of 2013 and 2014—with the aim of preventing the killing of non-human animals and assisting those who escape or are injured. These acts are currently often framed as humans saving, rescuing, or speaking up for other animals, which glosses over the agency of the non-human animals in the process and keeps intact a framework in which humans decide what is best. Viewing other animals as political groups, instead of simply as victims, not only challenges this, but also opens up new strategic, political, and legal channels to challenge their oppression. Comparisons to marginalized human groups can help to clarify what is at stake, and using political concepts as instruments to work towards justice opens up new possibilities for change. Using images and stories that highlight the perspectives of these non-human animals can also be a way to do justice to their individuality.

There are also forms of activism in which the main focus is translating, or bringing to light, non-human animal agency in interaction with other humans. For example, in the 1960s, Jane Goodall started to refer to the chimpanzees she studied as "her" or "him" instead of "it" in her scientific reports. Her colleagues saw this as anthropomorphism, but it changed the way that many humans thought about chimpanzees. More recent examples are the documentaries *Blackfish* (2013), about marine mammal park SeaWorld, which highlights orca whale Tilikum's agency by using footage in which he uses violence against humans, framing it as resistance,[7] and *Tyke Elephant Outlaw* (2015), about circus elephant Tyke's acts of resistance. Humans often present captive non-human animals as lovable and content, even happy, but these documentaries show that the subjects do not like performing tricks or living in captivity, that they can become depressed when they are held in solitary confinement, and that they can and do intentionally resist their oppression. Recognition of their agency works in two ways: the films can be seen as acts of solidarity with them and others in the same situation, and their acts make something clear that human advocates cannot, which strengthens the case the humans want to make.

In addition to these more explicitly political protests, taking non-human animal agency and subjectivity into account on a day-to-day basis also challenges anthropocentrism and can show new directions for interaction. In this context, Leslie Irvine (2001, see also Case Study 1) argues that play between humans and companion animals can be a site for political resistance, because, in play, humans and other animals challenge the current construction of the human/non-human animal divide. In play, humans acknowledge non-human animals' subjectivity and communication skills, which challenges "human disregard for non-human life" (2001, 1). Drawing on the work of Foucault, she argues that micro-practices—common everyday practices—are spaces in which power hierarchies and conflicts are shown, and in which common views about human/non-human animal hierarchies can be challenged. Humans who engage with other animals in this way can build new relations with them and can discuss these with other humans.

Finally, those who write about and educate others about non-human animals can, and should, also challenge anthropocentrism, not just by addressing questions regarding the lives of non-human animals, but also by taking their voices seriously and avoiding speaking for them whenever possible. Hribal (2012) signals a pressing problem in the growing field of animal studies, namely that theorizing often fails to take the animals' perspectives and their agency into account (see also Meijer 2016 and the Conclusion). This perpetuates the existing hierarchy and continues the silencing of non-human animals. While it is not always easy to know how we can best include the voices of other animals, we need to listen to them and learn from them, and not exclude them beforehand.

From Animals as Actors of Change to Interspecies Communities: Stray Dog Agency and Animal Activism

Viewing other animals as activists can help humans to see them in a different light. It can also point out injustices in human systems and help to imagine new ways of coexisting. This involves paying more attention to what they do and say. As discussed above, recent research on the cognition, languages, cultures, and politics of non-human animals shows that the worlds of non-human animals are much richer, and in some ways much closer, to those of humans than was previously thought (Bekoff 2007; Crane 2015; Smuts 2001; chapter 2). A stronger focus on this research is necessary in both activism and animal studies if we are to avoid repeating existing stereotypes about non-human animal cognition and behavior. This also means changing our own attitudes as humans, and being aware of our own privilege in being able to speak for other animals. Furthermore, we need to take their perspectives into account, not only in the ways in which we strive for change, but also in what we strive towards.

To conclude this chapter, I will discuss how the agency of stray dogs can function as a starting point for new relations and as an example of incorporating non-human animal agency into social change. Human interventions directed at helping stray dogs currently often focus either on neutering them and releasing them back onto the streets or capturing them and taking them to shelters where they must wait to be adopted. Although these types of interventions might sometimes be necessary because the dogs are in danger (see Case Study 1 on the situation in Romania), they also seem to imply that dogs can only be happy when they are living with a human family that takes care of all their needs. While stray dogs often suffer from many problems—disease, injuries, violence, hunger—they are not helpless victims waiting to be saved by humans. They form communities and carve out lives for themselves in which they instigate varying degrees of contact with humans.

Comparing the lives of street dogs in India and unwanted dogs in the United Kingdom, animal geographer Krithika Srinivasan (2013) questions whether the situation in the UK, which is generally perceived as more animal-friendly, is really better for the dogs. Apart from the fact that many dogs are put down in UK shelters, dogs who are brought to such shelters are always neutered, which limits their opportunities to have sexual relations and form families, and infringes upon their bodily integrity (see Driessen 2016 on the importance of sexual relations for other animals). Their freedom of movement is also severely limited. Indian dogs have freedom of movement, and live in packs in which family members can stay together, and that in some cases also live in harmony with the humans around them. Their lives are not free of danger and their situation could certainly be improved—they are marginalized, and sometimes the victims of great violence (Narayanan 2017).[8] But they do experience a great deal of freedom, and can live fairly good lives, especially if the humans in their area provide them with some care, such as rabies vaccinations. Street dogs in Istanbul also form their own communities; they are part of the city and co-shape it (Fortuny 2014). Their influence is not limited to spatial or geographical arrangements, and they also leave their mark on the lives and histories of humans. Dogs often seek out houses to guard, for which they are fed in return. These acts, and the relationships with humans that follow from them, play a role in many stories about the city (ibid.).

In Moscow, stray dogs have learned to use the subway. These dogs live in the suburbs because there is more space for them there and it is safer than the city center. There is, however, less food there, so they use the subway to go to the market during the day. They avoid ticket barriers by slipping through the gates when humans open them. They behave well while on the trains, and know when to get off because of the sounds and smells, and probably also because of the duration of the journey (Poyarkov 1991). By using public transport, these dogs show that non-human animals, who are often seen as part of nature (as opposed to humans who are seen as part of culture), can adapt to new inventions and circumstances and learn to use them for their own benefit.[9] These dogs challenge stereotypes with their behavior, and influence media as well as public opinion: photographs and videos of them waiting for the next stop circulate on the internet. When Moscow's city council threatened to kill the dogs, these images and stories were used by activists to generate goodwill amongst human citizens (Lemon 2015). While the dogs are not currently seen as full democratic actors, this process can be compared to Rancière's (2007) view of democratic action. The dogs claim a right— related to freedom of movement and using human infrastructure—and thereby make visible their own position in society. They trespass, and by doing so show that they are capable of participation within human structures.

While their existence should not be glamorized—most stray dogs die before their first birthday, winters are cold in Russia, and life is generally tough—they do show us something about the plurality of ways in which dogs and humans can coexist, as do the street dogs in Istanbul, India, and other places. Honoring dog agency does not simply mean leaving the dogs to their own devices. The Moscow dogs are descended from, and sometimes are, unwanted domesticated dogs who were abandoned on the streets. Not all of them have the physical and mental capacities needed to survive. Human infrastructure and architecture also influences the lives of animals of other species. Humans take up space and resources, and create situations that pose dangers to others, for example, with traffic, although we have seen that other animals can adapt and use this for their own purposes. For these and other reasons—such as forced processes of domestication—human societies have certain duties towards non-human animals. This does not, however, automatically lead to a duty to "rescue" dogs off the streets and discipline them into human society. Some dogs are the offspring of generations of feral dogs, and are closer to wild animals than to domesticated animals. They might value relations with members of their own species more than relations with humans, and they might prefer a life outside of the restrictions of a dog-human household, so instead of imposing a human rescue model on them, we need to think about other ways of improving relations with them.

There are many possible ways in which we could start to build new relations with stray dogs. Laws and policies should be changed to prohibit the killing and torturing of dogs, a major problem in India, Romania, and other countries. The architecture of public spaces could take their presence into account by building dog housing or other spaces, where they could rest and find some protection against the cold. Traffic and existing forms of infrastructure should be reconsidered; animal ambulances and hospitals should help those who are ill or injured because of human intervention, or who are part of shared societies.[10] Vaccination programs could prevent rabies. Education could teach dogs and humans about living with other animals, and promote respectful relations. Shelters could be opened during the days, so the dogs could come and go as they please, or they could install dog doors. Dogs who are persistent in seeking out human company could be adopted. How the situation might evolve would depend on the preferences of individuals and social groups, and also on external circumstances such as weather conditions. If humans stopped hurting street dogs, the dogs might want to be closer to them; if domesticated dogs could experience more freedom, they might prefer to live on their own.

Working towards change with stray dogs in the current situation can involve feeding them, building dog housing, participating in street protests—former street dogs also often take part in these protests—educating others, lobbying for political change, making documentaries, writing with dogs, or taking them into your home and letting them shape your life. The situation for other animals is often so bad that human activists cannot afford not to use all the options available to bring about improvement. It is, however, important to remember that other animals are subjects with their own perspectives on life; it is problematic to argue that their interests need to be taken into account because they are subjects, while at the same time determining for them how this should be done. In order not to repeat paternalism and anthropocentrism, we need to listen to other animals, and act, think, feel, and learn with them.

Conceptualizing other animals as activists and co-authors of change enables us to understand different interspecies practices as steps towards interspecies change. These practices correspond with, and often directly respond to, different forms of institutional oppression. In addition to further develop these critical practices, which can help us to frame the discourse differently and challenge the foundations of many existing liberal democratic institutions and practices, as humans we also need to look for ways to promote non-human animal political participation within given political structures and institutions. In the final two chapters of this book I address this movement from within human politics. I first focus on the more general question of non-human animal democratic participation, and discuss both the normative foundations for non-human animal political participation and ways to improve this participation based on examples of existing practices. In the final chapter, I integrate insights about non-human animal languages and non-human animal political participation by investigating how existing human-animal conversations can be incorporated in deliberative democratic systems.

8

Animal Democracy and the Challenges of Political Participation

Honeybees decide collectively where to build a new nest. When a new queen is born in the hive, half of the colony leaves with the old queen to find a new place to live. In order to survive, they need to find the best nest site, which might be a hollow tree or a chimney stack. The decision-making process works as follows: the transient colony swarm spends days hanging in a bush or tree, and scouts set out from this position to search for promising sites. As they return, they do a waggle dance, which means they move in the shape of a figure eight. The bees not only use movements and body postures in their dance, they also use sound and pheromones and influence electric fields, which passes social information to the other bees. They express the location and the quality of the site they have found by the intensity, direction, and shape of the dance they perform. The better the location, the longer the bees will dance, and so the scout who has found the best site will continue dancing when all the others have finished. Other scouts always verify the location. A unanimous decision needs to be made within a couple of days, because if they deliberate for too long they might lose the queen, or the colony may die (Seeley 2010). Biologist Thomas Seeley (2010) describes their decision-making procedures as democratic debates.[1] Bees are not the only non-human animals who make group decisions—deer, buffalo, pigeons, cockroaches, and many others do as well.[2] Humans and other animals also form communities in which group decisions are made.[3] We do, however, find a strict separation between humans and other animals in these communities when it comes to political participation and democratic agency (chapters 4 & 5). While it is generally accepted that other animals have some interest in influencing aspects of their life, it is generally assumed that they have no interest in co-shaping society and are not capable of democratic participation.

Most animal rights theorists (for example, Cochrane 2012; Garner 2013; Francione 1995; Regan 1983) share this opinion. While they argue that we should take non-human animal interests into account in existing human democracies, for example, in the form of parliamentary representation by designated groups of humans, they see the political participation of non-human animals as unnecessary, impossible, or inappropriate (Donaldson forthcoming). In this chapter, I argue that non-human animal democratic participation is important both in order to do justice to non-human animals and for democratic reasons. I first focus on the normative aspects of political participation. I then discuss why non-human animals should have the right to participate politically and which animals should have this right. In the final section, I explore ways in which existing political practices can be made more democratic, and how we can work towards new democratic practices with other animals.

Political Participation

Proponents of animal rights want to establish just treatment for other animals by instituting laws that would protect their basic liberties. In this scheme, humans would design the laws involved, and other animals would depend on humans to interpret these laws and speak for them. Even proposals that ask for extensive reformulations of animal representation—for example, in the form of trustees or proxies such as official advocates or ombudspersons supplemented by institutionalized systemic accountability by ethological experts, media, animal advocates and others who speak for animals—still start from the idea that humans should act on behalf of non-human animals, and do not involve any justification of their acts to the animals they represent. Most animal rights theorists see non-human animal political participation as unnecessary because humans can represent other animals, impossible because the animals concerned are thought not to have the capacity to be democratic actors, and inappropriate because they are not seen as members of interspecies communities (Donaldson forthcoming).

Sue Donaldson (forthcoming) argues that these dismissals of the right of non-human animals to political participation rely on an "impoverished conception of animals, of human-animal relations, and of democracy itself" (forthcoming, 4). With regard to non-human animals and our relations with them, this works as follows. Non-human animals are capable of living different types of lives, and there are many aspects of life that they can determine individually with regard to work, play, food, companionship, and various types of social relations. They do not depend on species-specific templates in the choices they make. Like humans, individual non-human animals are in the best epistemic position to recognize dimensions of their own flourishing, depending on their capacities, personalities, and identities. In order to find out what is best for other animals—given that humans currently decide everything for them—humans should provide them with a range of opportunities for self-realization, so that they can begin to make their own choices. Individual choice is closely interconnected here with societal constraints. If we consider freedom of movement for dogs, as discussed in the first case study, we find that even when an individual human is determined to let a dog companion choose the best life possible for themselves, both are still bound by a society in which traffic and rubbish make it unsafe for dogs to roam the streets. Current societies are designed to benefit humans at the cost of other animals.[4] Re-shaping societies while taking the good of non-human animals into account means creating space for them to articulate that good in their own ways. In this context, it is important to remember that other types of human-animal relations exist (chapter 3) and that non-human animals do already exercise agency and influence human practices. It is, however, up to humans to take the first steps towards making democracy more inclusive (chapters 4 & 5) and to begin to listen to other animals.

The right to political or democratic participation is not just any right, precisely because it concerns shaping the conditions under which one lives. Non-human animal interests have for a long time been shaped by subjection, and oppression of their agency and voice; power relations have not only played a role in how humans see them, but also in the space they have had to develop themselves. The epistemic problem with humans representing non-human animal interests on the basis of expert knowledge is that this knowledge is partly shaped by centuries of oppression and unequal power relations. More importantly, as Donaldson (forthcoming) argues, our good is not pre-political, and it cannot be traced back to species-specific attributes that can be measured scientifically (chapter 4). We come to know and revise our conception of the good through relations with the other human and non-human animals with whom we are tied up in political networks.

The Borders of the Democratic Community

According to Donaldson and Kymlicka (2011, chapter 5), we can and should distinguish between non-human animals who are part of shared human/non-human animal communities and non-human animals who are not in determining democratic rights and duties. Domesticated non-human animals have been brought into our communities by force, and have been deprived of living elsewhere through breeding programs, so for historical and moral reasons they have a right to be a part of our communities (see chapters 4 & 5). Because of the characteristics they have developed through living with humans and that humans have developed through living with them, domesticated animals and humans are also capable of forming close, responsive relations with each other. Donaldson and Kymlicka contrast this with those non-human animals who are not domesticated, and either live their lives as far away from humans as they can in their own sovereign communities, or who live amongst humans as liminal animal denizens. The last category poses the most problems for limiting democratic rights, and specifically rights to political participation, to domesticated animals. Donaldson and Kymlicka clearly show that humans and other animals can form communities, and they convincingly argue that other animals should be able to co-shape these communities. The categories they propose are not, however, fixed; some non-human animals move from one to the other over time: liminal animals can choose to live in a human home and be welcomed by the humans who live there, domesticated animals can leave, and so on. For some, it is unclear to which category they belong—Howard's birds (1952, 1956) are an example, and dog Merle (Kerasote 2008) as well (chapter 3). Relatedly, sharing certain spaces, such as gardens, warehouses, and even houses, with non-human animals who do not desire close relationships might still involve making common decisions. Consider a human who moves into a new house with a garden. In this garden stands a tree, and the birds who have lived in this garden for generations use this tree for nesting and feeding. If we view the birds as liminal animals, justice would require that the human does not cut down the tree, and that they should develop respectful ways of sharing the garden. However, these birds might also have an interest in clean air, the planting of more trees in the city, changes regarding the house and sharing the garden, and other issues that concern their habitat. Furthermore, some birds might be used to flying into the house, and they might develop new friendships with the owner of the house. Determining their rights of residence and participation would change as the relationship changes, but it would be appropriate to take their perspective into account democratically in many different circumstances.

Similar situations can occur with wild animals. Ralph Acampora (2004) discusses the example of beavers who built a bridge near a university in Alaska. This causes the parking lot of the university to flood when the bridge gets too high. The university has decided to respect the beavers as animal neighbors, and to allow them to build their bridge. Once the bridge gets too high and the car park floods, the humans take down the bridge, and the beavers have to start rebuilding it. Both parties suffer some inconvenience in this process of construction and destruction; the beavers have to keep rebuilding their bridge and the humans sometimes have no parking space. Both parties can, however, function well and they live their lives next to one another. Here we also find that beaver interests do not end with the building of their bridge. If we zoom out from the car park to the wider area, and consider human influence on the beavers' habitat, it would also make sense for them to be able to influence the way in which the surroundings are shaped, for example, concerning whether new buildings are erected in the area, when trees are taken down, pollution of air and water, or human use of the forests.

In addition to the fact that the lives of humans and non-domesticated animals are interconnected in many ways, there are also large differences within the group "domesticated animals" with regard to rights and to possibilities for political participation. Rabbits and horses can learn to take care of themselves fairly easily, and they might choose to leave human societies when offered the chance, whereas other non-human animals, such as goldfish, cannot make this choice, and others, such as dogs, might prefer to stay with humans. These different cases would all lead to different forms of membership, and to different forms of political participation. Within species there can also, of course, be large variations at an individual level, but also genetically and culturally. If we look at dogs, for example, we find that liminal dogs, such as stray dogs, can become members of human-dog households, as I showed in the first case study. Curious and outgoing domesticated dogs might, if offered the chance, choose to become liminal (Kerasote 2008; Marshall Thomas 2010). In both cases the dogs have shared interests with humans, especially with regard to determining the macro framework in which they live.[5] Topics for discussion might include spatial planning, division of goods, and rights of residence.

Concerning democratic decision-making, this means that we need not only to envision new procedures with other animals on the level of shared communities, but also between communities when interests overlap. In many cases this will require humans to take a step back: interaction about spatial planning with feral pigeons, negotiating sound pollution in seas with whale communities, or greening cities would all ask for a more respectful human attitude, more listening on the part of humans, and creativity in finding new ways to interact. It would, however, be a mistake to think that this would automatically lead to harmony: the interests of different groups of non-human and human animals might differ markedly. In democracies we always find a plurality of voices, and this will only increase when other animals also take part. Difference creates meaning, and paying attention to difference will make for a richer understanding of the world. While non-human animal participation would lead to new relations, and could lead to new forms of understanding, it will probably also lead to more conflicts.

Moving towards Interspecies Democracies

In order to think and work towards social change with other animals, we need to explore how existing democratic practices can be expanded to better include animal agency, and to search for new procedures, institutions, and encounters to further develop interspecies political processes and frameworks. To conclude this chapter, I will explore practical ways in which we can begin to do this. I do so first by discussing Donaldson's (forthcoming) proposals for "enabling voice" and "enabling space" as structural mechanisms for promoting non-human animal political participation. I then turn to two case studies in which democratic interaction between humans and other animals already takes place, and explore ways to improve these interactions.

In creating new democratic mechanisms for non-human animal participation, we can distinguish between proposals that aim to promote non-human animal participation and voice within the existing political framework, and proposals that challenge the framework itself. In this context, Donaldson (forthcoming) distinguishes between approaches that "enable voice" and those that "enable space." Enabling animal voice refers to fostering non-human animal democratic participation in existing democratic structures. Donaldson locates two levels of analysis: the home and work places. Humans currently determine most facets of life in these spaces, and other animals are dependent on the goodwill of one or two humans to lead a decent life. In order to avoid abuses of power, to foster domesticated non-human animal agency, and to get to know more about animals' individual wishes and desires, Donaldson proposes to use the so-called "microboard" structure for domesticated non-human animals who share households with humans. Microboards originated in the disability community and are small groups of individuals, such as the friends, relatives, and acquaintances of a disabled human with whom they have a relationship of trust. These boards incorporate different perspectives, skills, contacts, and mutual correctives that can help individuals to frame and pursue their good, and they offer advice and advocacy (similar structures have been proposed in relation to children, see Gheaus 2011). In shared human/non-human animal households, these structures could help to give non-human animals more of a voice in the processes in which decisions are made concerning their lives, and protect them from human harm. Donaldson also sees a role for microboards in interspecies workplaces, where they could attend to the wellbeing of individuals. Knowledge about these individuals could then be implemented into works councils. These works councils would function as follows: works council members whom the non-human animals in question demonstrably like and trust would work alongside working animals and map the good of these individuals within the workplace, as well as in decision-making procedures. Their observations could be fed into collective workplace decision-making processes, and this could lead to reshaping the workplace in ways that would benefit the more generalizable good of animal workers. These changes should then be communicated back to the working animals, and they should have a chance to respond in an ongoing process.

While these changes would certainly benefit non-human animal democratic participation, microboards and works councils still rely heavily on human assistance and intervention. Furthermore, they are built on human ideas and practices concerning other animals that were shaped through centuries of oppression and without consulting them. According to Donaldson (forthcoming), in order to address this, we need to create spaces in which other animals can make their own decisions, interact with humans on their own terms, and in which humans take a step back. She argues convincingly that the major obstacle to creating these spaces is not the unruliness of non-human animals, but private property: the public commons have systemically been enclosed, dismantled, and privatized, and this process has disproportionately affected non-human animals. They cannot buy land to live on or protect from ecological destruction. They often cannot even go outside when they want to. For social beings, this limits not only their freedom of movement, but also their options for self-realization. In order to adequately challenge this, private property should be severely restricted, and humans need to regard the sharing of space differently. The spaces that Donaldson envisions would, for example, be large areas in which traffic is severely restricted, where there are no laws requiring non-human animals to be on leads—individuals would have to prove that they could behave in such a setting—and in which non-human animals can interact with others of different species on their own terms. This does not mean abandoning them; in the beginning the process would be guided by humans, perhaps in interaction with certain other animals with good social skills. As a follow up to the microboard and works council structures, designated humans, again perhaps assisted by other animals, could begin to oversee the land instead of individual relations, as guides rather than police officers. Because other animals would be able to make more choices and have more freedom of movement, relations would change, and the commons would as well.

The rich new geography of citizenship that Donaldson sketches shows how new, more inclusive forms of political interaction with other animals can be envisioned. She rightly draws our attention to the inequalities with regard to space and freedom of movement. Her ideas about sharing space could, furthermore, be extended to include new forms of dealing with the non-domesticated animals who inhabit these spaces. In the new public commons, certain domesticated non-human animals could also choose to move further away from their human or seek out new humans—given that these humans would be interested in developing a relationship. Given the current state of political relations with other animals, however, the enabled space approach is also utopian. It is therefore also important to look for ways in which we can improve relations from the ground up. The idea of microboards in this context does, however, raise some problems. While it is an interesting tool for dealing with dependence, and could function as a check on human power, it might also run the risk of making too much of a stranger of non-human animals, i.e., at present, getting to know them is something that requires a lot of interpretation and care, but many humans can interpret the expressions of other animals correctly (chapter 3). This could reinforce ideas about them needing care, and prevent humans from seeing the agency that they already exercise. Non-human animals can express themselves in their own ways, and a high level of understanding is possible between human animals and domesticated non-human animals. Maybe the emphasis in this case should be on educating humans, and creating options for other animals to leave the household they have grown up in.[6] Another problem with using microboards is—and this is similar to the objections to dependent agency I raised earlier (chapter 5)—that in this model, non-human animals are supposed to interact closely with humans. While many domesticated non-human animals do indeed seek contact and even flourish because of their relations with humans, not all of them do. Furthermore, relations are often not harmonious, and other animals should have space to disagree and opt out of the frameworks they are part of, especially considering the fact that they were brought here against their will.[7] Finally, this would require a lot of intervention in the lives of companion animals and their humans. Donaldson recognizes these problems, and therefore argues that we should, in the end, aim to create spaces for other animals—but this leads us back again to the problem of improving relations within current power structures.

In thinking about new forms of political interaction, it is important to recognize that other animals already exercise agency, and to use this as the starting point for new relations. To conclude this chapter, I discuss two examples of political interaction with other animals, in which I investigate how we can further develop democratic procedures with them.

Material Interaction with Seagulls

In 2014, Dutch politician Rudmer Heerema declared war on the seagulls (NOS 2014). The seagulls in the Netherlands used to live near the coast, and twenty years ago they were hardly ever seen in other parts of the country. Due to the destruction of their nesting places by human activities such as farming and tourism, they have moved into urban areas, where they nest on houses with flat roofs and eat a diet that includes human foods. They can be found in most large cities in the Netherlands nowadays, particularly those in the west of the country, where they will eat any food thrown away by humans, from French fries to bread and fish. They also steal food and tear open rubbish bags. Because the population of seagulls is declining due to the aforementioned changes in habitat, they are protected by law. Heerema wanted to change this as soon as possible, because, as he argued, they open rubbish bags, damage cars, pollute neighborhoods, and keep thousands of people awake at night; according to Heerema, they also pose a danger to young children. Heerema is from Alkmaar, where seagulls apparently also steal the cheeses for which the city is famous.

De Vogelbescherming (the Dutch organization for the protection of birds) responded by strongly rejecting the idea of shooting the birds. Instead, they proposed a number of material interventions to persuade the birds to move elsewhere and change their behavior. The city of Leiden began an experiment with yellow rubbish bags that are much stronger than the normal black bags. The first series of stronger bags were still not strong enough, so they made new ones. The birds soon discovered that they could not tear open these bags and moved elsewhere. Other proposed measures included providing the seagulls with more natural food and creating islands for them to nest on near the coast. Because they will not just nest anywhere, the exact location of these islands will have to be determined together with the birds by offering them options and following their preferences. Finally, humans must stop feeding the seagulls. They do this either because they like the birds, or because they are afraid of them—seagulls are large birds, and people sometimes throw food towards them in order to get rid of them. They should learn to say no respectfully; both human and bird subjects will have to change their habits if they are to coexist more peacefully.

This example illustrates how we can experiment with interspecies decision-making. From a political point of view, one could argue that humans should simply accept the presence of the gulls, since it is human actions that caused them to move into towns, and since they have lived there for quite some time now. Humans have no right to kill the seagulls, and killing them will not solve the problem if the situation remains the same, because new birds will simply travel to the cities (like the geese in Case Study 2). In general, the map of the land that seagulls have is different to that of humans, and sometimes humans and seagulls inhabit the same spaces (ibid.); this will inevitably sometimes lead to conflicts (see also Nagy and Johnson 2013). When conflicts arise, communication is needed concerning who can live where and how; the recommendations from the Vogelbescherming can play a role in this. Small-scale experiments with negotiations about nesting and feeding spaces for seagulls— seen as a form of material deliberation (chapter 9)—could inform legislation in these circumstances. These experiments should be set up dialogically; humans can make proposals to which seagulls can respond, to which humans can in turn respond, and so on. While this might not lead to harmony, it will improve understanding on both sides and it could help humans to begin to see seagulls differently, and vice versa.[8]

Greeting as a Political Ritual

Humans also need to develop new institutions and procedures in order to improve non-human animal political participation. An example of this could be establishing interspecies political greeting rituals. Iris Young (2000) criticizes forms of political communication that are presented as universal, but that in fact merely reflect the preferences of the dominant group. She aims to remedy the exclusion that follows from these by discussing communicative practices that can work towards including others in the process of deliberation. One of the forms of interaction she discusses in this context is greeting. She argues that greeting is an important part of any political process, both ontologically and morally, because in greeting we acknowledge the other as an individual. Levinas (1981) distinguishes a process of "subject-to-subject recognition" from the expression of content; before we discuss thoughts and arguments, there is a moment of opening up to the other person. For Levinas, subjects respond to the physical vulnerability of the "other," without the promise of reciprocation.[9] The other, in his or her physical, material vulnerability, makes a claim on the subject that holds the subject hostage. Young argues that this moment of recognizing the other is implicit in greeting, because by greeting we are announcing that we take the other seriously as an individual and express our goodwill to communicate. Without the greeting rituals observed by Young in non-Western and traditional societies, as well as in Western societies—Maori societies for example, but also in Western political interaction, for example, in the act of introducing a speaker—the political process would not function well.

Smuts (2001) describes the relevance of greeting in baboon communities (chapter 2) and in interspecies contexts (chapter 3). In order to be able to study a group of baboons, she needed to learn their language: greeting was an important aspect of being accepted by them as a friendly stranger. Developing new greeting rituals can contribute to finding new forms of political interaction with different groups of animals. It can play a role in negotiations between humans and domesticated animals (Irvine 2001; Smuts 2001), but also in conflicts between human and non-human animal communities. An example of such a conflict in which greeting could play a role is the human-macaque interaction in urban Singapore. The population of native macaques in the Bukit Timah Nature Reserve in Singapore has been significantly affected by the encroachment of residential development into their habitat and the destruction of wildlife corridors (Yeo and Neo 2010). The National Parks Board has to continually negotiate between complaining residents and preserving the macaque population. In this conflict, both the macaques and the humans exert pressure, though to different degrees; the macaques usually draw the short straw. The residents knew that the macaques lived in the area before they moved there, and they often give a desire to be closer to nature as one of the reasons they chose to live there. They also feed the macaques, which has encouraged the animals to move closer to the human settlements, leading to problems; the macaques steal food and make noises, and there are often encounters that are experienced by the humans as problematic or frightening. However, the attitude of the humans is not purely negative; in addition to feeding the macaques, some of them like the way they look and the sounds they make, and many humans do not think they should be killed.

Yeo and Neo discuss different ways in which the macaques and humans interact, such as having eye contact, reading each other's body language, staying at a distance, or, on the other hand, making overtures. The macaques respond to human speech and tone of voice and humans respond to the sounds made by the macaques. In their recommendations at the end of their paper, Yeo and Neo mainly focus on what the humans can do. Humans should, for example, be educated about the consequences of their behavior (such as feeding the macaques) and about the macaques' behavior so that they know how to keep them at a distance. From a political perspective, taking interaction into account and focusing on both sides of the communication could strengthen the voice and position of the macaques in the conflict. The macaques already communicate with the humans, and they exercise political agency by questioning the borders between the communities and by challenging the human-animal hierarchy. Learning about each other's languages, developing a new shared language, and establishing (political) rituals could give the macaques a better understanding of the humans and vice versa.

A first step in improving interaction could be the development of forms of greeting as political rituals. Greeting can function as a way in which the humans acknowledge the macaques' existence as individual others and vice versa, and establishing greeting rituals might be helpful in determining borders between the two groups. Macaques are very sensitive to facial expressions and gestures (Maestripieri 1997) and responding to how they express themselves could make a significant difference to how the interaction evolves. In general, learning about the greeting rituals of other animals and respectfully engaging in new rituals with them can function as a gateway to increase political interaction and extended conversations. To further investigate the political significance of greeting in interspecies situations, we would need to conduct small-scale experiments. How and whether greeting works will depend on the animals involved—just as with humans, there is no guarantee that it will improve political processes or lead to consensus, but Smuts shows that it can lead to new ways of communicating and new forms of coexistence.

Conclusion

I began this chapter by arguing that the democratic participation of non-human animals is normatively important from the perspective of other animals and from the perspective of democracy. One of the main challenges for this project is that our current political practices and institutions seem to be too anthropocentric to be capable of incorporating non-human animal voices. In the former section, and in the discussion of non-human resistance and interspecies activism in chapter 7, I have shown that democratic interaction is already taking place, and have offered ways of further developing these interactions. In the next chapter, I further explore how this can be done by discussing how multi-species conversations can be translated into existing human democratic institutions, conceptualizing them as interspecies deliberation.

9

Deliberating Animals

From Multispecies Dialogues to Interspecies Deliberation

Dogs and humans co-shape each other's lives, goose communities interact with human communities concerning the use of land, macaques and humans argue about borders, earthworms and humans work together in laboratories. In all of these cases, humans and other animals communicate over time in processes that are, or that resemble, dialogues. In this final chapter, I investigate the value of using a deliberative model of democracy for institutionalizing different types of interactions and dialogues between human and non-human animals, and for promoting non-human animal political participation and voice. While non-human animal agency has become a topic of interest in a number of fields in recent years, the question of how to translate this agency, and political interactions between human and non-human animals more generally, into existing political institutions, practices, and structures has not received much attention. This is unfortunate, both from the perspective of the non-human animals who currently have very little voice in matters that concern them, and from the perspective of democracy (chapter 8).

Political animal philosophers sometimes use the concept of deliberation to conceptualize changes in human attitudes towards other animals (Garner 2016), but the concept is underexplored with regard to interspecies relations (exceptions are Driessen 2014; Gunderson 2016). This lack of attention for deliberation relates back to the idea that non-human animals cannot express themselves politically in the rational manner necessary to be able to speak of deliberation.[1] Rationalist interpretations of deliberation (Habermas 1994) have, however, been challenged in recent years by feminist (Young 2000), post-structuralist (Derrida 2008), constructivist (Driessen 2014), ecological (Dryzek 2000), and agonistic (Tully 2009) points of view. These approaches all criticize the image of the rational subject taken as standard and the image of political language and communication attaching to that image. This provides a good starting point for rethinking deliberation with non-human animals, because it questions capacities that are interconnected with a view of the human as superior to other animals, and asks for a broadening of the scope of political communication. In what follows, I draw on ideas about interspecies languages, non-human animal agency, and these critiques of an idealistic view of the human, to investigate what deliberation means and could come to mean in an interspecies context. I do so in order to bridge the distance between interspecies dialogues and human political systems, and to shed light on institutionalizing different types of political non-human animal acts. I also aim to contribute to the development of a different view of deliberative democracy by questioning existing views of deliberation as human rational political communication, and challenging the distinction between this type of deliberation and other forms of deliberation.

Non-Human Animal Agency and Interspecies Dialogues

Non-human animal agency is often discussed on the basis of personal interaction with individual non-human animals (Donaldson and Kymlicka 2013b; Srinivasan 2016). One of the most prominent examples of this approach is Haraway's (2003, 2008) work on dog-human interaction. As discussed above (chapter 3; Case Study 1), Haraway writes about her relationship with her dog companion Cayenne Pepper, and argues that through training for agility they not only came to understand each other better, but both their worlds changed. Through their interaction, something new came into being, influenced by the agency of both dog and human. Haraway describes agility as a "good in itself and also as a way to become more worldly" (2003, 61). She sketches a vivid picture of how a close relationship with a dog companion can have an impact on the way one views one's surroundings. She also successfully challenges the species boundary, showing that belonging to the same species is not necessary for understanding someone, building a close relationship, or creating a common framework of reference. There are, however, problems with her approach, and these become clear if we focus on the wider context (see also chapter 3; Case Study 1, Donaldson and Kymlicka 2013b; Weisberg 2009). Haraway critically addresses certain aspects of power relations between humans and dogs: she questions human exceptional-ism, and she challenges the image of dogs as incapable of meaningful communication. She also shows that dog agency can shape human lives. She does not, however, address the ways in which these power relations have been institutionalized, for example, at the level of the state, the mar-ket, or culture; neither does she discuss how this impacts the possibilities for exercising agency of most domesticated non-human animals. For example, the non-human animals subjected to the conditions of inten-sive farming cannot usually exercise agency in the way that Haraway describes—even those who find a way to escape their fate and make newspaper headlines because they have managed to flee the slaughter-house are usually shot and killed (Hribal 2007). Haraway and Cayenne Pepper even participate in certain practices involving non-human animal exploitation, for example, by eating the dead bodies of other non-human animals. Nor does Haraway question the wider framework in which she and Cayenne Pepper interact: while there is space for dog agency, the human in the relationship sets the borders for the framework in which this agency can be exercised; Cayenne Pepper cannot choose to leave the situation, nor can she set up a different life for herself. Not addressing these power relations is not just problematic from a normative point of view, it also sets limits on taking non-human animal agency seriously, because it neglects the possibilities for non-human animals to exercise macro-agency (see also chapter 3; Case Study 1).

A similar problem arises in Clemens Driessen's (2014) discussion of cow-human relations. Driessen discusses non-human animal agency in relation to technological innovations on the farm, and argues convinc-ingly that cow-human communication, involving material interventions, can be seen as a form of deliberation. An example of how this works can be found in the development of a mobile milking robot (Driessen 2014). A group of Dutch cows and farmers experimented with an outdoor milking robot, leading them to deal with technical and moral questions in a new way. The farmers interpreted the behavior of the cows in setting up the robot; the cows adapted to the robot and showed their prefer-ences, to which the farmers responded by changing the settings of the robot or its position, to which the cows again responded, and so on. The outcomes with regard to the position and use of the robot were the result of the agency of both the cows and the farmers. The robot thus enabled the cows to formulate their standpoint in a new way and the farmers to read them differently, and vice versa. Driessen sees this as a form of material interspecies deliberation. He proposes to view deliberative democracy not as the Habermasian "ideal, impartial and power-free antithesis to bargaining and voting" (2014, 96), but rather as an "ongoing attempt to find practical ways for making political processes more deliberative, stressing the importance of reasoned argument (in whatever form) and free and open discourse (in whatever space)" (ibid.). These processes take place between humans and other animals, which leads Driessen to use the term "animal deliberation," by which he means political interspecies communication around material interventions.

Theorizing interspecies deliberation in this way is promising for building new interspecies communities, and it could contribute to greater freedom for non-human animals, because their voices are brought to the fore and stereotypes about non-human animal agency are challenged. The cows can show what they want from a milking robot, which in turn shows humans that they do not need to make all the decisions for them. It also shows how interspecies understanding can grow through ongoing interactions, and that humans can adapt to non-human animal preferences. This type of experiment could very well inform government decisions; humans could create settings in which groups of non-human animals are enabled to make decisions with regard to aspects of their lives from which other humans can learn. The example of the milking robot is, however, also deeply problematic. In the dairy industry, cows are held captive and exploited for human benefit, which causes them, and their calves, physical and mental harm. They have no or very limited opportunity to address this abuse, let alone end or escape it. While suffering is not the only lens through which we should view non-human animals, something both Haraway and Driessen convincingly show is that not taking their suffering seriously keeps intact the worldview that allows for exploitation (see chapter 4 for an analysis of the relation between epistemic and institutional violence), and runs the risk of legitimating the practices attached to it. It is problematic to only conceptualize non-human animal agency at the level of individual relations, without also considering the broader political structures that shape these relations. It is also problematic to recognize non-human animal agency at an individual level and to not take into account the implications of this for political structures. Conceptualizing non-human animal agency at the micro-level only, while humans continue to determine the macro-framework in which it is enacted, reinforces the hierarchy between humans and other animals that Driessen aims to challenge. Developing an account of interspecies deliberation should involve investigating ways of moving beyond current power hierarchies on different societal and political levels.

For these reasons, it is important to explore the interconnections between interspecies dialogues—such as between Cayenne Pepper and Haraway, and cows and farmers—and existing political institutions and practices. Interspecies dialogues are important sites for engaging with other animals in new ways (chapter 3). These interactions can and should inform legislation, and offer starting points for new interspecies political institutions. In this context, it is important to recognize that different layers of political interaction are porous (Tully 2009), and that non-human animal agency already influences human cultures, spaces, and political structures—again, political non-human animal participation is not a matter of all or nothing. When we start from the idea that non-human animals are individuals with their own perspective on life and their own ways of expressing themselves, it becomes clear that it is not enough to let humans represent them in a deliberative human structure (as proposed by Garner 2016): we need to investigate how we can change this structure with them. A deliberative model of democracy can contribute to closing the gap between current highly symbolic, institutional human forms of interaction and the non-human animal agency we acknowledge at a micro-level, because it recognizes the relevance of interaction at different levels of society. It also captures the importance of recognizing relational agency for democratic participation: we are shaped by, and shape, common life-worlds and political structures in relations with others of different species.

Deliberation and Interspecies Political Communication

A deliberative approach to democratic theory has descriptive and normative value (Young 2000; chapter 1). Deliberative democracy is often contrasted with an aggregative model of democracy. In the aggregative view of liberal democracy, voting—understood as the expression of a given preference—is seen as the primary political act. In election processes, various groups declare their interests and compete for votes; citizens are seen as atomized private individuals, with more or less fixed opinions. Using this aggregative model to conceptualize democracy can only help to conceptualize some of the political processes in a democracy. It ignores the processes of discussion that take place in institutions and practices at different levels of society and politics, and the normative assumptions inherent in these. In current democracies, political discussions are often already viewed as a way of coming to a better judgment for all, and coming to informed judgments based on facts and reason is seen by many as better than simply expressing opinions loudly or voting for one's preferences, although it is well understood that voting and negotiation also inescapably form part of the democratic process. Seeing democracy simply as aggregative also fails to recognize the transformative character of these deliberative processes for individual political actors and society as a whole.

Furthermore, an exclusively aggregative model of democracy narrows both the goals of democratic interaction and its normative aims. The aggregative model primarily understands democracy as a protection against tyranny, and sees democratic interaction as a way of promoting and protecting human interests in the political sphere (Young 2000, 26). The deliberative model also includes these interests, but adds to this the relevance of other democratic values, such as cooperation, solving collective problems, and promoting justice. This model is interactive, and relies on a view of political actors as beings who do more than simply express their interests and form their opinions—which is a narrow and individualistic way of understanding rationality (Young 2000). It is based on the understanding that we always come to know and revise our conceptions of the individual and the public good in interaction with others (chapter 3; Donaldson forthcoming). Political activity is not simply a matter of expressing interests, but often also includes transforming those judgments, expressions, interests, and beliefs in interactions with others. This is an open-ended dialogic process, one in which judgments can always be refined and dialogues can take place at different levels of society and politics.

Human and non-human animals share a planet, and as discussed in detail in chapter 3, they share households, habitats, and communities.

We find a multitude of different relations and encounters between humans and other animals in which other animals exercise agency, some of which are political. In the first section of this chapter, and in chapters 2 and 3, I show that this interaction goes further than simply expressing preferences. Interspecies dialogues can transform all the parties involved. While these processes are not the same as human dialogues and human deliberative politics, they do show us the potential of interspecies deliberation. We can transform our judgments and our ways of understanding the world and others in dialogic processes with others of different species. In order to further conceptualize these as interspecies deliberation, we need to develop a more inclusive view of political communication and a better understanding of how different sites of deliberation can be related. I first turn to political interspecies communication.

Democratic Inclusion and Forms of Speech

Jürgen Habermas (1981, 1994), the most prominent theorist of deliberation, stresses the rationality of deliberative procedures. He puts forward an image of deliberation as informed by reason, which is tied to an image of the political actor as human and rational. Habermas argues that democratic procedures are not just collections of dialogues in which anything is allowed; decisions are improved through fair procedures in which the force of the better argument plays a central role. Habermas's influential views of rationality and rational communication do not, however, reflect universal values, but rather the preferences of the dominant group. To further elaborate on this, I now return to Young's (2000) critique of a rationalist view of deliberation. This critique sheds more light on how power relations are interconnected with our views of proper political communication, which is useful in further conceptualizing interspecies deliberation.

The democratic norm of inclusion, which is seen as necessary for the legitimacy of the outcome of a deliberative procedure and is interconnected with the democratic ideal of equality, is, according to Young (2000), frequently violated in deliberative practices. She also shows that forms of language use that are presented as neutral in deliberative practice and theory in fact often express social inequalities and exclusionary practices. To further explicate this, she distinguishes between two types of exclusion. External exclusion refers to forms of exclusion in which individuals or groups that ought to be included are left out of fora for discussion and decision-making. Internal exclusion occurs when groups are formally included in processes of discussion and decision-making, but the ideas or modes of expression of members of these groups are ignored, dismissed, patronized, or not taken seriously in other ways. In democratic deliberation, certain attitudes and attributes are favored, such as being dispassionate, articulate, orderly, unemotional, and focused on argument. These norms of good—i.e., rational and argumentative—political communication are presented as neutral, but they tend to reflect the preferences and style of the dominant group (usually educated, able-bodied, white men, see chapters 1, 4, & 7 for an analysis of this with regard to interspecies relations). Young argues that this image of proper political communication devalues the style of speech of humans who have not learned to argue in this manner or who do not speak the language well, who are less educated, who present their arguments in a more emotional manner, who use expressive body language, and so on. These humans are often members of groups that have historically been excluded from participating in political discourse. She therefore argues that working towards democratic inclusion asks for expanding our conception of political communication in order to identify new modes of inclusion, and to learn to attend to one another in new ways in order to reach understanding.[2] Identifying new modes of inclusion and learning to attend to others are also very important in building new relations with non-human animals.

The exclusion of non-human animals from human political discourse can currently be seen as a form of external exclusion; other animals have languages and express themselves in many ways, but they cannot make themselves heard in the dominant political discourse because they do not speak in the language of power (see chapters 1 & 2). To address this problem between humans, Jean-François Lyotard (1988) uses the concept "differend." Lyotard distinguishes between a plaintiff and a victim. A plaintiff becomes a victim if they have no means by which to prove the damage that has been done to them, or more specifically, if, because of how language is constructed, there is no representation possible in the language of the wrong suffered. "I would like to call a differend the case where the plaintiff is divested of the means to argue and becomes for that reason a victim. If the addressor, the addressee, and the sense of the testimony are neutralized, everything takes place as if there were no damages" (1988, 10). A "wrong" is a damage accompanied by the lack of the means to prove the damage (1988, 5). We find an example of this in situations where land has been colonized and indigenous peoples were unable to claim it on the grounds that their laws were not recognized as laws because they were not written down in the colonizer's language. Between human and non-human animals, the formal political discourse is constructed so that non-human animals are deprived of the possibility to address damages done to them on a very fundamental level: they cannot speak because speaking is understood as speaking in human language (chapters 1 & 4; Derrida 2008).[3] The problem is not that the non-human animals do not interact with humans or cannot draw attention to the wrongs done to them, but that a common epistemic and institutional framework in which these can be addressed is lacking.

In thinking about political communication with other animals, we therefore need to focus not only on institutional reform, but also on the epistemic dimensions of exclusion (chapter 4). Recognizing that other animals do speak is the first step to addressing Lyotard's problem; redefining what counts as "speaking" is the second (chapters 1 & 4). There is a strong connection between what is seen as proper political speech and the exclusion of marginalized groups, and, as Young's analysis also shows, it is not enough to formally include the voices of those who are excluded without changing the view of proper political communication associated with it. In other words, it is not enough to simply see a group as political and "give them voice"; acknowledging other groups as political should imply rethinking what we see as proper political communication on a deeper level. When we think about non-human animal political participation, we therefore also need to extend our views of political communication from the perspective of interspecies relations. Instead of arguing that other animals are as rational as humans, and living up to the Habermasian standards mentioned at the beginning of this section, we need to develop a view of deliberation—with them—that encompasses their forms of rationality and speech.

Embodied Political Communication

Deliberation is usually interpreted as encompassing more than having a conversation in which two or more individuals agree or disagree. It also demands more than expressing preferences and responding to the preferences of others, or sharing a common goal or plan. In deliberation, different parties mutually agree to normative claims, and can be held accountable on the basis of that agreement. The question of whether other animals are capable of this is usually answered in the negative. As we have seen above, this is because the view of language, rationality, and morality that underlies these ideas is based on humans, and therefore does not fit how other animals behave and express themselves.

An interspecies account of deliberation needs to incorporate the fact that other animals speak in other languages, and it needs to take the embodied and habitual aspects of political interaction into account. Much of human political communication also involves aspects other than rational linguistic speech that can't be completely controlled, as we are always also affected by pheromones, oxygen, and unintentional chemical processes (Dryzek 2000). Body language, gestures, rituals, and emotions (Bickford 2011) play a role in many forms of politics, as do stories and rhetoric (Young 2000). Referring to recent work in moral psychology, Donaldson and Kymlicka (2011, 2014b) argue that animal morality, including human morality, should be understood as primarily habitual. Humans are born with a certain social predisposition, which is developed in childhood. When confronted with situations that ask for a moral judgment, they often do not reflect extensively, but respond immediately. Non-human animals who display moral behavior are socialized in their group in a similar way (see Bekoff and Pierce 2009; Crane 2015; Peterson 2012), and we find a continuum of moral behaviors in different species, varying between species, communities, and individuals (compare chapter 2 on language). Domesticated non-human animals and humans can also form communities in which all are socialized and learn to respond to certain interspecies norms through the moral frameworks that structure social life (chapter 3; see also Hearne [1986] 2007). Moral agency is, in this conception, embodied and socially embedded; it is both subjective and intersubjective, as well as being something that is constantly learned and created with others. Donaldson and Kymlicka see this "norm responsiveness in intersubjective relationships—the ability to moderate behavior in accord with internalized norms when relating to other selves" (2014b, 14–15) as the basis of democratic citizenship.

A focus on the embodied and habitual aspects of moral behavior and political participation allows for a different interpretation of the requirements for deliberation. The process of revising reasons, coming to normative agreements, and holding someone accountable would not have to be expressed in human language. Processes could involve species-specific languages—including the use of movements and gestures—and material interventions (Driessen 2014; see also Case Studies 1 & 2). These processes might take more time than those between humans, and could lead to unexpected outcomes.

Political Interspecies Communication

While the precise characteristics of processes of interspecies political communication should be developed in interaction with non-human animals of other species, there are certain preconditions that we can already define as starting points for developing these processes. In what follows, I will outline these around four themes: time, space, relations, and physicality. These four aspects are not intended to be a full list, but taking them all into account offers a good starting point for further political communication.

Time: From Completed Conversations to Ongoing Processes of Deliberation

Political conversations between humans often take place in formalized settings, and are aimed at reaching final conclusions. Because interactions between humans and other animals are currently not yet formalized in this manner, and because political interspecies communication involves many uncertainties, with regard to non-human animal capacities, interspecies understanding, and so on, it is better to conceive of these interactions as open-ended processes (see also Donaldson forthcoming). In these processes, understandings can, of course, be reached, but new insights may always arise that can be used to improve these. As is the case with humans, consensus is worth striving for, but it is unrealistic to expect to reach full consensus because of the condition of plurality.

Throughout this book I have discussed examples of these processes of ongoing interaction between humans and other animals. They may have taken the form of cooperative relationships (chapter 3), of close friendships (ibid.), of ongoing conflicts (chapter 7; chapter 8), and of everything in between. While not all the examples discussed are political, they can shed light on the importance of taking temporal dimensions into account in relations with other animals. The example of Len Howard (1952, 1956), who shared her life with birds (chapter 3), shows how great tits taught each other not to be afraid of Howard, and that they also passed this knowledge on to younger generations. While the initial interaction with the birds was careful, once some of the birds found out that Howard could be trusted, others followed. In the example of Merle and Ted Kerasote (2008), we find that human acts, which were aimed at fostering the agency of a dog, initiated a process in which the dog became more independent, allowing the power structure to change. This did not happen overnight, but took a long period in which both parties could revise their position multiple times. Barbara Smuts's interaction with a troupe of baboons (2001; chapter 3) shows us that groups of non-human animals can adapt to a human presence in their midst, as long as the human participates in forms of interaction that are important to them. Again, getting to know each other's position and adjusting to each other takes time; Smuts describes how moving with the baboons through time changed not only their relationship, but also her perspective on the world.

These aspects play a role in political relations as well. The difference between resistance and a simple refusal to participate, for example, in the case of working animals, relies on this temporal dimension. When a non-human animal is asked to perform a job and they refuse, it does not necessarily mean they are resisting their oppression. When asked to work for humans every day, under harsh conditions, the refusal to work on a given day should be understood as intentional resistance; they know what is coming, and they know they do not want to cooperate in that situation anymore, even though they also know they will be punished (Hribal 2010). This is only one example of how time can play a role in interspecies political interactions; there are many others.

Space: Meeting Other Animals on Their Ground

Official political interaction often takes place in spaces that have been specifically designed for it, such as parliament buildings and city halls. In addition, different public and private (Tamura 2014) spaces can be used politically—for example, streets that are used for a demonstration, the internet when it is used for campaigning or activism, or museums when they exhibit political art—but these spaces are often not thought to have the same standing in political thought and practice (Tully 2009), and while their influence on official forms of politics is increasingly recognized (Hobson 2007), actual political decision-making is often located in official spaces.

Most non-human animals would feel uncomfortable in official human political spaces, because these are generally human buildings enclosed by stone walls. Certain domesticated non-human animals—dogs, for example—sometimes accompany humans into these settings, but even when they are present and can influence decision-making procedures with their presence, these spaces are not the spaces where human/non-human animal deliberation takes place. In order to further conceptualize processes of interspecies deliberation, we therefore need to think beyond these human political spaces. Here, as elsewhere, it is better to locate the spaces where political interspecies interaction already takes place and to work from there, rather than asking or expecting non-human animals to move into spaces designed by and for humans. This goes further than simply recognizing that political interactions do not only take place in official political institutions, or acknowledging the influence of other political practices on these institutions; it implies broadening the notion of official political spaces to include these other spaces. As we have seen above, examples of interspecies deliberation can be found in many different spaces, ranging from the meadows around Schiphol Airport to nature reserves in Singapore, cities, and farms.

In a discussion of donkey-human relations in Botswana, Geiger and Hovorka (2015) show that investigating the spatial dimensions of interspecies relations is not something additional to analyzing interspecies interactions, but an important component for understanding how other animals shape human lives and vice versa. In Botswana, for example, both donkeys and humans are affected by poverty, and are affected by a cultural understanding of what it means to be or have a donkey. This influences not only their relations, but also shapes their options for performing differently. In order to further develop political models that acknowledge the relevance of space, geographers and ethologists could locate and analyze the spatial dimensions of political interactions. This means both locating the actual spaces where these processes take place, and analyzing how they are connected to larger social and political structures. In further developing the spatial aspects of interspecies deliberation, humans should first acknowledge the political interspecies interaction where it takes place. They could then adopt new attitudes towards other animals and aim to find new answers with them, in tandem with developing ways of translating this interaction into existing political structures and using it to build new political interspecies institutions.

Physicality: Bodies, Objects, and Material Deliberations

Conversations are always about something. For humans, this "something" can often be captured in words. Interspecies deliberation often does not involve human words, but as we saw above, this need not mean that we cannot speak about things. Instead of viewing deliberation simply as a process in which arguments are used to revise judgments, we should also understand that our interactions with humans and other animals are always embodied (see also chapters 2 & 3). Furthermore, as discussed above, objects can play a role in deliberation. In dog-human relations, the lead can, for example, function as a tool in deliberation (Case Study 1), and in goose-human relations, land can function as a starting point for deliberation (Case Study 2).

As with the spatial dimensions of political encounters, in order to further investigate this, we should first focus on the material dimensions of existing interspecies communications (Driessen 2014), after which we can improve them and connect them to existing political practices. Understanding that encounters are embodied and that we send out physical signals to which other animals respond can contribute to change (chapter 8). We can also invent new methods and processes to further develop understanding and deliberation. A simple example can be found in a 2016 study, in which twenty-three horses of various ages and breeds were taught to use symbols boards to communicate with humans (Mejdell et al. 2016). They used these symbols to communicate whether they wanted a blanket left on, put on, or taken off, and they used the symbols correctly given the circumstances.[4] Instead of asking horses whether or not they want to wear blankets, humans could ask them whether or not they want to be ridden, whether they want to stay outdoors or use the stables, what kind of food they prefer, and so on. Humans could map these interactions, and the preferences could inform further studies. A symbols board is obviously a human invention, and there are many other options for investigating non-human animal perspectives; in the case of food or shelter, they could simply be given a choice. This example does, however, show that it is possible for horses to express their preferences in this manner, and that we can ask them about different aspects of their wellbeing in different ways. As long as we remain ignorant of many of the cues they use to communicate with us, this kind of invention can help to bridge the distance between their preferred styles of communication and ours.[5]

Relations: Taking into Account the Context of Deliberation

A focus on the temporal, spatial, and material aspects of interspecies deliberation helps us to understand how existing political dialogues are situated, and offers us a starting point for conceptualizing new forms of politics. In all of these aspects, humans are animals, and we should not see ourselves as rationally superior beings who ought to be supervising these processes, but rather as entangled in relations. Processes of change can begin with new human behaviors, and in the current state of affairs humans have a special obligation towards different groups of non-human animals (Donaldson and Kymlicka 2011). Both one-off individual encounters and daily group interactions are shaped by many historical, cultural, political, and other factors, and in understanding our rights and duties as humans, as well as in envisioning new forms of interaction, it is important that we take these into account. Hunting practices have caused wild animals to be shy, which often leads humans to assume that wild animals simply are shy. Howard's birds, and the fallow deer discussed in chapter 5, show that this does not need to be the case, opening up new possibilities for interaction. Certain domesticated non-human animals depend on humans for their survival, and understanding that humans have brought this about helps us to think about our duties towards them. Here we also find that the status quo is not a fixed truth: other animals can change individually and collectively once they are provided with new choices.

An important part of recognizing our obligations as humans is giving up control over other animals, and over the outcomes of processes of change. Beginning to interact with other animals differently and enabling them to take matters into their own hands might not lead to harmony, and might have unexpected results. We simply do not know. A suggestion for further research is therefore to develop new political experiments with other animals. These experiments can begin with existing sites for deliberation, as mentioned above; farmed animal sanctuaries (Donaldson and Kymlicka 2015a), understood as intentional communities, could also play a role in this (conclusion).

Interspecies Deliberation: A Systemic View

In addition to developing political experiments with other animals as a first step towards taking non-human animal voices into account in deliberative democracies, we have to find new ways to translate these into larger political structures. A systemic view of deliberation offers us a starting point for imagining how this might work, and can also function as a model for incorporating non-human animal agency into existing political structures. I will first briefly discuss what a systemic view of deliberation encompasses, and then discuss its relevance for the interspecies context.

A systemic approach to deliberative democracy turns the focus from single episodes of deliberation—in legislative bodies or small-scale initiatives in which citizens can deliberate under relatively favorable conditions—to the structure of the system (Mansbridge et al. 2012). This recognizes the complexity of democracies and the variety of associations, institutions, and sites of contestation—ranging from informal networks and schools to courts, organized advocacy groups, and the media—that foster and create political work. In this view, a democratic system is made up of a set of interdependent parts that are distinguishable and differentiated. These different parts are relationally interconnected, yet they function independently. A deliberative system encompasses a dialogue-based approach to political interaction through expressing, demonstrating, arguing, and persuading.

The systemic approach favors a focus on rational argument, but it also acknowledges that protest and other forms of disruptive communication can sometimes have a place in the larger scheme of things to put certain issues on the agenda, and allow the voices of those outside of hegemonic power to be heard. In this, it also suggests "looking for 'deliberative ecologies,' in which different contexts facilitate some forms of deliberation and avenues for information, while others facilitate different forms and avenues" (Mansbridge et al. 2012, 6). In the interspecies situation, we could take this to mean that certain sites consist of dog-human interactions, in which spatial arrangements play a role, or goose-human interactions, while others might consist of humans deliberating about other animals, informed by interactions with them. Focusing on the system of deliberation brings to light aspects that remain hidden if one only focuses on individual sites of deliberation. I will here discuss three, and show their relevance for interspecies interactions. First, a focus on the system allows us to think about deliberation on a larger scale and see connections between sites of deliberation. Second, it helps to analyze the division of labor among parts of a system; the deliberative qualities of some settings might be weak if we regard them autonomously, yet they might still contribute to the overall quality of deliberation. Third, regarding the entire system highlights larger systemic inadequacies and contextual issues that impact individual sites, but which remain hidden when we focus only on these.

Thinking on a large scale is important in interspecies relations. Face-to-face deliberations between humans and other animals have, up to now, only taken place in small settings, such as households, neighborhoods, and towns. On a larger scale, the focus usually shifts from humans interacting with non-human animals to humans discussing them. Investigating how we can strengthen the relations between these smaller settings of deliberation and institutionalized forms of human politics can give other animals more voice and lead to new forms of interspecies politics. Below, I discuss goose-human deliberation as an example of how this could work.

Second, the division of labor proposed by Mansbridge et al. (2012) can help in connecting and translating different forms of human and non-human animal knowledge. There are many matters that humans can discuss with other animals, and vice versa. We can and should further develop these ways of deliberating with other animals that take into account their species-specific expressions, but in the current state of empirical research it is unrealistic to expect to be able to deliberate with non-human animals in all political affairs and institutions, or to be able to discuss things with them in the same way that humans discuss with other humans. Non-human animals are experts with regard to their own lives, and they can be assisted by human experts, who can translate their standpoints for other humans. Humans can also take on certain political roles in the current system, allowing other animals to take on different roles; companion animals often are, for example, good teachers. Because power relations are currently unequal and the system is made to fit humans, humans have forms of knowledge that other animals do not have, and they do have a role to play in formulating change.

Third, when we look at the overall system of deliberative democracy, we find that non-human animals are underrepresented generally, but also that certain questions receive more attention than others. To give a few examples: in mainstream political thought, there is a strong emphasis on human fixed institutions and procedures, and not so much attention for the processes and practices that inform and shape these. The role of non-human animals in these is not adequately acknowledged; non-human animals are often not seen as a social group and are underrepresented in social justice movements. Finally, while non-human animal sentience is increasingly seen as relevant in, for example, Dutch and European legal and political decisions, their voices—in the wider sense—are not taken into account at all democratically.

The systemic approach has descriptive and normative potential for conceptualizing how to incorporate small-scale interspecies interactions in existing political mechanisms and institutions, because it focuses on relations between forms of deliberation. It also helps us see that non-human animals do not need to be able to represent themselves in human language in courtrooms or political settings for political participation to occur; there are many ways in which forms of deliberation already take place, and many ways in which these situations are related to, or bear a resemblance to, human political decision-making procedures. Tamura (2014) draws our attention to the deliberative potential in settings that are usually seen as non-deliberative, namely social movements and the intimate sphere. We can consider the deliberative potential of these in the light of their influence on the macro-deliberative structure, as proposed in the systemic view (Dryzek 2010; Mansbridge et al. 2012), without seeing them as sites for deliberation themselves. Tamura argues, however, that this view still seems to privilege the government as an "empowered space" above other spaces; when we focus on decision-making, we find that social movements also function as arenas for discussion, and in everyday life, everyday talk can be a locus for transforming ideas and opinions. He therefore proposes a nested view of deliberative systems, meaning that each part of a deliberative structure functions both as a deliberative system in itself and as part of a larger system.

If we modify our views of political communication and processes of deliberation, many of the interspecies dialogues discussed above can be compared to deliberation in the private sphere. The same applies to animal activism, in which non-human animals also take part (chapter 7). However, these forms of deliberation still need to be connected to other—currently exclusively human—political practices in order to work towards new interspecies political institutions and procedures. Mapping the relations between different sites of deliberation can be helpful in bridging the distance between the human-centered system we have now and a truly interspecies model developed with other animals. In order to further investigate how this could work in practice, I now briefly return to the example of goose-human deliberation in the Netherlands.

A Systemic Perspective on Goose-Human Deliberations

Goose-human conflicts arose as the Dutch goose population grew, for example, around Schiphol Airport, and between geese and farmers (Case Study 2). Humans have responded to these conflicts by killing the geese, which is morally problematic and ineffective in practice. Many parties play a role in these conflicts—including the media, farmers, politicians, and biologists—but the geese themselves are not consulted, even though they can exercise agency and interact with humans. Goose agency needs to be taken into account for normative reasons: the interests of the geese are affected and they should therefore be consulted in democratic procedures. It is also necessary for practical reasons: the current approach does not solve the problem. Part of the solution here is that humans need to accept the presence of the geese—but there will always be conflicts and interactions between groups of non-human and human animals, so we also need to look for new ways of dealing with this and similar situations. To do this, we need to improve deliberation with geese, and we also need to improve the relations between existing sites of interspecies deliberation and human politics as a starting point for reformulating democracy with them.

To connect different layers of goose-human politics and improve political goose participation, we can take the following steps. First, existing goose-human interactions need to be mapped, as do the political procedures and interactions that govern these interactions. We can then investigate how the relations between goose-human acts and human politics and legislation can be improved, and how goose agency can be taken into account in developing these improvements. A very first step towards the inclusion of goose voices in existing political decision-making could be for human politicians to meet the geese about whom they are making decisions. In the current situation, politicians often know nothing about the species and communities they are dealing with, which makes it easy for them to disregard their perspective and leaves stereotypes intact. More generally, interaction with the geese should inform the decisions made about them, and these decisions should be communicated back to the geese in a language they can understand— for example, through material interventions. They can then respond, for example, by leaving a certain spot or defending it, to which humans can then further respond. Existing communication can be a starting point for learning to communicate with the geese in better ways. Human experts in various fields, such as art, biology, and politics, could play a role in learning about the geese and finding new ways to live with them. Small-scale political experiments should be set up to further develop models of interacting and coexisting with geese.

The Importance of Beginning Now

In order to promote non-human animal political participation, we should improve existing sites where interspecies deliberation takes place, taking into account different forms of political communication. We should also look for ways to incorporate these in human political frameworks. Of course, such normative recommendations refer us back to the question of non-human animal exclusion, to the definition of language as exclusively human, and to the construction of the human as political actor, as discussed at the beginning of this book. While questions of language and politics are important and must be answered, it is also important to begin to act differently in non-ideal circumstances. Humans already influence, and often dominate, the lives of many other animals. Lobbying for their political inclusion and participation—through activism and official forms of politics, acting differently, and portraying them differently—can help individual non-human animals, and it can also create new beginnings. Given the profit that humans make from the exploitation of other animals—not to mention the more general reliance on animal products—it is unrealistic to expect society to change overnight, so for the time being, the possibility of creating change on a small scale is all we have. This does not mean that we cannot do or change anything. We can bring the perspectives of other animals to light, help individuals in need, advocate for them, and begin to take these new ways of living with them into account in political practices and institutions. For some non-human animals, this could mean everything.

Conclusion

Thinking with Animals

Political participation by non-human animals is not a matter of all or nothing, and non-human animals already participate in a number of political practices. However, non-human animals currently have little voice in political systems, nor do they have the opportunity to change this themselves; change must begin with humans. Existing human concepts and institutions can function as tools for change and disrupt systems of exploitation and domination. In working towards strengthening non-human animal political participation, ideas about justice between groups of humans—both insights from social justice movements and democratic views about equality and freedom—can help us think and act. If we are to avoid repeating anthropocentrism, however, we also need to challenge the human superiority in which these views are embedded. For the same reason, new models of political interaction should always be developed together with other animals.

Building new relations is an open-ended process; we do not know how other animals will behave when humans stop treating them so badly, or how communities might evolve. But we do know where it should start: with humans recognizing non-humans as curious and responsive persons with whom they are entangled in a multitude of relations—sometimes sharing their lives with them very intimately, sometimes in more symbolic or distant ways. This implies not only that humans should listen more carefully to other animals, it also means reconsidering the position of the human—no longer at the center of the universe, but entangled in a multitude of relations with other animals as part of a larger whole.

The work of Len Howard (1952, 1956) can offer inspiration in imagining new forms of interaction (chapter 3). Howard shows how relationships based on equality are possible with birds. By opening her house to wild birds and creating close relations with them based on trust and respect, she calls into question the distinction between domesticated, wild, and liminal: the birds trust her, but they are not domesticated. She also shows us that we do not need large areas of land or major societal reforms to begin building different relations and attending to other animals: a small house and garden are enough. The birds not only co-shape the relations they have with Howard, the course of her life, and the terms on which they interact—they also influence how the house is decorated, what grows in the garden, and their common habits.

Writing with Animals

Howard's work can also offer inspiration for those writing and thinking about other animals. Like Smuts (2001), she not only describes how the animals with whom she shares her life exercise agency and build relations, she also writes from a more-than-human perspective. By this I do not mean that she pretends to know all there is to know about the birds or to write from their perspective—although there is a great deal of understanding between them, (non-human and human) others always remain others, and can at times be a mystery. She does, however, allow herself to be changed by them, and writes from that position, acknowledging their influence on her life and writing.

Notwithstanding the work of Porphyry, Montaigne, and others, philosophy has long been a matter of humans thinking about humans. Animal ethics followed this schema by arguing for non-human animal rights on the basis of their resemblance to humans, valuing cognition over emotion and capacities over relations. Dinker and Pedersen (2016) discuss the ways in which educational institutions, such as universities, can become spaces for activism and resistance in the context of animal liberation. They draw our attention to the fact that theory and practice are interconnected, and to the fact that there are different ways of changing the university from within. One way of doing this is locating where non-human animals are exploited in or connected to universities, for example, where they are used in medical experiments or where they are eaten in university cafeterias. But their absence from philosophical texts and dialogues and their physical absence from academic spaces should also be considered. This might seem less urgent or relevant, but as we have seen, the production of knowledge is intertwined with power rela-tions (chapters 4 & 6). The recent focus on non-human animal agency and relations in animal scholarship is promising in this context, but we need to work harder to animalize universities. Other animals should be invited into processes of thinking and writing differently.

For these reasons, this book can only be a first step in developing a theory of political animal voices. If we are to take the next steps, we need to listen to other animals and engage with them differently.

Directions for Further Research

In order to further develop models of non-human animal political participation and voice, we need to create experiments that provide non-human animals with the opportunity to express themselves politi-cally. This means creating settings—in households, cities, sanctuaries, or elsewhere—where other animals are given the opportunity to make choices for themselves to which humans can respond, and so on, in open-ended dialogues. One way of doing this is by creating situations in which they experience as much freedom as possible, for example, in farmed animal sanctuaries (Donaldson and Kymlicka 2015a). It is particularly important in this context to search for ways in which non-human animals can determine the grounds for interaction. Experiments can also be more modest, taking place in interspecies households where humans can foster animal agency, learn to speak with and listen to their non-human companions in a better way, and find out how political par-ticipation can and should look. The problem in the latter case is that non-human animals are constrained in many ways such that humans must continuously make choices for them for reasons of safety or to comply with legal obligations, but again, this is not a matter of all or nothing, and more freedom is possible. In all of these cases, it is impor-tant to focus on the perspective of the non-human animals and the intersubjective dimensions of the interaction, and to understand that democratic participation is always something that is created in relations with, and in relation to, others. Acknowledging this means we must begin with the idea that other animals are subjects with whom we are entangled in relations, and about whom we learn in interactions that are also partly shaped by them. Taking steps towards interspecies politics is never a matter of "giving" other animals a voice, but rather of understanding and recognizing that they have been speaking to us all along.

While we can begin to experiment with political participation and new forms of living with other animals on a small scale, most of the non-human animals alive today are being held captive and will be killed by humans for human benefit. For the experiments that I have suggested to make sense, non-human animals need rights. Establishing rights is, of course, a political matter, but one that is interconnected with all kinds of cultural processes. Academics also have a role to play in these, for example, by investigating ways of making animal activism more mainstream to improve the position of those who are unable to do so themselves. This requires empirical research to determine which forms of activism are effective (Aaltola 2015; Leuven 2017), and seeking to establish collaborations between the different groups working towards change for animals, as well as those groups striving for social justice with regard to others (chapter 7). Moral and political philosophy has a role to play here, as does empirical research into the capacities of non-human animals. It also requires further investigation of the interconnections between academia and activism. We need to explore both how academia contributes to perpetuating non-human animal oppression, and how academic work can foster activism and different perspectives on non-human animals.

In addition to investigating the ties between academia and activism, there is a need to bridge the gap between certain fields of knowledge and political decision-making. The political experiments discussed above should inform larger political and social structures, as should recent empirical studies concerning non-human animal cognition, emotion, languages,[1] and cultures. Current political institutions and practices rely on specific forms of knowledge production that fit into the dominant discourse and keep intact forms of epistemic violence towards non-human animals. This epistemic construction is interconnected with institutional violence (chapter 4). In order to challenge animal oppression we need to address both forms of violence.

These are dark times for most other animals—something that should concern all who read this—and it is up to us to act differently. In order to improve the situation for other animals, we need to work in many areas, including lobbying for non-human animal rights in existing human political spheres, promoting veganism, caring for stray cats, writing novels, educating others, taking in non-human animals who need a home, and helping those in need in other ways. In all of this, we need to focus more strongly on listening to them and paying attention to their perspectives. This means learning about their languages and cultures, respectfully engaging with them to avoid repeating the exclusion on which current systems of knowledge are based, and working with them to find new pathways.

We can begin again. We should begin again.

ACKNOWLEDGMENTS

This book has benefited from many conversations with colleagues. For reading and responding to (parts of) this text, and discussing non-human animal agency, interspecies democracies, and all kinds of other animal philosophical topics with me, I want to thank Yolande Jansen, Robin Celikates, Bernice Bovenkerk, Clemens Driessen, Sue Donaldson, Will Kymlicka, the people from the OZSW Werkgroep Dierethiek, Elisa Aaltola, Ralph Acampora, Andrew Woodhall, Garmendia da Trindade, Angie Pepper, Marc Davidson, and Jody Emel. I also want to thank the anonymous reviewers of the manuscript for their very helpful comments and the kind people at NYU Press for their support.

For giving me the opportunity to do research and write for four years I want to thank the Amsterdam School for Cultural Analysis, most notably Eloe Kingma and Esther Peeren.

Most of all I want to thank Joy, Pika, Putih, Olli, Doris, Vera, Punkie, Dotje, Ronja, Kitty, Destiny, Poemelie, Witje, Mickey, Luna, Pino, and my other non-human friends, who taught me to listen and helped me think. This book would not be here if it weren't for you.

NOTES

INTRODUCTION

1 The idea that non-human animals are categorically different from human
animals is also increasingly challenged in other fields of study. Recent empirical studies in biology and ethology focusing on the cognition (Allen and Bekoff
1999), cultures (Smuts 2001) and languages (Gentner et al. 2006; Slobodchikoff
et al. 2009) of non-human animals argue that the difference between human
and non-human animals is, as Darwin (1872) already put it, a difference of
degree and not of kind. Poststructuralist and posthumanist thinkers challenge
the underlying hierarchy, questioning a binary opposition between humans and
other animals, as well as human exceptionalism (Calarco 2008; Derrida 2008;
Wadiwel 2015; Wolfe 2003).

2 Similarly, political philosophers and philosophers of language have focused
almost without exception solely on theorizing human language and politics (Donaldson and Kymlicka 2011).

3 It should be noted that understanding and speaking the languages of non-human
animals can also play a role in practices that are harmful to them. Hunters, for example, very often know how to read the traces left by non-human animals in the
landscape; they also understand their calls, and are often able to imitate them. The
problem here, however, is not language, but an abuse of power (see chapters 1 &
4 for a further discussion of the relation between language and power). Humans
also deceive other humans using language.

4 While Aristotle sees a morally relevant difference between humans and other
animals, it should be noted that he does not see non-human animals as a homogeneous group—on the contrary, belonging to a certain species is relevant for
an individual's way of flourishing and for becoming the best animal you can be.
While humans are a special species, so are other species. There is also much that
humans share with other animals in terms of basic capacities. Humans are similar
to other animals in that they eat and have the same organs, and in that they die
and have sex (Aristotle [350BC] 1991). Bees, wasps, ants, and cranes are social
creatures, as are humans; humans also share forms of communication with other
animals. However, forming political communities based on language and morality
is specific to the human species. Humans need the political community in order
to flourish and fulfil their *telos*, and humans are, simultaneously, the only animals
capable of living together in a political community, because they possess *logos*.

5 Various fields of study have focused on this, including ethology (Bekoff 2002; De
   Waal 2016), animal geography (Wolch and Emel 1998; Hobson 2007; Srinivasan
   2016), and history (Hribal 2010).
6 See, for example, Cochrane (2012), Cooke (2014), Hadley (2005), Regan (1983).
7 Speaking for other animals is sometimes unavoidable, the best option available,
   or simply a human duty as the more privileged party (Alcoff 1991), but it runs
   the risk of perpetuating anthropocentrism because it affirms an image of other
   animals as mute, and because it keeps intact the view of humans as the true political actors. Speaking for other animals should therefore always be accompanied by
   listening to them and looking for ways to let them speak for themselves within or
   outside given political and social frameworks.
8 Kohn discusses a similar movement in anthropology: "How other kinds of beings see us matters. That other kinds of beings see us changes things." Therefore,
   "anthropology cannot limit itself just to exploring how people from different
   societies might happen to represent them as doing so" (2013, 1). The perspective of
   those other beings also need to be explored.

CHAPTER 1. THE ANIMAL, WHAT A WORD!
1 I return to limiting the political to humans in chapter 4.
2 "For it is a very remarkable thing that there are no men, not even the insane,
   so dull and stupid that they cannot put words together in a manner to convey
   their thoughts. On the contrary, there is no other animal however perfect and
   fortunately situated it may be, that can do the same. And this is not because they
   lack the organs, for we see that magpies and parrots can pronounce words as well
   as we can, and nevertheless cannot speak as we do, that is, in showing that they
   think what they are saying. On the other hand, even those men born deaf and
   dumb, lacking the organs which others make use of in speaking, and at least as
   badly off as the animals in this respect, usually invent for themselves some signs
   by which they make themselves understood. And this proves not merely animals
   have less reason than men but that they have none at all, for we see that very little
   is needed to talk" (Descartes [1638] 1985, 42).
3 Calling non-human animals "it" is a common expression of viewing them as
   objects. The word "mistress," just as the contemporary variation "owner," of course
   also expresses a hierarchical relation.
4 "And 'tis not to be supposed that nature should have denied that to us which she
   has given to several other animals: for what is this faculty we observe in them, of
   complaining, rejoicing, calling to one another for succour, and inviting each other
   to love, which they do with the voice, other than speech? And why should they
   not speak to one another? They speak to us, and we to them. In how many several
   sorts of ways do we speak to our dogs, and they answer us? We converse with
   them in another sort of language, and use other appellations, than we do with
   birds, hogs, oxen, horses, and alter the idiom according to the kind" (Montaigne
   [1595] 1958, 334).

5 As Moore (2018) discusses in relation to horseshoe crabs, this problem is especially pressing in the case of invertebrates, who are less like humans than verte-
brates and therefore seen as only capable of reflexes, not responses.

6 "Der Stein ist weltlos, das Tier ist weltarm, der Mensch ist weltbildend."

7 See Derrida 2008, 142, for a discussion of *logos* and the as-such and Oliver 2007
for a discussion of language in relation to *logos* and the as-such.

8 We find the same mechanism in Heidegger's notion of *Mitsein*; see chapter 3.

9 Or, as Derrida expresses in "Eating Well": "More differences, yes. For at the
same time you will have to take into account other discriminations, for instance,
between human society and animal society. There are a lot of things to be said
and done. But there are also other partitions, separations, other than Auschwitz—
apartheid, racial segregation—other segregations within our Western democratic
society. All these differences have to be taken into account in a new fashion;
whereas, if you draw a single or two single lines, then you have homogenous sets
of undifferentiated societies, or groups, or structures. No, no I am not advocating
the blurring of differences. On the contrary, I am trying to explain how drawing
an oppositional limit itself blurs the differences, the difference and the differences,
not only between man and animal, but among animal societies—there are an
infinite number of animal societies, and, within the animal societies and within
human society itself, so many differences" (1994, 32).

10 "The strategy in question would consist in pluralizing and varying the 'as such,'
and, instead of simply giving speech back to the animal, or giving to the animal
what the human deprives it of, as it were, in marking that the human is, in a way,
similarly 'deprived,' by means of a privation that is not a privation, and that there
is no pure and simple 'as such'" (Derrida 2008, 160).

11 Derrida often refers to the act of naming others as a human capacity. Other animals, however, also use names for themselves and others. Dolphins and parrots
have names with which they introduce themselves, and to which they respond
(King and Janik 2013). Squirrel monkeys use a specific "chuck" sound for each
individual (Slobodchickoff 2012). Bats have names they use to call others in the
dark, which is particularly useful when flying in large groups (ibid.), and they
like to gossip and argue (Prat et al. 2016). Chickens who live with humans name
them (Davis 2012). Identity is, of course, not just expressed vocally; it can also, for
example, be expressed by using scents. Hyenas live in fluid social groups in which
the females are dominant. In order to communicate, they use smell signals from
their anal glands, forming up to 252 different combinations of smells, which form
an individual profile that can change over time. Other members of the group may
overwrite smells, which allows visitors to get an idea of both individuals in the
area (concerning gender, age, rank, and so on) and group compositions (Johnston
2008). Dogs and wolves also communicate by leaving scent markers from their
anal glands, and in urine and feces (Bekoff 2002).

12 Not addressing the difference between real and imaginary animals is problematic
as well.

13 This can be compared to Lyotard's (1988) concept "differend"; see chapter 9.

14 Seeing them as social groups does not need to imply obscuring all differences. Derrida is right in noting the dangers of using the word "animal" to describe all non-human animals, but if, for example, we investigate the use of violence against animals, or consider a concept such as "animal liberation," using this word can have political power precisely because the violence is directed towards them—the animals—as a group. Iris Young (1990) argues that individuals who share a characteristic (such as skin color, gender, or social class) can be made into a group by shared discrimination on the basis of that characteristic. This mechanism also applies to groups of non-human animals. We can, for example, think of working animals, the animals exploited by factory farming, or companion animals as being united by experiencing similar oppression.

CHAPTER 2. ANIMAL LANGUAGES

1 An extreme example of this concerns fish sentience. It was long assumed that fish could not suffer, and thus no research was undertaken to investigate this. Humans only started researching fish sentience around 2003 (Braithwaite 2010), and when they did, they found that fish do indeed suffer, that they use tools, form communities, play, and so on.

2 Nim had a difficult time in his foster home, which was unstable, and after several biting incidents he was brought back to Columbia University. When the experiment ended, Nim was taken to the Institute of Primate Studies in Oklahoma, and later sold to a pharmaceutical testing laboratory. He spent the last years of his life in a sanctuary, the Black Beauty Ranch, where he lived in solitude for ten years before being joined by other chimps.

3 Eye contact is also emphasized in the case of Washoe. One of her trainers had been away for a few weeks after suffering a miscarriage, and Washoe ignored her for having been absent. The trainer decided to tell Washoe what had happened. Washoe stared at her intently, then slowly made the sign for crying. Chimpanzees do not cry, but Washoe knew that this was what humans did when they were sad. The trainer said that Washoe's response to this told her more than all the words she ever spoke to her.

4 See also Derrida (2008, chapter 3) on capacities for pretending in non-human and human animals.

5 DeGrazia (1994) offers a list of examples but makes the mistake of reading them as statements about non-human animals by taking them out of context. There are certain points in the *Philosophical Investigations* where Wittgenstein does make claims about non-human animals, but these can be refuted by referring to recent empirical research.

6 Nigel Pleasants (2006) argues for the moral relevance of Wittgenstein's work for thinking about social and political relations with non-human animals. He specifically challenges the idea that "forms of life" only refers to a status quo in

which humans exploit other animals and does not allow for moral considerations of non-human animals, or for progressing insights about their capacities: critical and disputational practices have also always been part of our forms of life (2006, 332). Pleasants also briefly considers interspecies language games.

7 He does state that they are capable of certain language games (PI§25).

8 Sometimes non-human animals imitate human speech on their own initiative. For example, beluga whale Noc, who worked for the US army, copied human chatter (Meijer 2016). Elephants can use their trunks to manipulate the sounds they make, which enables them to pronounce human words. The Asian elephant Batyr started speaking in this manner in a zoo in Kazakhstan, where he was held captive for the whole of his life without other members of his species (ibid.). Scientists think that these animals use human language to connect with humans because they have no possibility of interacting with individuals of their own species. While this shows us that these animals are creative social beings (and very lonely), it again does not tell us much about the language skills of whales and elephants. Both elephants and whales have rich and complex languages that humans are only now beginning to decipher.

9 This is why humans and dogs start to look alike after sharing their lives for a certain time—mutual mimicry in facial expression and posture.

10 Their calls sound like birdcalls, and many of them sound like a dog barking, which is why they are called prairie dogs.

11 Sonograms are used for studying and understanding non-human animal languages; without computers we would not have been able to hear and understand the complexities of prairie dog languages, or bat or whale languages, in some cases because we are simply unable to hear them.

CHAPTER 3. FROM ANIMAL LANGUAGES TO INTERSPECIES WORLDS

1 In contrast to her contemporary, ethologist Konrad Lorenz. Like Howard, Lorenz believed in living with animals and getting to know them intimately as a basis for studying them; however, he held many of them in captivity, and often hand-raised young birds he had stolen from their parents. This is problematic from an ethical perspective, and, as Howard shows, not necessary for studying them.

2 A skeptical reader might ask whether Howard perhaps gave Star some sign that made her stop tapping at the right moment. Howard describes Star's tapping as really fast, which is why they never get to the number nine, so it could very well be that Star really understood what she was asked. However, even though the experiment could possibly be improved upon, the important thing Howard shows us is that it is possible to study birds in this manner, and on a voluntary basis.

3 Of course, developing a common language does not immediately lead to harmony or complete understanding: possibilities for misunderstanding are inherent in all forms of interaction, including between humans.

4 See Meijer (2016) for a longer discussion.

5 Contrary to popular belief, they also have a sense of time; it is now thought that they smell what time of day it is because smells change through the course of a day (Horowitz 2016).

6 I will discuss the political and moral consequences of this in chapter 5.

7 An illustration is found in the case of African elephant Buba, who was raised in a circus and lived there for over thirty-five years. Because wild animals are not allowed to work in circuses anymore in Germany and the Netherlands, she was relocated to a shelter but became severely depressed. She was allowed to go back to her circus life and family.

8 I was told about this practice in an animal ethics masterclass with horse professionals. Horses can, for example, be taught with clicker training to point their nose to the right foot of the rider if they want them to get off them, or, the other way around, to stand next to a stump or pole if they want them to climb onto their back.

9 Adult cats usually do not meow to each other; only kittens meow to get the attention of their mothers.

CASE STUDY 1. STRAY PHILOSOPHY

An earlier version of this chapter appeared in the *Journal for Critical Animal Studies* 5, no. 4: 105–35. Reprinted by permission from the *Journal for Critical Animal Studies*.

1 He weighs around twenty-five kilograms.

2 Really deep sleep came only after a few months. I do not think he ever slept like that in Romania.

3 Later on, I was also able to fulfil that role for him. I once gave him a piece of cucumber and he refused to eat it until I took a bite.

4 The only thing they had taught him in the shelter was to sit and give his paw, and in the first weeks he did this all the time to show he meant well.

5 Over the years this did change. We can now usually discuss things in peace.

6 He now likes to sit on a bench in the park, where he invites humans to sit next to him and pet him.

7 He also started to yawn when I yawn and to sigh when I sigh deeply.

8 Something similar happened with my horse Joy when I was younger. She was always slightly nervous in traffic, and I internalized her responses to the point that when I rode my bicycle, plastic bags also scared me.

9 Ideally, I would have left all choice of participation in our household with him. It took him only a few days to start to appreciate having a house, both in terms of safety and food, so I suspect he would have chosen to live with us.

10 See chapter 9 for a longer discussion and critique of this example.

11 He does not simply follow, and if I pull on the lead, he just pulls in the other direction. I need to convince him ("we are going home now").

12 Similarly, the lead makes some dogs feel more confident. Small dogs often feel confident knowing their human is at the other end of the lead, something they might express by barking loudly at dogs twice or three times their size.

13 In Olli's profile on their website, Dierenhulp Orfa described him as a very happy dog. Much of his "happy" behavior was actually an act to try and get attention and food. When he became more relaxed, he stopped acting in these ways. He still wags his tail, but not all the time; he can now lie somewhere without watching me all the time, and I sometimes see a really happy expression, for example, when I come home with groceries—like a smile.

14 In the case of non-human animals, the word "euthanasia" is often used as a euphemism for killing.

15 There are not many dogs in Dutch shelters, and no street dogs in the Netherlands, so many Dutch people choose to adopt dogs from abroad, mostly from Spain, Greece, Portugal, and Romania, where shelters are full and many dogs are treated badly—we find a similar situation in Germany, Belgium, and to some extent the UK. There are many small Dutch organizations that run shelters abroad and transport dogs to foster families in the Netherlands so they can be adopted here. Some Dutch shelters participate in this practice by taking in dogs from shelters—often kill shelters—from these countries, so they have a better chance of being adopted.

16 He makes Pika happy. He is very sweet, playful, and joyful and likes to make jokes. By "jokes" I mean acts that are meant to amuse me or to draw my attention to something in a joyful, playful way. Jokes are similar to games, but they refer to something outside of the situation. He and Pika also make jokes together. They like to roll in the dirt and sniff each other afterwards, wagging their tails as if giving the other a high five for smelling bad. And they form a team if they want to put pressure on me to give them food.

17 Although Olli and Pika understood each other well from the beginning, their contact still deepens. In the beginning, Olli lay next to Pika on the couch and the bed. Pika accepted this but was slightly indifferent. Later on, she also sought out his company. They often greet each other during the day, kissing and wagging their tails.

CHAPTER 4. ANIMAL POLITICS

1 Notifying rats of court orders by sending them letters, as well as sending them friendly letters of advice to leave certain houses because they would otherwise be poisoned, was a custom in various European countries and in parts of the US in the nineteenth and early twentieth centuries. The letters were pinned to the door of the house, and if the rats took no notice, they were rubbed with grease, rolled up, and put into their holes (Evans 1906, 129–31).

2 There was a distinction in criminal animal law between domesticated animals, who were seen as members of the community and sometimes actually brought to trial, after which they were often executed, and animals generally seen as pests, such as rodents and insects. Members of the latter group were not usually present at the hearings, although some randomly selected individuals were often brought to the court and killed after the trial to serve as an example. It was not possible to

excommunicate non-human animals of either group; they could only be anathematized. Like women, they had no legal standing of their own, so they could only be "waived" or abandoned (Evans 1906, 52).

3   There are now animal parties in many countries, such as the UK, Brazil, Spain, Portugal, Switzerland, Sweden, Germany, Australia, and Canada.

4   *Animal Liberation* is one of the few successful examples of how a philosophical work can influence a social justice movement.

5   The word "speciesism" was coined by psychologist Richard Ryder in 1970.

6   It is important not to confuse fundamental rights with improving animal welfare legislation. Changing the size of cages for battery hens from one A4 to one A4 plus 2 centimeters per hen might be seen as a step in the right direction, but does nothing to challenge the practice of keeping captive and killing hens, and makes it easier for humans to forget about their treatment and believe that things are not so bad or improving, which may even contribute to legitimizing these practices. In contrast, universal animal rights, like basic human rights, would in fact lead to great social change, and would also alter the position of other animals.

7   Donna Haraway (1991) rightly argues that dividing other animals into species is inherently political, drawing attention to the fact that primatology is concerned with a taxonomic and therefore political order, and that western primatology can be seen as a form of simian orientalism.

8   See also the feminist critiques of Regan and Singer, for example, Adams (2010), Donovan (1990), and Gruen (2015).

9   Of course, humans also participate in violence towards other humans through personal and communal choices.

10   Elisa Aaltola (2015) also turns to the concept of akrasia to conceptualize human attitudes, and draws attention to the role of emotion and cultivating one's character as an alternative. The animal rights movement should, according to her, focus more strongly on human emotions in trying to get humans to change their behavior, and emphasize the positive aspects of veganism and new, better relations with non-human animals.

11   In this context it is relevant to note that while the current scale of violence against non-human animals is unprecedented, and technological developments make their deaths more efficient than ever, there never was a "good old days" for other animals (Donaldson and Kymlicka 2011).

12   Grazian (2012) writes that zoo animals are not the exemplars of wild species that zoos want us to believe: they are part of a cultural construction that affects not only their circumstances, such as their enclosures and food, but also their relations with humans. They are used to humans in such a way that we can call many of them domesticated. This includes communication with keepers and visitors.

13   According to Donaldson and Kymlicka, this can function as the starting point for political representation, as I will discuss in more detail in the next chapter and in chapter 8.

14 A parrot's statement has been considered for use in a murder trial before. In 1993, a defence lawyer for Gary Joseph Rasp argued that an African grey parrot could tell the court who killed his human companion. The bird said repeatedly "Richard, no, no, no," suggesting Rasp was not guilty, but the judge ruled that the evidence could not be used and Rasp was convicted (Crilly 2016).

15 He sees examples of this approach in biopolitical theories that challenge the *zoe/ bios* distinction for groups of humans and other animals; in the work of Deleuze and Guattari (1988) that focuses on "becoming animal"; and in the work of eco-feminist Val Plumwood, who in her article "Becoming Prey" (2002) describes how she was attacked by an alligator and how this has deepened her understanding of predator-prey relations as well as human exploitation of non-human animals.

CHAPTER 5. ANIMALS AND THE STATE

1 Pit bulls are the most prominent example, but other breeds, including Rottweilers, Dobermanns, German shepherds, and Akitas are also mentioned.

2 All Dutch shelters are no-kill shelters.

3 Some dogs spend all day in a house or garden, waiting for their human to come back from work. Dogs are pack animals, and the emotional stress they suffer through being alone has long been underestimated (McMillan 2000).

4 This also applies to farmed animals; economic reasons are seen as good reasons.

5 As with humans, there will always be individuals who keep causing problems; we will need to devise programs to re-educate them and integrate them into society in a careful and responsible way.

6 Some experts argue that their presence benefits the biodiversity, and arguments have been going back and forth for years (see Partij voor de Dieren 2015 for an overview of the discussion).

7 Human groups have also colonized the land of other human communities on the grounds that their laws were not written down and could therefore not be recognized.

8 Hunting causes many species of non-human animals, including deer, to have more children (Bekoff 2009).

9 As the discussions about biodiversity I mentioned before (Partij voor de Dieren 2015) illustrate.

10 Complete harmony between communities is utopian and worth working towards, and achieving justice can be an important political goal, but unequal power relations are an ongoing reality that we have to deal with.

11 Legal scholar Steven Wise started the Nonhuman Rights Project to secure legally recognized fundamental rights for non-human animals. In his best-known case, he filed a petition for a writ of *habeas corpus* for chimpanzee Tommy in the state of New York in 2014. Because chimpanzees and other non-human primates are similar to humans in morally relevant respects such as cognition, emotion, and culture, Wise argues that they should be regarded as persons. Just as with human persons, non-human persons should have a right to liberty, life, and freedom

from torture; it is up to science to decide which non-human animals should be seen as persons. While Tommy has not yet been awarded personhood, the court has heard Wise, seriously considered the case, and declared that while they could not award Tommy personhood for now, there is a good possibility of this happening in the future. Wise does not challenge the distinction between persons and things, but rather wants to make use of it to improve legal conditions for non-human animals.

CHAPTER 6. WORM POLITICS

1 For a more recent defence of this view, see Herringshaw et al. (2017).
2 From the perspective of advocacy, worms are more difficult to "sell" because humans perceive them as less appealing, and they suffer less from the industrialized violence that other animals suffer (compare Driessen 2017 on fish).
3 Recent research on plants and fungi (Peeters 2016) shows that these exercise agency too, and form relations with one another and with humans (see also Wohlleben 2016 on trees). Because I concentrate on non-human animals in this book, I will not discuss these life forms in detail. Some of the thoughts developed in this chapter could perhaps contribute to further thinking about human-plant relations, or fungi-human relations, but for now these fall outside the scope of my project.
4 See also Moore (2018), who discusses similar entanglements in a variety of horseshoe crab-human relations, ranging from exploitation by humans for biomedical research and fishing to protection from the extinction they face because of that exploitation.
5 See also Tsing on the political economies of human-mushroom relations, conceptualized as assemblages in which humans are transformed, or "contaminated" (2015, 27).
6 Bennett draws on Dewey's concept of publics to further conceptualize this (Bennett 2010, 100).
7 Bennett (2010, 2012) also argues for using anthropomorphism as a way of understanding what is beyond the human perspective. While as humans we are always tied to a human lens, her interpretation of this concept shows an attachment to the human, versus the non-human. This is demonstrated further in her articulation elsewhere that ultimately "we" need to develop a new ontology for the humans involved, for "our" sake (Bennett 2012). This is problematic because it ultimately reduces the value of relations with others to a value for humans, and because precisely who belongs to this "us" is neither natural nor given, but is a cultural construction. We find a reflection of this in the distinction between human and non-human that Bennett and other object-oriented theorists use. While the focus on the non-human is used to challenge a liberal or Kantian view of the human, object oriented theories paradoxically run the risk of flattening social and political differences—exercising agency is not simply a matter of bodies having a certain capacity to move other bodies, because these operate in social and political relations. From the perspective of non-human animals, this focus on the

non-human as a broad category furthermore runs the risk of reinforcing human exceptionalism, something that can be seen in the fact that many actor-network theorists (most notably Latour) and new materialists (such as Bennett 2010; see also Coole and Frost 2010) hardly ever mention non-human animals as a relevant category, or as interlocutors (exceptions are Haraway 2008; Moore 2018), let alone discuss interaction with them on the same level as inter-human encounters. A similar problem arises in Morton (2017), who rightfully draws attention to the fact that humans are part of a larger whole, and argues this should lead to larger solidarity with the non-human world, but who in his writing fails to enter conversation with other animals.

8 For example, in American legislation to protect laboratory animals, mice are not seen as animals. Insects and other small animals are also usually not mentioned in this legislation at all.

9 See Thierman (2010) for an analysis of the relevance of this concept for thinking about non-human animals.

10 This raises the question of whether or not these worms are domesticated, or if they should perhaps be seen as a kind of cyborgs. While their bodies are changed, their social lives are not—they do not seek out human company, so this differs from the domestication of mammals or birds. It does, however, matter for thinking about justice, as I will discuss in the next section.

11 There is some research on emotions and subjectivity of social insects, for example, about pessimism in bees (Bateson et al. 2011) and the individual personalities of social spiders (Grinsted et al. 2013).

12 Gordon (1992), for example, describes how watching ants for a longer period of time can make you see them. Moore (2018) describes how watching horseshoe crabs allows them to answer you.

13 See also Kamphof (2017) on chicken-human relations.

CASE STUDY 2. GOOSE POLITICS

1 In 2015, plans were made for a new airport in the Flevopolder, which will probably lead to the killing of large numbers of geese in the Oostvaardersplassen.

2 245,000 geese are killed annually in the Netherlands.

3 Gassing is not a "humane" or painless method; see Faunabescherming (2013).

4 Different species are found in the Schiphol area, such as greylag geese, Canada geese, Egyptian geese, and white-fronted geese. Greylag geese are the most common, and the main target for hunters and pest control companies. This group consists of birds who nest here and stay all year long, birds who nest and migrate, and birds who nest further north in Europe and visit here in winter.

5 Not all geese can be seen as liminal animals; some are domesticated, and there are communities of wild geese. Geese also show that these categories are not fixed: wild geese can, under certain circumstances, start to seek out human company, and liminal geese can become more shy, for example, because they are hunted, and start avoiding humans.

6 Introducing this new category also shows us something about categorization itself: although concepts such as citizenship and sovereignty can clarify the rights and duties of non-human animals, provide a new perspective on animals, and help us imagine new forms of living together, the wide spectrum of human/non-human animal relationships and the major differences between different animals—species, communities, and individuals—make it difficult to draw lines.

7 Such as Schiphol and pest control companies like Duke Faunabeheer, who have an economic interest in killing geese.

8 In the words of Dutch biologist Maarten Loonen, who has studied geese for over thirty years.

9 The mother goose nests, although Lorenz (1991) describes one occasion where the father took over nesting and raising the children when the mother died.

10 See Lorenz (1991) for an extensive description of the different calls and their functions.

11 Imprinting is highly problematic from an ethical and political point of view, even when geese are taught goose behavior and can live without being dependent on humans, because it usually involves taking young animals away from their families in order to benefit humans.

12 See Hirschman (1970) for an analysis of the relation between "voice" and "exit." Here it should be noted that many non-human animals do not have an option to leave because they are held captive in farms, laboratories, or zoos.

13 See also Narayanan (2017) on colonialism and street dogs in India.

14 Geese remember maps of the land as they see it from the sky, and can find their way around if they are walking on the ground (Lorenz 1991).

15 It is important to note that geese cross national borders: more than half of the geese in the Netherlands spend part of the year in Antarctica or other places; the question of land needs to be dealt with on different institutional levels.

16 Leading to situations in which trespassing immediately leads to death; a recent example in the Netherlands is the rescue of a group of wild boars who had fallen into a canal and were rescued by firefighters only to be immediately killed by hunters, because they were not allowed on that side of the water.

CHAPTER 7. ANIMAL ACTIVISM AND INTERSPECIES CHANGE

1 Sue Donaldson and Will Kymlicka (2011) criticize the animal rights movement for focusing too strongly on negative rights, and even argue that this partly explains why the animal rights movement has failed to be successful; see also Leuven (2017).

2 Research into non-human animal consciousness is progressing fast. Recent studies show, for example, that manta rays (Ari and D'Agostino 2016) and ants (Cammaerts and Cammaerts 2016) recognize themselves in the mirror.

3 On an individual level, of course, not all non-human animals are activists, and being an activist is not necessary to be taken into account morally or politically, similar to the way in which this works in the human case. Also, not all forms

of activism can be grounded in animal agency. But in many cases, non-human animal agency is ignored, and this has consequences for how non-human animals are portrayed and treated.

4 See, for example, Cochrane (2010).

5 See also Kim (2015) on interconnections between the oppression of human groups and non-human animal groups, and see Elder, Wolch, and Emel (1998) for an analysis of how cultural ideas about humans and animals have been used to produce and reproduce cultural differences and legitimize violence towards subaltern human groups.

6 See, for example, Cooke (forthcoming), who unambiguously denies that non-human animals speak, or Cochrane (2012), who argues that other animals cannot exercise meaningful political agency.

7 It is a successful example: following the release of the documentary, SeaWorld lost 15.9 million dollars in 2013 and its market value dropped by half. In November 2015 they announced they were planning to phase out their use of orca whales. See Coldwell (2015) for an overview.

8 Research on dingos shows that killing wild dogs probably only makes conflicts worse because it breaks up families and social structures, leaving dogs traumatized (Keim 2017).

9 These dogs also use traffic lights and know which humans to turn to for food— women who are over forty.

10 Whether or not medical intervention would be required or permitted would depend on the circumstances.

CHAPTER 8. ANIMAL DEMOCRACY AND THE CHALLENGES OF
POLITICAL PARTICIPATION

1 He concludes that humans can learn from bee democracy: in order to be most efficient, decision-making groups should consist of individuals who share interests; debate should be taken seriously; different solutions should be offered; leaders should not have the last word; and the majority of the group should play a role in finding a good resolution.

2 Herds of red deer move when over 62% of the adult members of the group stand up (Conradt and Roper 2005). In African buffalo communities, females dictate their travel preferences by standing up, staring in one direction, and then lying back down (Wilson 1997). It took scientists some time to understand that this behavior was not stretching, but voting. When the cows differ sharply in the direction of their gaze, the herd splits up and grazes in different places. In yellow baboon communities, high-ranking males and females have the final say about troop movement, but all the baboons influence decisions (Norton 1986). Pigeons have complex social hierarchies in which low-ranking birds also vote on the flock's next flight. They have a flexible system of rank, in which some birds are more likely to lead and others to follow, which according to researchers makes for a particularly efficient form of decision-making (Nagy et al. 2010). African bees

use pheromones to warn each other, and when they attack collectively they can and do kill humans (Collins et al. 1982). Cockroaches do not have complex social structures like bees and ants, but are still capable of collective decision-making (Amé et al. 2006). Non-human animals of many other species, ranging from birds, bats, and fish to different species of insect, also make collective decisions (Conradt and List 2009).

3 In the next chapter I further theorize these forms of decision-making as deliberation.

4 Drawing on recent work in disability studies, Donaldson (forthcoming) describes this as a "lack of fit" between groups of non-human animals and the societies in which they live. This lack of fit is not there because there is something wrong with them, it is because the current system is designed to fit humans (and as disability theorists show, for example, not all humans).

5 Dogs who have close relations with humans could, under certain conditions, function as advocates for other members of their species; they can let us know about their preferences, and we can develop new forms of living with them in a process of revising reasons.

6 There is, of course, the problem of adaptive preferences, which we have to be careful about, especially in the transition to a different form of living with other animals.

7 Some dogs do not want to be touched or even looked at, and can feel the need to defend themselves when humans approach them. It would be problematic to ask them to ignore this as a citizenship requirement.

8 It is important to recognize that, in this example and others, other animals can also choose to simply refuse relations or refuse certain aspects of the relations within communities—they might, for example, ignore human orders or their presence, or refuse to leave territories. These acts of refusal often operate within other knowledge systems, and might not therefore challenge human power in terms of power, but in other terms (for a parallel in the human case, see Wood and Rossister (2017) on indigenous politics of refusal).

9 For Levinas, this only takes place between humans; see Derrida (2008) and Wolfe (2003) for problems with this view.

CHAPTER 9. DELIBERATING ANIMALS

1 See chapters 1–5 for a critique of this image of non-human animals and an alternative.

2 Young explicates the political functions of three modes of communication in addition to making arguments: greeting (see chapter 8 for interspecies political greeting), rhetoric, and narrative. In doing so, she focuses not only on words but also on body language, signs, symbols, and other forms of expression.

3 See Spivak (1988) for an analysis of this movement in the case of subaltern humans.

4 One horse, however, often wanted to change, regardless of the weather; it was assumed that she liked the interaction with humans.

5 Horses use referential communication to direct the behavior of humans, and humans are only just beginning to understand how complex and refined this communication is (Malavasi and Huber 2016).

CONCLUSION. THINKING WITH ANIMALS

1 As discussed above, there is still very little knowledge about non-human animal languages. More empirical research into this is needed, especially research that moves beyond studying one aspect of the language of one species, as is still common in biology and ethology.

WORKS CITED

Aaltola, Elisa. 2013. "Empathy, Intersubjectivity, and Animal Philosophy." *Environmental Philosophy* 10, no. 2: 75–96.

———. 2015. "Politico-Moral Apathy and Omnivore's Akrasia: Views from the Rationalist Tradition." *Politics and Animals* 1, no. 1: 35–49.

Acampora, Ralph. 2004. "Oikos and Domus: On Constructive Co-Habitation with Other Creatures." *Philosophy & Geography* 7, no. 2: 219–35.

Adams, Carol. (1990) 2010. *The Sexual Politics of Meat: A Feminist-Vegetarian Critical Theory.* London: Continuum.

Adams, Carol, and Josephine Donovan, eds. 1995. *Animals and women: Feminist theoretical explorations.* Durham, NC: Duke University Press.

Alcoff, Linda. 1991. "The Problem of Speaking for Others." *Cultural Critique* 20: 5-32.

Alger, Janet, and Steven Alger. 2013. "Canine Soldiers, Mascots, and Stray Dogs in U.S. Wars: Ethical Considerations." In *Animals and War*, edited by Ryan Hediger, 77–104. Leiden, Netherlands: Brill.

Allen, Colin, and Marc Bekoff. 1999. *Species of Mind: The Philosophy and Biology of Cognitive Ethology.* Cambridge, MA: MIT Press.

Allen, Daniel. 2014. "Justice for Romanian Stray Dogs." *Huffington Post*, September 22, 2014. www.huffingtonpost.co.uk.

Amé, J., M. Halloy, J. Rivault, C. Detrain, and J. Deneubourg. 2006. "Collegial Decision Making Based on Social Amplification Leads to Optimal Group Formation." *Proceedings of the National Academy of Sciences* 103, no. 15: 5835–40.

Andics, A., A. Gábor, M. Gácsi, T. Faragó, D. Szabó, and A. Miklósi. 2016. "Neural Mechanisms for Lexical Processing in Dogs." *Science* 353: 1030–32.

Aplin, Lucy. 2015. "Experimentally Induced Innovations Lead to Persistent Culture via Conformity in Wild Birds." *Nature* 518: 538–41.

Arendt, Hannah. (1958) 1998. *The Human Condition.* Chicago: University of Chicago Press.

Ari, Csilla, and Dominic D'Agostino. 2016. "Contingency Checking and Self-Directed Behaviors in Giant Manta Rays: Do Elasmobranchs Have Self-Awareness?" *Journal of Ethology* 34, no. 2: 167–74.

Aristotle. (350BC) 1991. "History of Animals." Translated by David Balme. In *Books VII–X.* Cambridge: Loeb Classical Library.

Azeredo, Sandra. 2011. "Multispecies Companions in Naturecultures: Donna Haraway and Sandra Azeredo in Conversation." In *Pensar/Escrever o Animal - Ensaios de*

Zoopoética e Biopolítica, edited by Maria Esther Maciel, 2–29. Florianópolis, Brazil: EdUSC.

Bakels, Jet. 2003. "Perceptions of Wildlife Among the Kerinci of Sumatra." In *Wildlife in Asia: Cultural Perspectives*, edited by John Knight, 147–65. London: Routledge.

Barua, Maan. 2014. "Bio-geo-graphy: Landscape, Dwelling, and the Political Ecology of Human–Elephant Relations." *Environment and Planning D: Society and Space* 32: 915–34.

Bastiaansen, Maarten. 2013. "On the Possibility of Diminishing the Egyptian Goose (*Alopochen aegyptiacus*) Population through Intervention in the Adult Geese in Sabi River Sun Golf Estate and White River Country Estate." Thesis, Utrecht University.

Bateson, Melissa, Suzanne Desire, Sarah Gartside, and Geraldine Wright. 2011. "Agitated Honeybees Exhibit Pessimistic Cognitive Biases." *Current Biology* 21, no. 12: 1070–73.

BBC. 2013. "Nottinghamshire's Police Dogs to Receive Pensions." September 22, 2013. www.bbc.com.

Beach, Frank. 1955. "The Descent of Instinct." *Psychological Review* 62, no. 6: 401–12.

Bekoff, Marc. 2002. *Minding Animals: Awareness, Emotions, and Heart*. Oxford: Oxford University Press.

———. 2007. *The Emotional Lives of Animals: A Leading Scientist Explores Animal Joy, Sorrow, and Empathy and Why They Matter*. Novato, CA: New World Library.

———. 2009. "Stalking, Hunting, Stress and Emotion." *Psychology Today*, July 6, 2009. www.psychologytoday.com.

Bekoff, Marc, and Jessica Pierce. 2009. *Wild Justice: The Moral Lives of Animals*. Chicago: University of Chicago Press.

Belcourt, Billy-Ray. 2015. "Animal Bodies, Colonial Subjects: (Re)locating Animality in Decolonial Thought." *Societies* 5, no. 1: 1–11.

Bennett, Jane. 2010. *Vibrant Matter: A Political Ecology of Things*. Durham, NC: Duke University Press.

———. 2012. "Powers of the Hoard: Further Notes on Material Agency." In *Animal, Vegetable, Mineral: Ethics and Objects*, edited by Jeffrey Jerome Cohen. New York: punctum books.

Bentham, Jeremy. (1823) 1907. *Introduction to the Principles of Morals and Legislation*. Oxford: Clarendon Press.

Berg, Karl, Soraya Delgado, Kathryn Cortopassi, Steven Beissinger, and Jack Bradbury. 2011. "Vertical Transmission of Learned Signatures in a Wild Parrot." *Proc. R. Soc. B* 0932: 1471–2954.

Bertoni, Filippo. 2013. "Soil and Worm: On Eating as Relating." *Science as Culture* 22, no. 1: 61–85.

Bickford, Susan. 2011. "Emotion Talk and Political Judgment." *Journal of Politics* 73, no. 4: 1025–37.

Bijlsma, Rob, Fred Hustings, and Kees Camphuysen. 2001. *Avifauna van Nederland 2*. Soest, Netherlands: KNNV Uitgever.

Bohman, James. 1998. "Survey Article: The Coming of Age of Deliberative Democracy." *Journal of Political Philosophy* 6, no. 4: 400–425.

Bradshaw, Isabel Gay. 2004. "Not by Bread Alone: Symbolic Loss, Trauma, and Recovery in Elephant Communities." *Society and Animals* 12, no. 2: 143–58.

Bradshaw, Isabel Gay, Allan Schore, Janine Brown, Joyce Poole, and Cynthia Moss. 2005. "Elephant Breakdown." *Nature* 433: 807–9.

Bradshaw, John. 2016. "Sociality in Cats: A Comparative Review." *Journal of Veterinary Behavior: Clinical Applications and Research* 1, no. 11: 113–24.

Braithwaite, Victoria. 2010. *Do Fish Feel Pain?* Oxford: Oxford University Press.

Brentari, Carlo. 2016. "Behaving Like an Animal? Some Implications of the Philosophical Debate on the Animality of Men." In *Thinking about Animals in the Age of the Anthropocene*, edited by Morten Tønnessen, Kristin Armstrong Oma, and Silver Rattasepp, 127–45. New York: Lexington Books.

Breure, Abraham. 2015. "The Sound of a Snail: Two Cases of Acoustic Defence in Gastropods." *Journal of Molluscan Studies* 81, no. 2: 290–93.

Bröer, Cristian. 2006. *Beleid vormt overlast, hoe beleidsdiscoursen de beleving van geluid bepalen (Policy Annoyance, How Policy Discourses Shape the Experience of Aircraft Sound)*. Amsterdam: Aksant.

Brooks Pribac, Teja. 2013. "Animal Grief." *Animal Studies Journal* 2, no. 2: 67–90.

Broom, Donald. 2010. "Cognitive Ability and Awareness in Domestic Animals and Decisions about Obligations to Animals." *Applied Animal Behavior Science* 126, no. 1–2: 1–11.

Burger, Joanna. 2002. *The Parrot Who Owns Me: The Story of a Relationship*. New York: Random House.

Burghardt, Gordon. 2005. *The Genesis of Animal Play: Testing the Limits*. Cambridge, MA: MIT Press.

Calarco, Matthew. 2008. *Zoographies: The Question of the Animal from Heidegger to Derrida*. New York: Columbia University Press.

———. 2015. *Thinking Through Animals: Identity, Difference, Indistinction*. Stanford, CA: Stanford University Press.

Cammaerts, Marie-Claire, and Roger Cammaerts. 2016. "Are Ants (Hymenoptera, Formicidae) Capable of Self Recognition?" *Zoology* 5, no. 7, 521–32.

Candea, Matei. 2013. "Habituating Meerkats and Redescribing Animal Behavior Science." *Theory, Culture & Society* 30, no. 7–8: 105–28.

Carrington, Damian. 2016. "World on Track to Lose Two-Thirds of Wild Animals by 2020, Major Report Warns." *The Guardian*, October 27, 2016. www.theguardian.com.

Cavalieri, Paola. 2001. *The Animal Question: Why Non-Human Animals Deserve Human Rights*. Oxford: Oxford University Press.

Cavalieri, Paola, and Peter Singer, eds. 1993. *The Great Ape Project: Equality beyond Humanity*. London: Fourth Estate.

CBC Radio. 2016. "The Current Transcript for November 30, 2016." November 30, 2016. www.cbc.ca/radio.

Ceballos, Gerardo. 2015. "Accelerated Modern Human–Induced Species Losses: Entering the Sixth Mass Extinction." *Science Advances* 1, no. 5: e1400253.

Celikates, Robin. 2016. "Rethinking Civil Disobedience as a Practice of Contestation— Beyond the Liberal Paradigm." *Constellations* 23, no 1: 37–45.

Clark, Jonathan L. 2014. "Labourers or Lab Tools? Rethinking the Role of Lab Animals." In *The Rise of Critical Animal Studies: From the Margins to the Centre*, edited by Nik Taylor and Richard Twine, 139–64. London: Routledge.

CLM. 2011. "Pilot gansveilig Schiphol: ganzen en graan. Monitoring ganzen en animo." September 22, 2011. www.clm.nl.

Cochrane, Alasdair. 2010. *An Introduction to Animals and Political Theory*. New York: Palgrave Macmillan.

———. 2012. *Animal Rights Without Liberation: Applied Ethics and Human Obligations*. Columbia: Columbia University Press.

———. 2016. "Labour Rights for Animals." In *The Political Turn in Animal Ethics*, edited by Robert Garner and Siobhan O'Sullivan, 15–31. London: Rowman and Littlefield International.

Cochrane, Alasdair, Robert Garner, and Siobhan O'Sullivan. 2016. "Animal Ethics and the Political." *Critical Review of International Social and Political Philosophy* 19: 1–17.

Cohen, Ari. 2015. "We Support Circus Animals Who Kill Their Captors: Non-human Resistance, Animal Subjectivity, and the Politics of Democracy." In *Tiere—Texte— Transformationen*, edited by Reingard Spannring. Bielefeld, Germany: Transcript.

Coldwell, Will. 2015. "Brancheau, Blackfish and San Diego Shutdown: A SeaWorld in Turmoil Timeline." *The Guardian*, November 11, 2015. www.theguardian.com.

Coles, Romand. 1992. *Self/Power/Other: Political Theory and Dialogical Ethics*. Ithica, NY: Cornell University Press.

Collins, A. M., T. Rinderer, J. Harbo, and A. Bolten. 1982. "Colony Defense by Africanized and European Honey Bees." *Science* 218, no. 4567: 72–74.

Conradt, Larissa, and Christian List. 2009. "Group Decisions in Humans and Animals: A Survey." *Philosophical Transactions of the Royal Society of London B: Biological Sciences* 364, no. 1518: 719–42.

Conradt, Larissa, and Timothy Roper. 2005. "Consensus Decision Making in Animals." *Trends in Ecology & Evolution* 20, no. 8: 449–56.

Cooke, Steve. 2014. "Perpetual Strangers: Animals and the Cosmopolitan Right." *Political Studies* 62, no. 4: 930–44.

———. 2017. "Animal Kingdoms: On Habitat Rights for Wild Animals." *Environmental Values* 26, no. 1: 53–72.

Coole, Diana, and Samantha Frost. 2010. "Introducing the New Materialisms." In *New Materialisms: Ontology, Agency, and Politics*, edited by Diana Coole and Samantha Frost, 1–43. Durham, NC: Duke University Press.

Coulter, Kendra. 2016. *Animals, Work, and the Promise of Interspecies Solidarity*. New York: Palgrave Macmillan.

Crane, Jonathan, ed. 2015. *Beastly Morality: Animals as Ethical Agents*. Columbia: Columbia University Press.

Crilly, Rob. 2016. "Parrot May Be Used as Witness in Murder Trial After Repeating 'Don't Shoot.'" *The Telegraph*, June 28, 2016. www.telegraph.co.uk.

Daniel, Raik, Len Carpenter, Jhon Organ, and Tania M. Schusler. 2005. "Collabouration for Community-Based Wildlife Management." *Urban Ecosystems* 8, no. 2: 227–36.

Darwin, Charles. 1872. *The Expression of the Emotions in Man and Animals*. London: John Murray.

———. 1881. *The Formation of Vegetable Mould, through the Action of Worms, with Observations of Their Habits*. London: John Murray.

Davis, Karen. 2012. *The Social Life of Chickens*. Columbia: Columbia University Press.

De Bruijn, Paulien. 2015. "Context-Dependent Chemical Communication, Alarm Pheromones of Thrips Larvae." PhD thesis. University of Amsterdam.

DeGrazia, David. 1994. "Wittgenstein and the Mental Life of Animals." *History of Philosophy Quarterly* 11, no. 1: 121–37.

Deleuze, Gilles, and Félix Guattari. 1988. *A Thousand Plateaus: Capitalism and Schizophrenia*. London: Bloomsbury Publishing.

De Putter, Jos. 2015. "Ganzen ruimen voor de grote vakantie doe je zo." *De Correspondent*. May 16, 2015. www.decorrespondent.nl.

Derrida, Jacques. 1991. *Of Spirit: Heidegger and the Question*. Chicago: University of Chicago Press.

———. 1994. "'Eating Well,' or the Calculation of the Subject." In *Points . . . : Interviews, 1974–1994*, edited by Elizabeth Weber, 255–87. Stanford, CA: Stanford University Press.

———. 2008. *The Animal That Therefore I Am*. New York: Fordham University Press.

———. 2009. *The Beast and the Sovereign, Volume I*. Chicago: Chicago University Press.

———. 2011. *The Beast and the Sovereign, Volume II*. Chicago: Chicago University Press.

Descartes, René. (1638) 1985. "Letter to R. P. Vatier, 22 February 1638." In *The Philosophical Writings of Descartes*, vol. 3, translated by John Cottingham, Robert Stoothoff, Dugald Murdoch, and Anthony Kenny. Cambridge: Cambridge University Press.

———. (1646) 1991. "Letter to (the Marquess of Newcastle) 23 November 1646." In *Descartes: Philosophical Letters*. Cambridge: Cambridge University Press.

Despret, Vinciane. 2004. "The Body We Care For: Figures of Anthropo-Zoo-Genesis." *Body & Society* 10: 111–34.

———. 2006. "Sheep Do Have Opinions." In *Making Things Public: Atmospheres of Democracy*, edited by Bruno Latour and Peter Weibel, 360–70. Cambridge, MA: MIT Press.

———. 2008. "The Becoming of Subjectivity in Animal Worlds." *Subjectivity* 23: 123–39.

De Waal, Frans. 2016. *Are We Smart Enough to Know How Smart Animals Are?* New York: W.W. Norton & Company.

Diamond, Cora. 1978. "Eating Meat and Eating People." *Philosophy* 53, no. 206: 465–79.

———. 2003. "The Difficulty of Reality and the Difficulty of Philosophy." *Partial Answers: Journal of Literature and the History of Ideas* 1, no. 2: 1–26.

Dinker, Karin Gunnarsson, and Helena Pedersen. 2016. "Critical Animal Pedagogies: Re-Learning Our Relations with Animal Others." In *The Palgrave International Handbook of Alternative Education*, edited by Helen E. Lees and Nel Noddings, 415–30. London: Palgrave Macmillan.

Dolgert, Stefan. 2015. "Animal Republics: Plato, Representation, and the Politics of Nature." *Politics and Animals* 1, no. 1: 75–88.

Donaldson, Sue (forthcoming). "Animals Citizens and the Democratic Challenge."

Donaldson, Sue, and Will Kymlicka. 2011. *Zoopolis: A Political Theory of Animal Rights.* Oxford: Oxford University Press.

———. 2013a. "A Defense of Animal Citizens and Sovereigns." *Law, Ethics and Philosophy* 2013, no. 1: 143–60.

———. 2013b. "A Defense of Animal Citizenship. Part 1: Citizen Canine: Agency for Domesticated Animals." Unpublished manuscript.

———. 2014a. "Animal Rights, Multiculturalism, and the Left." *Journal of Social Philosophy* 45, no. 1: 116–35.

———. 2014b. "Unruly Beasts: Animal Citizens and the Threat of Tyranny." *Canadian Journal of Political Science* 47, no. 1: 23–45.

———. 2015a. "Farmed Animal Sanctuaries: The Heart of the Movement?" *Politics and Animals* 1, no. 1: 50–74.

———. 2015b. "Rethinking Membership and Participation in an Inclusive Democracy: Cognitive Disability, Children, Animals." *Disability and Political Theory*, edited by Barbara Arneil and Nancy Hirschman, 168–98. Cambridge: Cambridge University Press.

Donovan, Josephine. 1990. "Animal Rights and Feminist Theory." *Signs: Journal of Women in Culture and Society* 15, no. 2: 350–75.

Doremus, Holly. 2000. "Rhetoric and Reality of Nature Protection: Toward a New Discourse." *Wash. & Lee L. Rev* 57: 11–41.

Driessen, Clemens. 2014. "Animal Deliberation." In *Animal Politics and Political Animals*, edited by David Schlosberg and Marcel Wissenburg, 90–104. London: Palgrave Macmillan.

———. 2016. "Comment: Caring for Captive Communities by Looking for Love and Loneliness, or Against an Overly Individual Liberal Animal Ethics." In *Animal Ethics in the Age of Humans: Blurring Boundaries in Human-Animal Relationships*, edited by Bernice Bovenkerk and Jozef Keulartz, 319–32. Dordrecht, Netherlands: Springer.

———. 2017. "Een kleine filosofie van de visstick." *Wijsgerig Perspectief* 57, no. 1: 24–34.

Dryzek, John. 2000. *Deliberative Democracy and Beyond: Liberals, Critics, Contestations.* Oxford: Oxford University Press.

———. 2008. "Green Reason." *Environmental Ethics* 12, no. 3: 195–210.

———. 2010. *Foundations and Frontiers of Deliberative Governance.* Oxford: Oxford University Press.

Eisenman, Stephen. 2015. "The Real Swinish Multitude." *Critical Inquiry* 42, no. 2: 339–73.

Elder, Glen, Jennifer Wolch, and Jody Emel. 1998. "Race, Place, and the Bounds of Humanity." *Society & Animals* 6, no. 2: 183–202.

Elephant Listening Project. http://www.birds.cornell.edu/brp/elephant/index.html.

Emel, Jody, Chris Wilbert, and Jennifer Wolch. 2002. "Animal Geographies." *Society & Animals* 10, no. 4: 407–12.

Evans, Edward Payson. 1906. *The Criminal Prosecution and Capital Punishment of Animals*. London: William Heinemann.

Fagot, Joël, and Robert Cook. 2006. "Evidence for Large Long-term Memory Capacities in Baboons and Pigeons and Its Implications for Learning and the Evolution of Cognition." *PNAS* 103, no. 46: 17564–67.

Faria, Catia. 2015. "Disentangling Obligations of Assistance: A Reply to Clare Palmer's 'Against the View That We Are Usually Required to Assist Wild Animals.'" *Relations: Beyond Anthropocentrism* 3, no. 2: 211–18.

Faunabescherming. 2013. "Schipholganzenfolder." www.faunabescherming.nl.

Fletcher, Thomas, and Louise Platt. 2016. "'(Just) a Walk with the Dog? Animal Geographies and Negotiating Walking Spaces." *Social & Cultural Geography* 2016: 1–19.

Flower, Tom. 2011. "Fork-Tailed Drongos Use Deceptive Mimicked Alarm Calls to Steal Food." *Proceedings of the Royal Society of London B: Biological Sciences* 278, no. 1711: 1548–55.

Flower, Tom, Matthew Gribble, and Amanda Ridley. 2014. "Deception by Flexible Alarm Mimicry in an African Bird." *Science* 344, no. 6183: 513–16.

Fortuny, Kim. 2014. "Islam, Westernization, and Posthumanist Place: The Case of the Istanbul Street Dog." *Interdisciplinary Studies in Literature and Environment* 21, no. 2: 271–97.

Foucault, Michel. (1975) 2010. *Discipline & Punish: The Birth of the Prison*. London: Penguin.

———. 1998. *The History of Sexuality, Vol. 1: The Will to Knowledge*. London: Penguin.

Francione, Gary. 1995. *Animals, Property, and the Law*. Philadelphia: Temple University Press.

Francis, Leslie, and Anita Silvers. 2007. "Liberalism and Individually Scripted Ideas of the Good: Meeting the Challenge of Dependent Agency." *Social Theory and Practice* 33, no. 2: 311–34.

Gaita, Raimond. 2002. *The Philosopher's Dog*. Melbourne: Text Publishing.

Garner, Robert. 2013. *A Theory of Justice for Animals*. Oxford: Oxford University Press.

———. 2016. "Animal Rights and the Deliberative Turn in Democratic Theory." *European Journal of Political Theory*. First published online: 1474885116630937.

Geiger, Martha, and Alice Hovorka. 2015. "Animal Performativity: Exploring the Lives of Donkeys in Botswana." *Environment and Planning D: Society and Space* 33, no. 6: 1098–117.

Gentner, T., K. Fenn, D. Margoliash, and H. Nusbaum. 2006. "Recursive Syntactic Pattern Learning by Songbirds." *Nature* 440, no. 7088: 1204–7.

Genty, Emilie, and Klaus Zuberbühler. 2014. "Spatial Reference in a Bonobo Gesture." *Current Biology* 24, no. 14: 1601–5.

Gheaus, Anca. 2011. "Arguments for Nonparental Care for Children." *Social Theory and Practice* 37, no. 3: 483–509.

Gillam, Erin, and Brock Fenton. 2016. "Roles of Acoustic Social Communication in the Lives of Bats." In *Bat Bioacoustics*, edited by M. B. Fenton, A. D. Grinnell, A. N. Popper, and R. R. Fay, 117–39. New York: Springer.

Goodall, Jane. 1986. *The Chimpanzees of Gombe: Patterns of Behavior.* Cambridge, MA: Harvard University Press.

Goodin, Robert, Carole Pateman, and R. Pateman. 1997. "Simian Sovereignty." *Political Theory* 25, no. 6: 821–49.

Gordon, Deborah. 1992. "Wittgenstein and Ant-watching." *Biology and Philosophy* 7, no. 1: 13–25.

Glendinning, Simon. 1998. *On Being With Others: Heidegger, Derrida, Wittgenstein.* New York: Routledge.

Grazian, David. 2012. "Where the Wild Things Aren't: Exhibiting Nature in American Zoos." *Sociological Quarterly* 53: 546–65.

Grinsted, Laura, J. Pruitt, V. Settepani, and T. Bilde. 2013. "Individual Personalities Shape Task Differentiation in a Social Spider." *Proceedings of the Royal Society of London B: Biological Sciences* 280, no. 1767: 1–8.

Gruen, Lori. 1993. "Dismantling Oppression: An Analysis of the Connection Between Women and Animals." In *Ecofeminism: Women, Animals, Nature*, edited by Greta Gaard. Philadelphia: Temple University Press.

———. 2015. *Entangled Empathy: An Alternative Ethic for Our Relationships with Animals.* New York: Lantern Books.

Guerrini, Anita. 2003. *Experimenting with Humans and Animals: From Galen toAanimal Rights.* Baltimore: Johns Hopkins University Press.

Gunderson, Ryan. 2016. "Sympathy Regulated by Communicative Reason: Horkheimer, Habermas, and Animals." In *The Persistence of Critical Theory: Culture & Civilization*, edited by Gabriel Ricci. Piscataway, NJ: Transaction Publishers.

Habermas, Jurgen. 1981. *The Theory of Communicative Action, Volume 1: Reason and the Rationalization of Society.* Boston: Beacon Press.

———. 1994. "Three Normative Models of Democracy." *Constellations* 1, no. 1:1–10.

Hadley, John. 2005. "Non-Human Animal Property: Reconciling Environmentalism and Animal Rights." *Journal of Social Philosophy* 36, no. 3: 305–15.

Haraway, Donna. 1991. *Simians, Cyborgs and Women: The Reinvention of Nature.* New York: Routledge.

———. 2003. *The Companion Species Manifesto: Dogs, People, and Significant Otherness.* Chicago: Prickly Paradigm Press.

———. 2008. *When Species Meet.* Minneapolis: University of Minnesota Press.

Hardt, Michael, and Antonio Negri. 2011. "The Fight for 'Real Democracy' at the Heart of Occupy Wall Street." *Foreign Affairs.* www.foreignaffairs.com.

Hare, Brian, and Vanessa Woods. 2013. *The Genius of Dogs: How Dogs Are Smarter than You Think*. New York: Penguin.

Haysom, Keith. 2009. "Communicating Depth: Habermas and Merleau-Ponty on Language and Praxis." *Political Theory* 37, no. 5: 649–75.

Hearne, Vicki. (1986) 2007. *Adam's Task: Calling Animals by Name*. New York: Skyhorse Publishing.

Heberlein, Marianne, Marta Manser, and Dennis Turner. 2017. "Deceptive-Like Behavior in Dogs (Canis familiaris)." *Animal Cognition* 1: 1–10.

Heidegger, Martin. 1927. *Being and Time*. Malden, MA: Blackwell Publishing.

———. (1929) 1995. *The Fundamental Concepts of Metaphysics*. Bloomington: Indiana University Press.

———. (1947) 1993. "Letter on Humanism." In *Basic Writings*. San Francisco: HarperCollins.

Herringshaw, Liam, Richard Callow, and Duncan McIlroy. 2017. "Engineering the Cambrian Explosion: The Earliest Bioturbators as Ecosystem Engineers." *Geological Society, London, Special Publications*, SP448–18.

Herzing, Denise. 2016. "Interfaces and Keyboards for Human-Dolphin Communication: What Have We Learned." *Animal Behavior and Cognition* 3, no. 4: 243–54.

Hickman, Pamela, and Pat Stephens. 1998. *Animal Senses: How Animals See, Hear, Taste, Smell and Feel*. New York: Kids Can Press Ltd.

Higgins, Polly, Damien Short, and Nigel South. 2013. "Protecting the Planet: A Proposal for a Law of Ecocide." *Crime, Law and Social Change* 59, no. 3: 251–66.

Hillix, William Allen, and Duane Rumbaugh. 2004. *Animal Bodies, Human Minds: Ape, Dolphin, and Parrot Language Skills*. New York: Springer Science & Business Media.

Hinchcliffe, Christopher. 2015. "Animals and the Limits of Citizenship: Zoopolis and the Concept of Citizenship." *Journal of Political Philosophy* 23, no. 3: 302–20.

Hinchliffe, Steve, and Sarah Whatmore. 2006. "Living Cities: Towards a Politics of Conviviality." *Science as culture* 15, no. 2: 123–38.

Hirschman, Albert. 1970. *Exit, Voice, and Loyalty: Responses to Decline in Firms, Organizations, and States*. Cambridge, MA: Harvard University Press.

Hobaiter, Catherine, and Richard W. Byrne. 2014. "The Meanings of Chimpanzee Gestures." *Current Biology* 24, no. 14: 1596–1600.

Hobson, Kersty. 2007. "Political Animals? On Animals as Subjects in an Enlarged Political Geography." *Political Geography* 26, no. 3: 250–67.

Honneth, Axel. 2014. *Freedom's Right: The Social Foundations of Democratic Life*. New York: Columbia University Press.

Hopkins, William, Jamie Russell, and Jennifer Schaeffer. 2012. "The Neural and Cognitive Correlates of Aimed Throwing in Chimpanzees: A Magnetic Resonance Image and Behavioral Study on a Unique Form of Social Tool Use." *Phil. Trans. R. Soc. B* 367, no. 1585: 37–47.

Horowitz, Alexandra. 2016. *Being a Dog: Following the Dog Into a World of Smell*. New York: Scribner.

Horta, Oscar. 2010. "What is Speciesism?" *Journal of Agricultural and Environmental Ethics* 23, no. 3: 243–66.

Howard, Len. 1952. *Birds as Individuals*. London: Collins Press.

———. 1956. *Living with Birds*. London: Collins Press.

Hribal, Jason. 2003. "Animals are Part of the Working Class: A Challenge to Labour History." *Labour History* 44, no. 4: 435–53.

———. 2007. "Animals, Agency, and Class: Writing the History of Animals from Below." *Human Ecology Review* 14, no. 1: 101.

———. 2008. "The Story of Ken Allen and Kumang: Orangutans, Resistance and the Zoo," *Counterpunch*, December 16, 2008. www.counterpunch.org.

———. 2010. *Fear of the Animal Planet: The Hidden History of Animal Resistance*. New York: AK Press.

———. 2012. "Animals are Part of the Working Class Reviewed." *Borderlands* 11, no. 2: 1–37.

Hughes, Christina, and Celia Lury. 2013. "Re-turning Feminist Methodologies: From a Social to an Ecological Epistemology." *Gender and Education* 25, no. 6: 786–99.

Huys, Maarten, and Maarten Kroesen. 2009. "A Foucaultian Contribution to the Study and Transformation of Fixated Policy Discourses." Conference presentation, *Discourse, Power, and Politics 4th International Conference in Interpretive Policy Analysis*.

Irvine, Leslie. 2001. "The Power of Play." *Anthrozoos: A Multidisciplinary Journal of The Interactions of People & Animals* 14, no. 3: 151–60.

Iveson, Richard. 2010. "Animals in Looking-Glass World: Fables of Überhumanism and Posthumanism in Heidegger and Nietzsche." *Humanimalia: a Journal of Human/Animal Interface Studies* 2010, no. 2: 46–85.

———. 2012. "On the Importance of Heidegger's Anthropogenesis, and of Moving Beyond It." Conference presentation, *Unruly Creatures 2: Creative Revolutions*, Natural History Museum, London, June 18, 2012.

Jenkins, Peter. 1978. "Cultural Transmission of Song Patterns and Dialect Development in a Free-Living Bird Population." *Animal Behavior* 26: 50–78.

Jerolmack, Colin. 2008. "How Pigeons Became Rats: The Cultural Spatial Logic of Problem Animals." *Social Problems* 55, no. 1: 72–94.

Johnston, Robert. 2008. "Individual Odors and Social Communication: Individual Recognition, Kin Recognition, and Scent Over-Marking." *Advances in the Study of Behavior* 38: 439–505.

Joy, Melanie. 2011. *Why We Love Dogs, Eat Pigs, and Wear Cows: An Introduction to Carnism*. New York: Conari Press.

Kamphof, Ike. 2017. "Lichamelijke resonantie tussen mens en kip." *Wijsgerig Perspectief* 57, no. 1: 34–42.

Keim, Brandon. 2017. "Is Kindness the Solution to Conflicts with Wild Dogs?" *Anthropocene Magazine*, February 2017. www.anthropocenemagazine.org.

Kelley, Laura, and John Endler. 2012. "Masters of Illusion: [Bowerbirds Construct Bowers Which Include Visual Illusions to Attract Potential Mates.]" *Australasian Science* 33: 5–30.

Kerasote, Ted. 2008. *Merle's Door: Lessons from a Freethinking Dog*. New York: Houghton Mifflin Harcourt.

Kershenbaum, Arik, Ann Bowles, Todd Freeberg, Dezhe Jin, Adriano Lameira, and Kirsten Bohn. 2014. "Animal Vocal Sequences: Not the Markov Chains We Thought They Were." *Proc. R. Soc. B*. 281, no. 1792: 1471–2954.

Kheel, Marti. 2004. "Vegetarianism and Ecofeminism: Toppling Patriarchy with a Fork." In *Food for Thought: The Debate over Eating Meat*, edited by Steve Sapontzis, 327–41. New York: Prometheus.

Kim, Claire Jean. 2015. *Dangerous Crossings: Race, Species, and Nature in a Multicultural Age*. Cambridge: Cambridge University Press.

King, Stephanie, and Vincent Janik. 2013. "Bottlenose Dolphins Can Use Learned Vocal Labels to Address Each Other." *Proceedings of the National Academy of Sciences* 110, no. 32: 13216–21.

Kittay, Eva Feder. 2005. "At the Margins of Moral Personhood." *Ethics* 116: 100–131.

Ko, Aph, and Syl Ko. 2017. *Aphro-Ism: Essays on Pop Culture, Feminism, and Black Veganism from Two Sisters*. Herndon: Lantern Books.

Kohn, Eduardo. 2013. *How Forests Think: Toward an Anthropology Beyond the Human*. Berkeley: University of California Press.

Kunst, Jonas, and Sigrid Hohle. 2016. "Meat Eaters by Dissociation: How We Present, Prepare and Talk about Meat Increases Willingness to Eat Meat by Reducing Empathy and Disgust." *Appetite* 105: 758–74.

Kymlicka, Will. 2017. "Social Membership: Animal Law beyond the Property/Personhood Impasse." *Dalhousie Law Journal*, no. 40: 123–38.

LaCroix, Travis. 2014. "Wittgenstein and the Animals." *Hemlock* 1: 59–67.

Latour, Bruno. 1993. *We Have Never Been Modern*. Cambridge, MA: Harvard University Press.

———. 1999. *Pandora's Hope: Essays on the Reality of Science Studies*. Cambridge, MA: Harvard University Press.

Latour, Bruno, and Peter Weibel, eds. 2005. *Making Things Public: Atmospheres of Democracy*. Cambridge, MA: MIT Press.

Laude, Jennifer, C. W. Daniels, J. C. Wade, and T. R. Zentall. 2016. "I Can Time with a Little Help from My Friends: Effect of Social Enrichment on Timing Processes in Pigeons (Columba livia)." *Animal Cognition* 19, no. 6: 1205–13.

Leahy, Michael. 1994. *Against Liberation: Putting Animals in Perspective*. London: Routledge.

Lemon, Alaina. 2015. "MetroDogs: The Heart in the Machine." *Journal of the Royal Anthropological Institute* 21, no. 3: 660–79.

Leuven, Joost. 2017. "The Theory and Practice of Contemporary Animal Rights Activism." *Krisis* 2017: 2.

Levinas, Emmanuel. 1981. *Otherwise than Being or Beyond Essence*. Dordrecht, Netherlands: Springer.

List, Clarissa. 2004. "Democracy in Animal Groups: A Political Science Perspective." *Trends in Ecology & Evolution* 19, no. 4: 168–69.

Lorenz, Konrad. 1949. *King Solomon's Ring: New Light on Animal Ways*. London: Routledge.

———. 1991. *Here I Am—Where are You?: The Behavior of the Greylag Goose*. New York: HarperCollins.

Lynch, Joseph. 1996. "Wittgenstein and Animal Minds." *Between The Species* 12: 47–52.

Lyotard, Jean-François. 1988. *Le différend*. Minneapolis: University of Minnesota Press.

MacKinnon, Catharine. 2004. "Of Mice and Men: A Feminist Fragment on Animal Rights." In *Animal Rights: Current Debates and New Directions*, edited by Martha Nussbaum and Cass Sunstein, 263–67. Oxford: Oxford University Press.

Maestripieri, Dario. 1997. "Gestural Communication in Macaques: Usage and Meaning of Nonvocal Signals." *Evolution of Communication* 1, no. 2: 193–222.

Malavasi, Rachele, and Ludwig Huber. 2016. "Evidence of Heterospecific Referential Communication from Domestic Horses (Equus caballus) to Humans." *Animal Cognition* 19, no. 5: 899–909.

Mansbridge, Jane, James Bohman, Simone Chambers, Thomas Christiano, Archon Fung, John Parkinson, Dennis F. Thompson, and Mark E. Warren. 2012. "A Systemic Approach to Deliberative Democracy." In *Deliberative Systems: Deliberative Democracy at the Large Scale*, edited by John Parkinson and Jane Mansbridge, 1–26. Cambridge: Cambridge University Press.

Manser, Marta. 2001. "The Acoustic Structure of Suricates' Alarm Calls Varies with Predator Type and the Level of Response Urgency." *Proceedings of the Royal Society of London B: Biological Sciences* 268, no. 1483: 2315–24.

Marshall Thomas, Elisabeth. 2010. *The Hidden Life of Dogs*. New York: Houghton Mifflin Harcourt.

Massumi, Brian. 2014. *What Animals Teach Us About Politics*. Durham, NC: Duke University Press.

McDonald, Mark, Sarah Mesnick, and John Hildebrand. 2006. "Biogeographic Characterization of Blue Whale Song Worldwide: Using Song to Identify Populations." *Journal of Cetacean Research and Management* 8, no. 1: 55–65.

McMillan, Franklin. 2000. "Quality of Life in Animals." *Journal of the American Veterinary Medical Association* 216, no. 12: 1904–10.

Meijer, Eva. 2013. "Political Communication with Animals." *Humanimalia: A Journal of Human/Animal Interface Studies* 5, no. 1.

———. 2016. "Speaking with Animals: Philosophical Interspecies Investigations." In *Thinking about Animals in the Age of the Anthropocene*, edited by Morten Tønnessen, Kristin Armstrong Oma, and Silver Rattasepp, 73–88. New York: Lexington Books.

Mejdell, Cecilie, T. Buvik, G. Jørgensen, and K. Bøe. 2016. "Horses Can Learn to Use Symbols to Communicate Their Preferences." *Applied Animal Behavior Science* 184: 66–73.

Melehy, Hassan. 2006. "Silencing the Animals: Montaigne, Descartes, and the Hyperbole of Reason." *symploke* 13, no. 2: 263–82.

Merleau-Ponty, Maurice. 1962. *Phenomenology of Perception*. London: Routledge.

———. 1968. *The Visible and the Invisible.* Evanston, IL: Northwestern University Press.

———. 2003. *Nature: Course Notes from the Collège de France.* Evanston, IL: Northwestern University Press.

Messenger, Stephen. 2012. "The Incredible Story of an Elephant Who Derailed a Train to Defend His Herd." *Treehugger.* www.treehugger.com.

———. 2013. "Elephants Take Revenge on Village after Herd Member is Killed by Train." *Treehugger.* www.treehugger.com.

Milburn, Josh. 2017. "Nonhuman Animals as Property Holders: An Exploration of the Lockean Labour-Mixing Account." *Environmental Values* 26, no. 5: 629–48.

Milligan, Tony. 2015. "The Political Turn in Animal Rights." *Politics and Animals* 1, no. 1: 6–15.

Mitchell, Brian. 2006. "Information Content of Coyote Barks and Howls." *Bioacoustics* 15, no. 3: 289–314.

Montaigne, Michel de. (1595) 1958. "Apology for Raymond Sebond." In *The Complete Works of Montaigne,* translated by Donald Frame. Stanford, CA: Stanford University Press.

Montgomery, Sy. 2016. "Are Your Chickens Talking About You?" *Globe Correspondent,* September 22, 2016. www.bostonglobe.com.

Montreal Gazette. 1954. "Little 'Chimp' Proves Smarter than Human Baby after One Year." July 28, 1954. https://news.google.com.

Moore, Lisa Jean. 2018. *Catch and Release: The Enduring Yet Vulnerable Horseshoe Crab.* New York: NYU Press.

Morton, Timothy. 2017. *Humankind: Solidarity with Non-Human People.* New York: Verso Books.

Moynihan, Martin. 1991. "Structures of Animal Communication." In *Man and Beast Revisited,* edited by Michael H. Robinson and Lionel Tiger, 193–202. Washington, DC: Smithsonian Institution Scholarly Press.

Nagasawa, M., S. Mitsui, S. En, N. Ohtani, M. Ohta, Y. Sakuma, and T. Kikusui. 2015. "Oxytocin-Gaze Positive Loop and the Coevolution of Human-Dog Bonds." *Science* 348, no. 6232: 333–36.

Nagy, Kelsi, and Phillip David Johnson II, eds. 2013. *Trash Animals: How We Live with Nature's Filthy, Feral, Invasive and Unwanted Species.* Minneapolis: University of Minnesota Press.

Nagy, M., Z. Ákos, D. Biro, and T. Vicsek. 2010. "Hierarchical Group Dynamics in Pigeon Flocks." *Nature* 464, no. 7290: 890–93.

Narayanan, Yamini. 2017. "Street Dogs at the Intersection of Colonialism and Informality: 'Subaltern Animism' as a Posthuman Critique of Indian Cities." *Environment and Planning D: Society and Space* 35, no. 3: 475–94.

Norton, Graham. 1986. "Leadership Decision Processes of Group Movement in Yellow Baboons." In *Primate Ecology and Conservation,* edited by J. Else and P. Lee, 145–56. Cambridge: Cambridge University Press.

NOS. 2014. "VVD verklaart meeuw de oorlog." August 20, 2014. http://nos.nl.

Nussbaum, Martha. 2006. *Frontiers of Justice: Disability, Nationality, Species Membership.* Cambridge, MA: Harvard University Press.

Oliver, Kelly. 2007. "Stopping the Anthropological Machine: Agamben with Heidegger and Merleau-Ponty." *PhaenEx* 2: 1–23.

———. 2010. "Animal Ethics: Toward an Ethics of Responsiveness." *Research in Phenomenology* 40, no. 2: 267–80.

———. 2015. "Witnessing, Recognition, and Response Ethics." *Philosophy and Rhetoric* 48, no. 4: 473–93.

———. 2016. "Service Dogs: Between Animal Studies and Disability Studies." *philoSOPHIA* 6, no. 2: 241–58.

Osborn, Ferrel, and Guy Parker. 2003. "Towards an Integrated Approach for Reducing the Conflict between Elephants and People: A Review of Current Research." *Oryx* 37, no. 1: 80–84.

O'Sullivan, Siobhan. 2011. *Animals, Equality and Democracy.* London: Palgrave Macmillan.

Otjes, Simon. 2016. "The Hobbyhorse of the Party for the Animals." *Society & Animals* 42, no. 4: 383–402.

Pachirat, Timothy. 2011. *Every Twelve Seconds: Industrialized Slaughter and the Politics of Sight.* New Haven, CT: Yale University Press.

Palacios, Vicente, Enrique Font, and Rafael Márquez. 2007. "Iberian Wolf Howls: Acoustic Structure, Individual Variation, and a Comparison with North American Populations." *Journal of Mammalogy* 88, no. 3: 606–13.

Palmer, Clare. 2003a. "Placing Animals in Urban Environmental Ethics." *Journal of Social Philosophy* 34, no. 1: 64–78.

———. 2003b. "Colonization, Urbanisation and Animals." *Philosophy & Geography* 6, no. 1: 47–58.

———. 2010. *Animal Ethics in Context.* New York, Columbia University Press.

———. 2013. "Companion Cats as Co-Citizens? Comments on Sue Donaldson's and Will Kymlicka's *Zoopolis.*" *Dialogue* 52, no. 4: 759–67.

Partij voor de Dieren. 2015. "Dossier Damherten." September 22, 2015. https://amsterdam.partijvoordedieren.nl.

Pederson, Helena. 2017. "Learning to Change the System from Within? Two Cases of Education for Animal Liberation." *Animal Liberation Currents,* January 20, 2017. www.animalliberationcurrents.com.

Peeters, Norbert. 2016. *Botanische Revolutie.* Zeist, Netherlands: KNNV Uitgeverij.

Pepper, Angela. 2016. "Political Agency in Humans and Other Animals." Conference presentation, *Political Animals: Agency, Participation, and Representation* workshop, Montreal, March 5, 2016.

Pepperberg, Irene. 1995. "Grey Parrot Intelligence." *Proceedings of the International Aviculturists Society* 1995, no. 1: 11–15.

Peterson, Dale. 2012. *The Moral Lives of Animals.* New York: Bloomsbury Publishing.

Pika, Simone, and Thomas Bugnyar. 2011. "The Use of Referential Gestures in Ravens (Corvus corax) in the Wild." *Nature Communications* 2011, no. 2: 560–73.

Pilley, John. 2013. "Border Collie Comprehends Sentences Containing a Prepositional Object, Verb, and Direct Object." *Learning and Motivation* 44, no. 4: 229–40.

Pilley, John, and Allison Reid. 2011. "Border Collie Comprehends Object Names as Verbal Referents." *Behavioral Processes* 86, no. 2: 184–95.

Planinc, Emma. 2014. "Democracy, Despots and Wolves: On the Dangers of Zoopolis's Animal Citizen." *Canadian Journal of Political Science* 47, no. 1: 1–21.

Pleasants, Nigel. 2006. "Nonsense on Stilts? Wittgenstein, Ethics, and the Lives of Animals." *Inquiry, An Interdisciplinary Journal of Philosophy* 49, no. 4: 314–36.

Plumwood, Val. 2002. "Prey to a Crocodile." *Aisling Magazine*, September 22, 2002. www.aislingmagazine.com.

Porphyry. (268–70 BC) 1823. *On Abstinence from Animal Food*, translated by Thomas Taylor. London: T. Rodd.

Poyarkov, A. D. 1991. "From the Lives of Wandering Dogs." In *What Dogs Bark About*, edited by E. Kotenkova and A. Surov, 97–111. Moscow: Patriot.

Prat, Yosef, Mor Taub, and Yossi Yovel. 2016. "Everyday Bat Vocalizations Contain Information about Emitter, Addressee, Context, and Behavior." *Scientific Reports* 6, no. 39419.

Proops, Leanne, Kate Grounds, Amy Victoria Smith, and Karen McComb. 2018. "Animals Remember Previous Facial Expressions that Specific Humans have Exhibited." *Current Biology*. First published online: https://doi.org/10.1016/j.cub.2018.03.035.

Rancière, Jacques. 2007. *Hatred of Democracy*. New York: Verso Books.

Rawls, John. 1971. *A Theory of Justice*. Oxford: Oxford University Press.

RDA. 2017. "Zienswijze hondenbeten." February 23, 2017. http://rda.nl.

Regan, Tom. 1983. *The Case for Animal Rights*. Berkeley: University of California Press.

Ringhofer, Monamie, and Shinya Yamamoto. 2017. "Domestic Horses Send Signals to Humans When They Face with an Unsolvable Task." *Animal Cognition* 20, no. 3: 397–405.

Robinson, Margaret. 2013. "Veganism and Mi'kmaq Legends." *Canadian Journal of Native Studies* 33: 184–96.

Rowlands, Mark. 1997. "Contractarianism and Animal Rights." *Journal of Applied Philosophy* 14, no. 3: 235–47.

——. 2011. "Animals that Act for Moral Reasons." In *The Oxford Handbook of Ethics and Animals*, edited by Tom Beauchamp and Richard Frey. Oxford: Oxford University Press.

——. 2017. "Making Light of the Ethical? The Ethics and Politics of Animal Rights." In *Ethical and Political Approaches to Nonhuman Animal Issues*, edited by Andrew Woodhall and Gabriel Garmendia da Trindade, 21–38. New York: Palgrave Macmillan.

Seeley, Tom. 2010. *Honeybee Democracy*. Princeton: Princeton University Press.

Seeley, Tom, and Susannah Buhrman. 1999. "Group Decision Making in Swarms of Honey Bees." *Behavioral Ecology and Sociobiology* 45, no. 1: 19–31.

Seyfarth, Robert, Dorothy Cheney, and Peter Marler. 1980. "Vervet Monkey Alarm Calls: Semantic Communication in a Free-Ranging Primate." *Animal Behaviour* 28: 1070–94.

Sherry, David, and Bennett Galef. 1984. "Cultural Transmission Without Imitation: Milk Bottle Opening by Birds." *Animal Behavior* 32, no. 3: 937–38.

Shukin, Nicole. 2009. Animal Capital: Rendering Life in Biopolitical Times. Minneapolis: University of Minnesota Press.

Singer, Peter. 1975. *Animal Liberation*. New York: HarperCollins.

Slabbekoorn, Hans, and Ardie den Boer-Visser. 2006. "Cities Change the Songs of Birds." *Current Biology* 16, no. 23: 2326–31.

Slobodchikoff, Con. 2012. *Chasing Doctor Dolittle: Learning the Language of Animals*. New York: Macmillan.

Slobodchikoff, Constantine Nicholas, Bianca Perla, and Jennifer Verdolin. 2009. *Prairie Dogs: Communication and Community in an Animal Society*. Cambridge, MA: Harvard University Press.

Smuts, Barbara. 2001. "Encounters with Animal Minds." *Journal of Consciousness Studies* 8, no. 5–7: 293–309.

———. 2002. "Gestural Communication in Olive Baboons and Domestic Dogs." In *The Cognitive Animal: Empirical and Theoretical Perspectives on Animal Cognition*, edited by Marc Bekoff, Colin Allen, and Gordon M. Burghardt. Cambridge, MA: MIT Press, 301–6.

———. 2006. "Between Species: Science and Subjectivity." *Configurations* 14, no. 1: 115–26.

Smuts, Barbara, Dorothy Cheney, and Robert Seyfarth. 1986. "Social Relationships and Social Cognition in Non-Human Primates." *Science* 234, no. 4782: 1361–66.

Smuts, Barbara, and John Watanabe. 1990. "Social Relationships and Ritualized Greetings in Adult Male Baboons (*Papio cynocephalus anubis*)." *International Journal of Primatology* 11: 147–72.

Soltis, Joseph, Lucy King, Iain Douglas-Hamilton, Fritz Vollrath, and Anne Savage. 2014. "African Elephant Alarm Calls Distinguish between Threats from Humans and Bees." *PLoS ONE* 9, no. 2: e89403.

Somin, Ilya. 2014. "Foot Voting, Federalism, and Political Freedom." In *Federalism and Subsidiarity: NOMOS LV*, edited by James E. Fleming and Jacob T. Levy, 110–54. New York: NYU Press.

SOVON. 2017. "Vogelinfo Grauwe Gans." September 22, 2017. https://www.sovon.nl.

Spivak, Gayatri Chakravorty. 1988. "Can the Subaltern Speak?" In *Marxism and the Interpretation of Culture*, edited by Cary Nelson and Lawrence Grossberg, 271–313. Urbana: University of Illinois Press.

Srinivasan, Krithika. 2013. "The Biopolitics of Animal Being and Welfare: Dog Control and Care in the UK and India." *Transactions of the Institute of British Geographers* 38, no. 1: 106–119.

———. 2016. "Towards a Political Animal Geography?" *Political Geography* 50: 76–78.

Steiner, Gary. 2010. *Anthropocentrism and its Discontents: The Moral Status of Animals in the History of Western Philosophy*. Pittsburgh, PA: University of Pittsburgh Press.

Stel, Mariëlle, and Roos Vonk. 2010. "Mimicry in Social Interaction: Benefits for Mimickers, Mimickees, and Their Interaction." *British Journal of Psychology* 101, no. 2: 311–23.

Suzuki, Ryuji, John Buck, and Peter Tyack. 2006. "Information Entropy of Humpback Whale Songs." *Journal of the Acoustical Society of America* 119, no. 3: 1849–66.

Tamura, Tetsuki. 2014. "Rethinking Grassroots Participation in Nested Deliberative Systems." *Japanese Political Science Review* 2: 63–87.

Taylor, Sunaura. 2017. *Beasts of Burden: Animal and Disability Liberation*. New York: The New Press.

Teunissen, Paul. 2016. "Het tuig van de waterleidingduinen." *Vrij Nederland*. www.vn.nl.

Thierman, Stephen. 2010. "Apparatuses of Animality: Foucault Goes to a Slaughterhouse." *Foucault Studies* 9: 89–110.

Tiebout, Charles. 1956. "A Pure Theory of Local Expenditures." *Journal of Political Economy* 64, no. 5: 416–24.

Tsing, Anna Lowenhaupt. 2015. *The Mushroom at the End of the World: On the Possibility of Life in Capitalist Ruins*. Princeton: Princeton University Press.

Tully, James. 2009. *Public Philosophy in a New Key: Volume 1, Democracy and Civic Freedom (Ideas in Context)*. Cambridge: Cambridge University Press.

Tyler, Tom. 2012. *CIFERAE: A Bestiary in Five Fingers*. Minneapolis: University of Minnesota Press.

Van Baaren, Rick, R. W. Holland, K. Kawakami, and A. Van Knippenberg. 2004. "Mimicry and Prosocial Behavior." *Psychological Science* 15, no. 1: 71–74.

Vogelbescherming. 2014. "Afschieten meeuwen zinloos." September 22, 2014. www.vogelbescherming.nl.

Von Essen, Erica, and Michael Allen. 2016. "The Republican Zoopolis: Towards a New Legitimation Framework for Relational Animal Ethics." *Ethics & the Environment* 21, no. 1: 61–88.

Wadiwel, Dinesh. 2015. *The War Against Animals*. Leiden, Netherlands: Brill Publishers.

———. 2016. "Fish and Pain: The Politics of Doubt." *Animal Sentience: An Interdisciplinary Journal on Animal Feeling* 1, no. 3: 31.

Warkentin, Traci. 2010. "Interspecies Etiquette: An Ethics of Paying Attention to Animals." *Ethics & the Environment* 15, no. 1: 101–21.

Watson, Matthew. 2014. "Derrida, Stengers, Latour, and Subalternist Cosmopolitics." *Theory, Culture & Society* 31, no. 1: 75–98.

Weil, Simone. 2002. *Gravity and Grace*. London: Routledge.

Weisberg, Zipporah. 2009. "The Broken Promises of Monsters: Haraway, Animals and the Humanist Legacy." *Journal for Critical Animal Studies* 7, no. 2: 22–62.

Weiss, Gail. 2006. "Can an Old Dog Learn New Tricks? Habitual Horizons in James, Bourdieu, and Merleau-Ponty." In *Intertwinings: Interdisciplinary Encounters with Merleau-Ponty*, 223–40. Albany: State University of New York Press.

Whatmore, Sarah, and Lorraine Thorne. 1999. "Elephants on the Move: Spatial Formations of Wildlife Exchange." *Environment and Planning D: Society and Space* 18, no. 2: 185–203.

Wilson, David. 1997. "Altruism and Organism: Disentangling the Themes of Multilevel Selection Theory." *American Naturalist* 150, no. 1: S122–S134.

Wise, Steven. 2010. "Legal Personhood and the Non-Human Rights Project." *Animal Law* 17, no. 1: 1–11.

————. 2014. *Rattling the Cage: Toward Legal Rights for Animals.* Cambridge, MA: Da Capo Press.

Wittgenstein, Ludwig. 1958. *Philosophical Investigations.* Oxford: Blackwell.

————. 1969. *Uber Gewißheit. On Certainty.* Oxford: Blackwell.

————. 1978. *Lectures and Conversations on Aesthetics, Psychology and Religious Belief.* Oxford: Blackwell.

Wohlleben, Peter. 2016. *The Hidden Life of Trees: What They Feel, How They Communicate—Discoveries from a Secret World.* Vancouver: Greystone Books.

Wolch, Jennifer. 2002. "Anima Urbis." *Progress in Human Geography* 26, no. 6: 721–42.

————. 2010. "Zoöpolis." In *Metamorphoses of the Zoo: Animal Encounter after Noah,* edited by Ralph Acampora, 221–45. Plymouth: Lexington Books.

Wolch, Jennifer, and Jody Emel. 1998. *Animal Geographies: Place, Politics, and Identity in the Nature-Culture Borderlands.* New York: Verso Books.

Wolfe, Cary. 2003. *Animal Rites: American Culture, the Discourse of Species, and Post-humanist Theory.* Chicago: Chicago University Press.

————. 2012. *Before the Law: Humans and Other Animals in a Biopolitical Frame.* Chicago: Chicago University Press.

Wood, Patricia Burke, and David Rossiter. 2017. "The Politics of Refusal: Aboriginal Sovereignty and the Northern Gateway Pipeline." *Canadian Geographer/Le Géographe canadien* 61, no. 2: 165–77.

Wright, Timothy, and Gerald Wilkinson. 2001. "Population Genetic Structure and Vocal Dialects in an Amazon Parrot." *Proceedings of the Royal Society of London B: Biological Sciences* 268, no. 1467: 609–16.

Wyckoff, Jason. 2014. "Linking Sexism and Speciesism." *Hypatia* 29, no. 4: 721–37.

Yeo, Jun-Han, and Harvey Neo. 2010. "Monkey Business: Human-Animal Conflicts in Urban Singapore." *Social and Cultural Geography* 11, no. 7: 681–700.

Young, Iris. 1990. *Justice and the Politics of Difference.* Princeton: Princeton University Press.

————. 2000. *Inclusion and Democracy.* Oxford: Oxford University Press.

Zeder, Melinda, D. G. Bradley, B. D. Smith, and E. Emshwiller. 2006. *Documenting Domestication: New Genetic and Archaeological Paradigms.* Berkeley: University of California Press.

Zirbes, Lara, Jean-Louis Deneubourg, Yves Brostaux, and Eric Haubruge. 2010. "A New Case of Consensual Decision: Collective Movement in Earthworms." *Ethology* 116, no. 6: 546–53.

Zuberbühler, Klaus. 2001. "Predator-Specific Alarm Calls in Campbell's Monkeys, Cercopithecus campbelli." *Behavioral Ecology and Sociobiology* 50, no. 5: 414–22.

————. 2002. "A Syntactic Rule in Forest Monkey Communication." *Animal Behavior* 63, no. 2: 293–99.

INDEX

Aaltola, Elisa, 72–73, 252n11
abolitionist animal rights theory,
    116–17
Acampora, Ralph, 161–62, 206
Adams, Carol, 120
African bees, 52
African grey parrot, 129–30, 253n15
agency, 4, 9, 11, 75, 79–82; democratic
    political, 136; dependent, 139; of
    dogs, 197–201, 218, 227; of domesti-
    cated animals, 124–25, 139; of earth-
    worms, 155–56; of geese, 180, 234–35;
    habits and, 93, 95; honoring, 105;
    interspecies dialogues and, 217–20;
    macro-, 105; micro-, 105; political,
    123–29, 136, 139, 155–56; of stray dogs,
    197–201
alarm calls: chicken, 51; goose, 172–73; lan-
    guage games and, 50–53; prairie dogs,
    53; vervet monkey, 51
Alcoff, Linda, 194
Alex, 48–49
animal activism, 118–19, 256n3; academia
    and, 240; interspecies change and,
    185–201; new directions for, 191–97;
    practices, 195–96
animal advocacy movement, 194–95
animal citizens, 135–40
animal experimentation, 21–22; behavior-
    ism and, 62; human language, 36–38,
    41–42, 47; problems with, 41; solitary
    confinement and, 41
animality: Blackness and, 192–93; human-
    ity and, 123; of humans, 131

Animal Liberation (Singer), 26, 114,
    252n5
animal politics, 111–32
animal rights, 2, 144–49; abolitionist,
    116–17; anthropocentrism of, 25, 115–18;
    for chimpanzees, 253n11; citizenship
    theory of, 117–18; concept of, 33; criti-
    cism of, 256n1; Donaldson on, 256n1;
    establishing, 240; habitat, 147–49;
    Kymlicka on, 256n1; labor, 145–47;
    morality and, 114, 115; negative rights
    and, 115–18; Nonhuman Rights Project,
    253n11; political participation and, 203;
    political theory of, 4; property, 147–48;
    reciprocal, 168; relational approach to,
    118; of residence, 168; social member-
    ship, 146; territorial, 147–49; theories,
    26; traditional theories of, 115–17;
    welfare regulations and, 252n7
animals: categorizing, 138; circus, 186,
    250n7; citizenship, 135–40; cogni-
    tion, 39–40, 48, 187; companion,
    196–97, 233; human representation of,
    140; laboratory, 22, 36, 158; liminal,
    167–69, 205–6, 255n5; multiplicity of,
    27–28; oppression of, 240; speaking
    for, 194–95, 246n7; thinking with, 60;
    treatment of, 2; urban, 149–51; word,
    27; working, 185, 189–90; zoo, 186–87,
    252n13. *See also* domesticated animals;
    non-human animals; wild animals;
    specific animals
animal welfare regulations, 158, 252n7
animot, 27

279

ABOUT THE AUTHOR

EVA MEIJER is Postdoctoral Researcher at Wageningen University & Research in the project Anthropocene Ethics: Taking Animal Agency Seriously. She taught (animal) philosophy at the University of Amsterdam and is the chair of the Dutch Study Group for Animal Ethics. Her novels and nonfiction books have been translated into twelve languages. www.evameijer.nl.

Lightning Source UK Ltd.
Milton Keynes UK
UKHW011550181120
373391UK00011B/350